THE
COUNTRY MUSIC
MESSAGE:
Revisited

Jimmie N. Rogers

THE
COUNTRY MUSIC
MESSAGE:
Revisited

The University of Arkansas Press
Fayetteville   1989   London

Designer: *Chang-hee H. Russell*
Typeface: *Linotron 202 Fournier*
Typesetter: *G&S Typesetters, Inc.*
Printer: *Thomson-Shore, Inc.*
Binder: *John H. Dekker & Son, Inc.*

The paper used in this publication meets the minimum requirements
of the American National Standard for Permanence of Paper
for Printed Library Materials Z39.48-1984. ∞

Library of Congress Cataloging-in-Publication Data

Rogers, Jimmie N.
The country music message: revisited.

Includes index.
1. Country music—History and criticism.
2. Country music—Texts—History and criticism.
I. Title.
ML3524.R65 1989   784.5'2'009   88-17176
ISBN 1-55728-051-7 (alk. paper)
ISBN 1-55728-052-5 (pbk.)

To Jean
who is still my best friend

Contents

PART III
The Country Music Audience:
The People Who Listen to the Folks

Preface

The history of country music is interesting, but this is not a history. The stars of country music are fascinating "folks," but this book is not primarily a description of men and women who make the music and the history live. This book focuses on the message of country music—what the folks are communicating to an audience that has increased in size dramatically since the late 1950s. In 1983, *The Country Music Message* examined the predominant themes or ideas found in the fifty most popular songs for each year from 1960 to 1980. Much has happened in the music since 1980, and these happenings call for another visit. This book will consider an additional 350 songs and expand the first view by one-third. It is an examination of the messages in the most popular country songs from 1960 to 1987.

Although the history is important and the performers are interesting, the lyrics are the key to country music. It requires almost seventy hours to listen to more than 126,000 words in these 1,400 songs, and although they may contain 1,400 individual themes most of them can be placed in broad categories according to their predominant ideas. Most commercially popular country songs speak of love between men and women. Three major types of relationships can be identified within the love category: the songs of "hurtin' love" are the most numerous; "happy love" is celebrated less than hurtin', but a large number of these songs find their way to the charts; and a specific type of relationship called "cheatin'" is very prevalent. Although nearly three of every four popular country songs are about love, a significant number can be described as songs about "livin'"—how a person wishes to live, is living, or plans to live.

A few people believe all that is necessary to explain the country music message is a slight familiarity with a couple of songs, a few biases, and a naive audience. This book takes a different approach by employing a technique known as content analysis to identify the themes in the songs and place them in categories and subcategories. There is little description of the method developed in a study of the music, for most people are more interested in the message than in the method. However, several references are offered for those interested in how the analysis was conducted.

For a better understanding and appreciation of why and how we receive the messages, the process by which they are created, produced, and disseminated is outlined in Part I of this book. Using the human communication process as a framework, the songwriter, singer, recording companies, radio stations, jukebox industry, live performances, and other elements of the process are described according to how they act, interact, and react to determine the message delivered to the audience.

The predominant characteristics of the message are described for each category. The characteristics are identified according to the situation, people, and behaviors described in the songs. A country song is treated as a special form of communication—communication that more closely resembles interpersonal or face-to-face interaction between two people than do other types of mass appeal music. The close bond that exists between audience and performers, as well as the unique treatment of the song topics, fosters the acceptance of what is described here as a "sincerity contract" and helps to make the music, the performers, and the audience special. After the characteristics are reviewed, observations are made about the audience that accepts and approves these messages. The topics, and the approach to those topics by the songwriter and by the singers, tell us much about the audience that chooses to listen to country music.

Although the book is not a history of commercial country music, some historical background is offered. Even though this book is not about the lives of the performers, the communication techniques of the entertainers are highlighted. The book is not a compilation of lyrics; however, almost ninety partial and full sets are offered to allow the reader to get a feel of the language in the music. If you are familiar with the music of the 1960s, 1970s, and 1980s, you can certainly add songs to support (or to contradict) some of the observations made in the following pages. In some cases, different examples might have been offered, but a few owners of popular songs make it virtually impossible to obtain permission to reprint them.

If you are a newcomer to country music, perhaps this book will increase your interest in and understanding of the music. Reading the songs is not as fulfilling as hearing them, but this book may identify some songs you might want to seek out. The book offers a view of what commercial country music is communicating to its growing audience, and it is hoped that, after reading it, you will better understand and appreciate the music that a few folks are performing for a large number of people.

Acknowledgments

A number of people contributed to this project, and I am happy to be able to thank them at this time. Many people provided recordings and lyrics for the songs examined in this book, but I would especially like to thank Pat Demaree, general manager of radio station KFAY, Fayetteville, Arkansas, and the staff who were extremely patient and helpful in supplying resource materials. I would also like to thank Warren Schleiff, Dave Vaughn, and Delbert and Hazel McConnell for supplying a large number of difficult-to-locate recordings and lyrics for the first book.

Raymond Rodgers and Peggy Beasley-Rodgers helped develop the research design and procedure for the parent study that led to this project, and their contributions are greatly appreciated. Mike Flynn and Candy Clark located, transcribed, and catalogued many sets of lyrics and also served as coders to test the categories.

Three songwriters must be singled out for special appreciation: Willie Nelson, for taking time to talk about songwriting and performing; Tom T. Hall, for allowing me to glimpse a songwriter at work; and Wayland Holyfield, for his insights into creating a successful country song.

Several colleagues offered support during this and the original study. Richard Rea gave initial encouragement, and Preston Magruder encouraged me to finish it. Miller Williams supplied encouragement and more. I am deeply indebted to him for the suggestions, guidance, and time he gave to this project, for without his expert advice this book would not have taken shape.

Steve Smith, a frequent co-author and gifted titler, offered many suggestions for the improvement of this book, guided me to see the music in a better perspective, and insured that I live out a country song. Shari Guinn removes the bugs that Steve puts into my program. She catalogued and indexed over 10,000 recordings and sets of lyrics and is in harmony with the world and her computer. She made this visit through the music an easier trip and knows the difference between the Statler Brothers and the Oak Ridge Boys. Steve's and Shari's friendship and assistance helped me make it through the nights and days spent on this book.

I am, as always, grateful to my family for their support: Jean, who has given too much to the project; Barry, who has found Jill and no longer hears the sound of typing in his sleep; Robin, who will be glad to get the computer back; and Renee, who wants to see her name in print again. They still love the music, endure an obsessed writer, and furnish the melody for this message.

THE
COUNTRY MUSIC
MESSAGE:
Revisited

PART I

Commercial Country Music:

Where More People Came to Hear Fewer Folks

The Country Music Process:

How the Folks
Send the Message to the People

The film *Nashville* was released to a primed public in June of 1975. Robert Altman, according to some publicity, intended to direct an epic describing the country music scene with all its foibles and fables fully bared. Altman, whose knowledge of country music must have been obtained from Stan Kenton, allowed the actors to write and perform what they thought were country songs. The film's effect is questionable; however, it did demonstrate that writing a country song is much more difficult than it appears on the surface.[1] Altman had the finances and facilities to portray his misconceptions of country music and all that is required to create, write, and perform a country song, but he is not alone in his perceptions. Many people who encounter the music, whether in a three-minute episode or exposure over many years, seldom consider the complications faced by anyone who has a message and wishes to present it to the public.

"I Dreamed of a Hillbilly Heaven"

The stories of how some people go to Nashville, Bakersfield, or Austin and make it "big" provide incentive to those who want to be part of commercial country music. The hopeful hear how Dolly Parton caught a bus and rode to Nashville and fame, or how Loretta Lynn cut a record for a small independent recording label and then drove to Nashville to become a success. These stories are partly true, but most are vast oversimplifications. Parton and Lynn were each blessed with unique talent, drive, and intelligence, and each was noticed by the right people at the right time. Moving to the city is much easier to visualize than the work, anguish, and frustration these two endured before they "made it."

The determined ones with a message will almost always persevere and do what is necessary to survive while waiting for the big break. The few who make it provide fuel for those who hope to make it, and little is known of those who try and fail. It is generally assumed that those who fail do so for a variety of reasons: lack of talent, lack of perseverance, or the inability or unwillingness to adapt to the system for producing the country music product. The successes are far fewer than the failures, but this does not deter those with a message to tell—and for that we can be thankful.

The struggle to find "heaven" must be, for a large number of people, similar to the description painted by two songwriters who have made it. Bob McDill and Wayland Holyfield provide a picture of what it must be like for many who seek an opportunity in the country music system and find instead "Hillbilly Hell."

My friends and my mother they all like my songs
They said boy in Nashville is where you belong
And I agreed the music world prob'ly needed me
Well Music City here I am
But I don't think anybody gives a damn.

In the cold cold heart of Tennessee
There's ten thousand dreamers just like me
With a song and a guitar and a message to tell
Come to find heaven in hillbilly hell.

Another day of watchin' the Cadillacs go past
Writin' songs in my head while I'm pumping gas

Eatin' beans and wearin' jeans and sleepin' in my car
I hope the folks back home will understand
It's gonna take a little longer than I planned.

As the speaker in McDill and Holyfield's song discovered, one must have more than "a song and a guitar and a message to tell" to find a niche in commercial country music. It is a long and often tortuous route from the idea for a song to the accolades of a large and adoring public, and to make that trip one must somehow master an intricate and often confusing system.

"Mother Country Music"

The commercial music world can be compared with the human communication process. Larry Barker defines the communication process as "a system that involves an interrelated, interdependent group of elements working together as a whole to achieve a desired outcome or goal."[2] The similarity between the communication process and the music system is striking when one understands that the ultimate goal of the music industry is the same as in any other business: to earn money. The weakness in the analogy is the "working together" segment of the definition, for it certainly seems that cohesion is not a mark of the industry. The goal may be reached with or without cohesion, but without it friction is often created between the various parts of the system.

We can turn to the six elements of the communication process to see how the goals of the country music industry are pursued. These are: "(1) a source/encoder of communication, which sends (2) a message (3) through a channel(s) to (4) a receiver/decoder, who (5) responds via feedback with (6) possibilities of communication breakdowns in each stage of communication."[3] These elements, most often used to describe interpersonal communication (interaction between two individuals), are easily expanded to include mass communication, as mass communication is an extension of that at the interpersonal level. While mass communication maintains all six elements, it emphasizes the channel (how a message is distributed to the receiver). For example, when a book is written, there is the hope that it will be produced and distributed in large quantities, but it is normally read by one person at a time. A book is a form of mass communication, but the receiver does not read it in mass. The same situation occurs with a country song. Even if a record is a million-seller, it will be, in most cases, heard by one person at a time. It is easier to listen to a song as part of a group than to have others join you in reading a book, but country music does require some isolation. A person must listen, understand, and react to the words in order to receive the full impact of most country songs. This procedure necessitates some concentration and can be done best when one is alone or is able to isolate his or her thoughts in order to suppress competing messages. When this occurs, the act of listening becomes an interpersonal experience between the singer and the listener.

Even though the experience of listening to a country song must be a private or semi-private one, the system for channeling a message to an extended audience by way of a relatively inexpensive recording places it on the level of mass communication. When communicating at this level, it is necessary to add another element to a description of the process. Seldom does a source in a mass communication system have complete control over the form or content of a particular message. Usually there is a person, organization, or other influence that can make various modifications in that message. This individual, or group of individuals, is described as a "gatekeeper"—something through which the message must flow in order to get from the source to the receiver.[4]

We can follow the path through the commercial country music system that seems so simple to those "ten thousand dreamers" by using the elements of the communication process as a guideline.

The Source

A country song can be, and often is, a message from at least two sources. Most listeners recognize a song as sung by the artist performing it, although a number of fans do notice and follow the original source—the songwriter. A significant number of entertainers write and record their own country songs and reap several benefits from this dual role. Writing and recording one's own material certainly increases the value of any release (the writer earns a few cents per song for each record sold as well as certain performance fees) and in addition helps ensure that the song will be interpreted in the way it was originally intended. The number of performers who write and sing has declined since the 1960s, but it is still rather common to find them.[5] Willie Nelson, Merle Haggard, Loretta Lynn, Tom T. Hall, and Dolly Parton, to name a few, are known as both songwriters and singers of fine country songs.

The tradition of the songwriter/singer has made a great impact upon commercial country. This tradition was developed and honed to perfection by Ralph Peer, a pioneer in commercial country music. Peer came to the south in search of talent to record in the 1920s and was the first to record a number of "folks" including the original Carter Family and Jimmie Rodgers—the first "star" of commercial country music. Peer realized that the ownership of the publication rights of a song established by control of a copyright would be of great value.[6] The enterprising publisher was so confident of the economic advantages of possessing the rights to songs that in 1925 he offered to work for a recording company (the Victor Talking Machine Company) for no salary if they would allow him to hold the copyrights of the "new" songs he recorded. This practice of recording singers capable of creating their own material was so financially successful that it encouraged others to attempt the same procedure; as a result, singers who could compose their own songs became and still are a premium commodity in the country music industry.

Since the writer of country songs is often the performer of

those songs, and because the listener ordinarily identifies a particular song as a message from the interpreter, it is useful to distinguish between the "real" or original source and the "perceived" or readily identifiable source and then treat them as one—the songwriter/singer.

"Hank Williams, You Wrote My Life"

It is difficult to look at some systems and select the key part. A system, by its nature, is composed of interrelated and interdependent elements. There is no doubt, however, that without the songwriter there would be no country music system, for the song is the raw material of the industry. A few observers suggest that some entertainers could record short sections of the Yellow Pages and still sell records, and there is a bit of truth to this. When an artist is "hot," the buying public will purchase the latest single or album on faith alone. Unfortunately, some performers have discovered that even loyal followers (and the country fan can be exceptionally loyal) will begin to falter if the singer habitually records "turkeys." A hard core of fans will continue to support an artist no matter what the quality of the songs, but the size of that group may become so small that recording companies will discontinue making and distributing his or her records. As difficult as it must be for all those people with a "message to tell" to believe, the search for a hit song is a continuing and all-consuming effort for most professional performers.

"Make Mine Country"

The creators of country songs are sometimes criticized (directly or indirectly) for writing songs of little merit. These objections typically come from those outside the primary audience for the material and are normally aimed at the topics of the songs, although the subject matter for the successful country songwriter appears to vary little from that used by composers of other types of songs. For example, a study of the top ten country songs from 1965 to 1980 showed that seventy-three percent of them contained the predominant theme of love, a subject that permeates all music.[7]

The topics country songwriters are most likely to have in their repertoire will be discussed more fully when we examine the message element of this process, but for now it is important to consider the topics from the writer's point of view. Anyone who wishes to communicate must have something to tell the receiver, and if the source is concerned with having the receiver react to the message, then it must be of some interest. The average age of the country music fan is an important consideration when selecting a subject that will appeal to the audience. Mature men and women make up the largest group of listeners for this music; therefore, it does little good to attempt to interest them by describing the pleasures or problems encountered in junior high school or speaking of rebelling against parental authority. Understanding that they have an older audience and realizing that this type of listener will probably be interested in situations they normally encounter, it is natural for songwriters to describe adult relationships. Practically anything one would ever want to know about an adult interpersonal relationship can be found in country music.

A songwriter knows that it is possible to write about anything he or she wishes, but to be successful the song must attract and hold the attention of the audience. Willie Nelson, when asked if he wrote songs designed to appeal to a particular audience, stated that he wrote about his own experiences because that is what he knew, and it was usually impossible to know enough details about other people to write about their lives.[8] This statement highlights an important point to remember when writing for any audience. The selected parts of Nelson's personal experiences that he writes about are not very much different from those of his audience. People are often lonely, depressed, happy, satisfied, or displeased about their relationships just as Nelson has obviously been with some of his. Surely many individuals have had a "Bloody Mary Morning," have been distraught enough over an unhappy romance to feel "Crazy," or have been lonely enough after being deserted by a lover to lie on a bed and say "Hello Walls." The key to a songwriter's success is his or her ability to articulate these feelings in a message that appeals to an audience. While some people might lose the ability to form complete thoughts as a result of an intense emotional feeling, the songwriter appears to become more lucid. In fact, it can be extremely profitable for some writers to have stormy relationships. When this idea was suggested to Nelson, he just smiled and said, "Maybe that's why we have so many of them."

A perceptive and creative person does not have to live an experience in order to write about it, as Nelson demonstrated on his *Red Headed Stranger* album. The ability to place people, events, and emotional reactions in imaginary situations and make all these elements conform to a design is a key to the creative process. In other words, some songwriters live their experiences and write about them while others get their ideas by observing the experiences of others. Probably most do both, by designing situations out of isolated bits of life, either from their own past or that of someone else, and by creating surrounding events as they might have been.

An interesting item mentioned by Nelson in the discussion of songwriting involved the manipulation of a creative person in order to make him think along certain lines. As Nelson tells it, a friend of his was tricked into writing a specific type of song. A record producer needed a "cheating" song for a recording session and was unable to find one that satisfied him, so he started rumors that he and the songwriter's wife were having an affair. According to Nelson, the producer's tactics worked; the writer went off and wrote a fine cheating song.

"The Words Still Rhyme"

Once a writer has a subject that will interest the audience, the second major consideration is the language to be used to tell the message. The choice of language is determined in part by the form of the song. A songwriter who grows up listening to the music may instinctively place a message in the proper form. As Nelson said, "I just think that way." Loretta Lynn relates in her autobiography that she bought a copy of *Country Song Roundup,* the magazine that publishes country lyrics, and decided after reading the songs that she could write some of her own.[9] Tom T. Hall, in *The Songwriter's Handbook* advises anyone interested in country songwriting to first become familiar with this type of song; in addition, he decides the elements of poetry and song that all would-be songwriters should know.[10]

"Simple Little Words"

To say that the words used in most country songs are easy to understand is an overstatement. To say that those words are easy to write because they are easily understood is a misstatement. The songwriter must get the audience's attention, set the scene for a situation, describe that situation, and make certain the story is told, in a message that normally lasts less than three minutes. It is no small task, even with a five-piece band, to tell about a problem, a moment of joy, a bit of history, a lifestyle, or even curse a flat tire in three minutes, using words that require no amplification or qualification, are instantly recognizable, and mean what you intend them to mean. When you attempt this exercise, remember that you are trying to instill a desire in the listener to actively seek out this particular message to hear again. The author of a country song, therefore, must be a master of successful communication techniques.

The use of simple words in uncluttered patterns allows for the expression of much information or emotion in a few lines, but it also provokes some unfavorable comments. For instance, country songwriters have been accused of filling songs with clichés that fail to offer the power of eloquence found in most "sophisticated" lyrics.[11] The restrictions of time and form are two reasons for the use of simple words. The effectiveness of many country songs derives from the clever selection of words and phrases to produce emotional reactions in the listener.[12] An additional tool for expressing multiple meanings in lyrics is the ambiguity in our language—something that is both a blessing and a curse to most communicators. One way to depict this characteristic is to note one of many songs that deliberately use a key word in an uncommon manner. For instance, Roy Head recorded a regionally popular song called "The Most Wanted Woman in Town," and neither the title nor the lyrics referred to a fugitive from justice.

"Something Strange Got into Her Last Night"

Turning words and/or phrases into lines that draw attention because of the novel way in which they express an idea is described as a "play on words," a truly appropriate description of both the intent and outcome of the maneuver. The process itself is play, or at least is enjoyable, for both the source and receiver. One of the most interesting traits of both the songwriter and the listener in country music is a good sense of humor. The novelty or comedy song has long been a trademark of country music, and even though these songs are not as popular as they were in the past, the sense of having a good time is still found in much of the music. Perhaps the secure feeling the source and receiver have about their music enables both to relax and enjoy it. No music can be more serious than country, but none can be as irreverent.

Ordinarily, words and phrases containing double meanings and farfetched metaphors appear in the treatment of sexual activities. Some people have expressed displeasure at the explicit language found in country music, but the language is not as explicit as the meaning, and that meaning is often derived from stylistic manipulations of the language rather than the use of graphic words. Just as the type of humor found in country songs is often an inside joke between the source and certain receivers (you need to know something about the lack of indoor plumbing to fully appreciate "Ode to the Little Brown Shack Out Back"), the allusions to sexual activities require a prior knowledge and understanding of the subject.

Perhaps the reluctance of the gatekeepers to allow the transmission of certain language hinders the songwriters' use of it; certainly popular country music is less "vulgar" than some of the songs recorded in the 1930s or 1940s.[13] There was a resurgence of more explicit language in songs in the early 1970s and again in the early 1980s, but the number of songs in which this occurred was relatively small.

"Three-Chord Country Song"

An essential ingredient of a country song is the melody that accompanies the lyrics. Most observers agree that the lyrics overshadow the melody and the interpretation of the melody in a country song. The major focus of the message in some genres of music is the melody and instrumentation, and the lyrics are relegated to secondary status. Country music, on the other hand, has long been characterized by its lyrics and a melody designed to transport and complement the lyrics, not to clutter or hinder those messages. This does not mean that the accompaniment is an insignificant part of the message, for without the proper musical accompaniment the lyrics would have little opportunity to succeed. In fact, some country songs are recognized for their distinctive musical arrangement. Johnny Cash's "I Walk the Line" gains much from the unique music that is an integral part of the message.

The musical sound serves functions other than the transporting of the lyrics. It gets the attention of the audience and announces the intent of the lyrics by setting the tone or mood of the material under normal conditions. A soft, simple melody prepares a listener for a ballad or love song; an up-tempo sound alerts the listener to a happy, lively message. In the early 1980s a trend seemed to develop that ran counter to the usual pattern of allowing the accompanying sound to set a mood. For instance, some lyrics filled with sadness were transported by upbeat instrumentation. A few of these songs were successful, but by the mid-eighties the tendency was more prevalent on album cuts than on successful singles. Most of us are acutely aware of a melody that fails to complement the lyrics, but when it does what it is supposed to do, the melody combines with the lyrics to become a complete message.

Some of the conflict in country music has developed over the melodies, instrumentation, and background singers used in recording the songs. Since much of the change, or the desire to change, the overall sound of country music has been because of, or in spite of, those who control the recording of country music, the conflicts will be discussed more fully when we look at those channels for sending the country message.

"Ghost-Written Love Letters"

The listener must perceive the singer as the prime source of the message to ensure that the act of listening to a country song is an interpersonal experience. Many people know that some love letters, a great number of speeches, and more than a few books and songs are written by someone other than the apparent author, but at the moment of listening or reading, the one who presents the message is considered the source. In fact, if a source is questionable during the reception of the message, it causes confusion and will probably lead to a breakdown in communication. The first priority of a country singer, therefore, is to assure the listener that he or she is an acceptable source.

A singer must establish a certain credibility to accomplish this objective, and one important technique is to present what is (or appears to be) his or her own personal statements in the song. In other words, these statements are offered with no indication that the singer lacks faith in the listener. This act suggests that the singer wishes to foster a close relationship with the listener.

Mark Knapp reports that two people who are close friends share personal, self-disclosing information during the early stages of their relationship, and many successful country songs fit nicely into this framework.[14] While outside observers might think that some of the comments in country songs are rather maudlin, the singer and the listener, by developing a close bond, know what is allowed in their personal communication. When a country singer describes an intense emotional episode, there is an intuitive feeling that the disclosure will be accepted with no denigration of the message's source.

The audience must accept the source's attitudes and treatment of the topic in the song if the singer is to be credible. Credibility can only be given by the audience and is most often bestowed on the singer who has, or appears to have, a sincere approach to the lyrics. Hank Williams stated that sincerity is the key element for any country singer.[15] What Williams left unstated is that the audience has to recognize and approve such sincerity. John Ciardi and Miller Williams label this type of emphatic response a "sympathetic contract" when describing how a reader forms a bond with the poet by accepting the writer's attitudes and tone toward a subject.[16] They explain, for instance, that a poet may view love as a major consequence and adopt a tone of self-pity toward it; for the poem to succeed, the reader must agree with this approach. This contract must also exist between a country singer and the listener, but for our purposes we might combine the ideas of these three poets and call it a "sincerity contract."

Perhaps the contract between the listener and the singer is one reason for some of the stereotypes of country singers. Some successful singers are known for possessing less than fine voices. A singer of country music does not use his or her voice as an instrument to be judged separately from the song; a country singer uses the voice to project a feeling toward the material. The vocal characteristics might be more accurately compared to those suitable for interpersonal relationships than to the grand style found in some types of music. What is required to sing a country song is the ability to communicate a thought or feeling without dis-

17

tracting the listener from the message by calling undue attention either to artificial vocal techniques or to the inability to carry a tune.

"(How Can I Write on Paper) What I Feel in My Heart"

Some singers put such an imprint on a song that it has little chance of becoming a hit for anyone else. An example is George Jones's version of "He Stopped Loving Her Today," a song that won the award for Best Song in both 1980 and 1981 from the Country Music Association (CMA). Jones wears a mantle that is not passed around lightly—he is a singer's singer. The sincerity that marks his version of this song is an excellent example of the quality a singer contributes. Reading the lyrics, one might be unimpressed with the image of a heartsick man who has been pining over an absent lover for years. The man in the song has stopped loving the woman only because he is dead, and the smile on the face of his corpse is one of the few he has displayed in the last twenty years. Such a story might not be new to country music, but George Jones makes it very special. It is always hoped that a singer will take a song and mold it into an individual expression filled with statements that are not embarrassing to the singer and cause no discomfort to the listener. Jones can take material loaded with such pathos and express it in a way that an audience feels is appropriate and can relate to in a positive manner.

This song also serves to demonstrate another quality that a country singer should have—the ability to step outside a situation and describe it convincingly. Jones is telling a story about someone else and, even though he makes it personal by wondering if the woman will come to the funeral, he is, for the most part, serving only as the narrator. Much country music is written in this style. The art of good storytelling is one that a country singer must master.[17]

18

As noted earlier, the most obvious advantage of being a song-writer/singer is the additional income earned from such a dual role; however, a song's intended meaning is also important to some songwriters. A singer is able to exercise some control over the lyrics on a record, but modern technology allows for the mixing and remixing of a tape and seems to encourage the producer, engineer, or anyone else with access to a multitrack recording console to mold the overall sound of a song. A songwriter has less control over the final product than does a singer, as demonstrated in those instances where a singer changes the intent of a song. Tom T. Hall experienced this situation when Jeannie C. Riley changed the word "that" to "my" during the recording of "Harper Valley PTA." As a result of this alteration, Hall was reluctant to record or sing it in concert because Riley had made it a woman's song.[18]

Words, lines, and entire verses are sometimes altered or deleted to enable a singer to feel more comfortable with a song. But there are subtle changes that can be even more significant and may modify the song's original meaning.[19] Willie Nelson wrote "It's Not Supposed to Be That Way" as a poignant statement about a daughter growing up in his absence. Waylon Jennings's interpretation of the lyrics encourages the listener to visualize a woman about to visit her lover, rather that a girl growing up without the guidance and support of a father. When Nelson was asked about the variance between the two versions, he said, "I don't know what Waylon was thinking about when he recorded the song, but I know I wrote it about my daughter." A writer can never control what a singer is thinking about when approaching a set of lyrics, and no singer can know the exact meaning intended by a songwriter. What we do know is that neither matter without the approval and acceptance of the country music audience.

The Message

In Part II we will examine what the "folks" have to say in many of those songs the audience has accepted and approved of from 1960 (when country music began its recovery from the damage caused in the late 1950s when Elvis Presley was changing the direction of all commercial music) to 1987, when country had grown to be one of the most widely sold types of music in the United States. The top fifty records on *Billboard* magazine's year-end charts are used to select the most popular songs for each of those years. Approximately 1,400 songs will be surveyed. (Some songs appear more than once and there are ties when the people who compile the lists cannot, or will not, decide which side of a single is the more popular.) It would be tedious to describe all of these songs, so only the top twenty-five for each year are used to determine general characteristics and provide most of the examples. Some songs from the second half of each list as well as some that appear in the top ten on weekly charts are used for examples as well as supplementary data.

Several observers have written about country lyrics, but few have dealt exclusively with the most popular songs.[20] Although these writers do make some perceptive and interesting comments about certain segments of the music, we will concentrate here on the messages contained in popular country songs. These most widely accepted songs have made it through an intricate and difficult process and contain not only the messages "some had to tell" but, more importantly, the messages that a large number of people wanted to hear. Whether these popular songs are good or bad, or perhaps not country as some people contend, is not an issue. It is the judgment of the listeners that make them important.

The method used to analyze the songs is a form of content analysis.[21] The songs are arranged in categories according to their predominant themes. (These broad categories are named in the titles of chapters 2 through 5.) After the songs are grouped by theme, the messages are examined. First, the situations articulated in these three-minute stories are identified to see if there are any common characteristics; second, the people involved in those situations are studied to discover if the stereotypical roles and behaviors often attributed to characters in the songs are found in these particular lyrics; third, the attitudes expressed toward the situations (scenes), the people in those situations (actors), and the behaviors found in them (actions) are determined. Finally, the special language used to describe the situations, people, and behaviors is noted.

The Channel(s)

It is impossible to fully describe here the various channels disseminating the country message. This section will be a brief description of how these channels act upon the message and not a history of their role in country music.[22] Four primary channels act and interact to accomplish the aim of the country music system. The channel that has received the most attention is the recording industry. Radio, the second channel, has received some attention and deserves more. The third channel, and the one that has received the least attention, is the jukebox industry. The fourth channel, of greatest financial importance to the performer, is the personal appearance. Two additional channels that are gaining in significance are the films and television programs that utilize country music.

"Old Records"

The recording industry began when Thomas Edison patented the first recording equipment in the United States, but it was the recording of Fiddlin' John Carson in June of 1923 that is generally recognized as the bellwether of commercial country music. Even if some recording company executives failed to grasp the esthetic merit of the rural music, they did not fail to note that the records were selling.

Although the early records were distributed primarily in the South, they sold rather well and encouraged the companies to continue making them. The first million-selling country music recording was "The Prisoner's Song," recorded in 1924 by Vernon Dalhart. This light opera singer, whose real name was Marion T. Slaughter, took the name of two towns from his home state of Texas as a pseudonym to record "folk" music. Dalhart might have been the "father of country music" if he had not been reluctant to acknowledge his offspring. He is reported to have recorded under approximately 180 different names in his career. Late in life he was reduced to giving singing lessons to earn a living, but he made no mention of his tenure as one of the all-time great folk singers when advertising for prospective students.[23]

One phenomenon noticed by the recording companies was the healthy sales of early country records during difficult economic times. Good taste is often modified by financial reality, and so it was by the executives in the recording industry. Sales for all types of music were reported to be over $100 million in 1921, and by 1933 they had dropped to less than $6 million because of the Depression.[24] During the Depression, country records held their markets better than most other music, and it was a less than vibrant economy in 1979 when country records became the second most popular genre of music sold.[25] The stable market for country records and the low cost of producing them (compared to other types of music) make it an important part of the business.[26]

"The Tennessee Waltz"

The search to widen the market for country music has created some of the greatest tension in the industry.[27] The market for pop and rock music is larger than that for country, and if a company can produce a product that appeals to all these markets the amount of return will obviously be significantly greater. This has produced the "crossover," a recording that is usually called country, but makes (or hopes to make) an inroad into the larger market. Such efforts are condemned by the "traditional" entertainers and fans of those performers and their music, and this reaction is understandable.

There is another way to view the crossover phenomenon, although it will not satisfy the people who are harmed or offended by the development. If a person chooses to listen to country music because of crossover recordings, there is the possibility that the same person will be led to traditional country. Polydor is selling Hank Williams's recordings and probably a number of new fans are drawn to them after being exposed to crossover artists. The ebb and flow of the industry can be seen in the early 1980s as tending toward the smooth crossover recording, but by the mid-eighties the traditional music was again having an impact.[28]

Changes in the music have always occurred, with or without the consent of the recording companies. The development of bluegrass music is an example of one such change. Country music has split as often as some rural churches have. Just as a new church opens down the road because the members feel the true message is not being delivered by the original church, country performers often make such a decision about the path of their music. Many new churches, as well as country music practitioners, quickly trace their roots back to the beginning of time, rather than back to the time of the split. Most bluegrass performers and fans see little relationship between their music and amplified commercial country music, and they believe they are the only ones still carrying the true country message.

A significant change in country music was brought about by the recording companies because of increased technology and an exceptionally talented and cohesive group of pickers who were brought together in the Nashville studios. Chet Atkins is given the credit for combining and using these properties to create the "Nashville Sound." Atkins assembled these pickers when he was producing records for RCA, and together they created a smooth, jazzy, and mellow sound. The problem was that other people tended to imitate Atkins's success and therefore created a product that lost much of its individuality. Whether it is called "modern," "Nashville," or "pop-country," it moved country from a narrowly focused path to what is mistakenly called the "mainstream." In this case, mainstream is not simply middle of the road; it is the road. It is a product intended for all buyers, not just a dedicated and relatively small audience.

The best and most distinctive sound is produced by allowing a singer to use his or her "road" band rather than "session" pickers, a practice that was once an important part of recorded country music. When studio musicians are employed to cut a record, it is possible to do it quickly and inexpensively, but the songs often lack originality. The road band comes into a studio and provides the "feel" the singer is accustomed to and encourages the creation of a special sound. The so-called "Outlaws," who gained so much attention in the mid-1970s, were not rebelling against the music; they were rebelling against the lack of control they had over the way the music was recorded.[29] The right to control the final product allows the performer to make the music on a recording similar to that heard during a live concert.

"Two Minutes Thirty Seconds"

Some of the important gatekeeping functions of the recording companies relate to the length and content of the messages. Most country songs are approximately three minutes in length, though some are longer. Marty Robbins's "El Paso" was four minutes and thirty-seven seconds long, but this was and still is unusual. The three-minute length was originally determined by the amount of material that could be placed on a single recording, and it still survives even though it is possible to include much more on a long-play record or compact disc. Presently, the length of a song seems to be dictated by a desire to have it played on AM radio and jukeboxes. Songs recorded in the late 1970s started to creep up on the four-minute period, but the tendency is still to keep them relatively short.

Another gatekeeping function is the insistence that the material be suitable for air play. The recording companies know that, for most recordings to be successful, they must receive extensive air play and, traditionally, the program or music directors at radio stations will not allow a song to be played if it contains a topic or language that might be offensive to their audience. Loretta Lynn encountered much difficulty with her recording of "The Pill" because of negative reactions from some radio stations.[30] The song was banned by several stations, but it achieved success because Lynn had the power to overcome these objections. If a singer with less fan support than Lynn had attempted to record such a song, it might never have made it to the stations much less found its way to the listening public. An example of another singer facing what she considered to be a similar problem occurred in 1982. A song written and recorded by K. T. Oslin entitled "Younger Men" was released and received little or no air play. Oslin felt that the lack of play was due to the fact that the lyrics described the inability of older men to perform sexually. Noting that this was no problem for a young woman, it became one as she matured and men her age displayed a lack of interest in or an inability to satisfy her needs. The solution described in the song (a younger man) was one that Oslin could accept, but programmers and disc jockeys would not present to their audiences. Oslin was unable to overcome the restrictions imposed by the gatekeepers and the song was heard by very few until it was included on an album in 1987.[31]

Although it may be difficult to believe, it is not the recordings that earn the greatest income for most professional country performers. The recordings are used to attract an audience to concerts. Some naive artists think that once they cut a record they can sit back and reap the benefits, but it will only take a short time for them to discover that this is untrue. Even if the record sells fairly well, there is no guarantee that the performer will earn much from the sale; therefore, it is incumbent upon the artist to work at promoting the record, but most of all, to work on the road to gain the maximum benefit from any recording venture.[32]

It is not within the scope of this book to discuss all the intricate interworkings of the people and agencies that earn a living from the country music product. Kenny Rogers and Len Epand have written an excellent book covering this aspect of the music business.[33]

"Every Time I Turn the Radio On"

Country music has always been a part of commercial radio, but the role has been ever changing.[34] The most constant factor continues to be the stations' use of live and then recorded music to attract customers for the advertisers, and the entertainers' discovery of radio as an excellent medium for promoting their music. The changes in radio that had the greatest impact upon the country music message were the increase in the number of stations programming the music, the relationship between the recording companies and radio stations, and the approach the stations take toward programming the music.

"Country Music Time"

When radio began twisting on the spit of the TV tuner, the stations moved away from block programming toward the concept of programming for a specific audience. This action was taken to convince advertisers interested in reaching a target audience that radio stations would best serve their needs. Before 1960 most stations playing country were small, low-powered operations, usually located in rural areas and not too troubled by television.[35] On the other hand, those radio stations located in metropolitan areas felt the heat and needed relief. In 1961, according to the CMA, only eighty-one stations in the United States and two in Canada programmed country full-time; but in 1981 there were 1,785 stations programming it exclusively. The number was 2,212 in late 1987. It would seem, then, that with such a tremendous increase in outlets, the country message would flow much more freely. This was not the case.

Just as the recording companies act as gatekeepers to restrict the flow of some country messages to the audience, so do the radio stations. The primary method the recording companies use to promote their latest releases is to send singles (and some albums) to radio stations for possible inclusion on playlists. A radio playlist is composed of those records the disc jockey is allowed to play on the air and is usually compiled by a person designated as the music or program director. The normal procedure for promoting a record can only be highlighted here, but it follows a general pattern.[36] First, a performer records enough songs to fill an album. Normally, the second step is to select a song (sometimes more than one) that the recording company feels has the best chance to be a hit and forward it to the stations as a promotional single. The first act of gatekeeping by radio takes place when the single reaches the station. Even though some companies have reduced the number of records they send to stations, a station in a medium-sized market will receive a large quantity each week. A recording company's problem boils down to a simple question that is easy to ask but difficult to answer: How can a particular song get the attention of the persons who make the decision to play a record on the air?

"D. J. for a Day"

The number of outlets has increased, but this did not increase the width of the gate. The stations located in smaller markets are still the ones that are likely to program a wider variety of country music, and the stations in the larger areas are apt to feature today's hits.[37] The major reason for what appears to be the bilevel of country music offerings on radio can be traced to the impact of the playlist, since it is most rigidly adhered to by the larger, metropolitan stations. The playlist acts as a funnel, and it seems to become shorter as the number of large country stations increases.[38]

The second problem arises in how the playlist is compiled, a factor that also relates to the quantum jump in the number of country stations. Richard Peterson has identified this problem in a perceptive article on contemporary country music, where he points out that with the great switch to the country format there developed a shortage of qualified country programmers and an excess of pop, rock, and middle-of-the-road programmers out of work because of the number of stations rushing to country.[39] The "staff gap" was filled by the unemployed programmers and on-air personalities assuming positions on the new stations. This staffing decision created several problems that affect the presentation of country music: (1) a staff with little or no background in the music turned to another page in the trade magazines and designed a playlist from the records that were on the country chart at the time of the switch; (2) since members of the staff were more likely to recognize those artists on the charts at the time of the switch, few other performers are able to gain their attention; (3) the personalities and roles developed in a staff that had been programming other formats were retained by the people who suddenly (and probably unhappily) were working with country music; (4) these newcomers were attuned to the country singers who had previously appeared on rock or pop charts. It might be added that people are apt to gravitate toward the country music that bears a closer resemblance to the music they once played.

"Tiny Blue Transistor Radio"

The stations that make up the radio community are constantly searching for an expanded audience by manipulating playlists and changing formats. Undoubtedly, the rush to embrace a country format will not solve the inherent problems that cause a station to desert an unsuccessful format, and when they fail with country, they will proclaim that "the music is dead."

A worry for some observers is the possibility that a message distributed to a mass audience will tend to lose its unique qualities in order to gain wide acceptance. In 1975, Richard Peterson and Paul DiMaggio reported that country music had not suffered this fate.[40] Since that time there has been a further development of a type of radio programming that might encourage the homogenization of country music, as the movement toward packaging country to be distributed over normal lines, or by satellite, would seem to encourage a national approach and thereby diminish the regional or local input into the music. With the increase in the number of automated stations and dependency upon a few national program sources, it is certain that the "funnel" will become even more constricted and possibly will come to affect the country music message.

Another development that could alter the message is the increase in the number of FM stations (a 29 percent increase between 1980 and 1981) that are programming country music.[41] Some of these have deserted the approach utilized on many AM stations and play the music with little interruption, several songs with the same theme, or several cuts from the same album, and they are not so concerned with the length of the selections. This approach is more like the way the music is heard in the home or wherever the listener controls the selection process. It is attractive to many listeners, for radio is a medium most often heard alone. Much of radio listening is done in the automobile, or radio is used as background while a person performs some other activity.[42] Country music radio certainly serves the first half of this role, but rarely is the music treated as background unless it is the type recorded by Henry Mancini. (It would take some totally oblivious and dedicated people to make love with country music in the background for undoubtedly one, or both, of the activities will suffer from a lack of attention.)

Whatever the impact of the changes that have been made or are likely to be made in the future, country radio has not significantly altered the country music message. As Willie Nelson stated, there is little difference between his music and that of Roy Acuff— only the beat is different. So it is with country radio. There may

29

be more stations, tighter gatekeeping, various means of presentation, or music with a different beat in different locales, but the message has remained fairly stable.[43]

"There's a Song on the Jukebox"

The 45-rpm record is used by most recording companies as a promotional device to gain attention for the more lucrative albums; however, singles have long maintained a strong position in country sales, and with the steady increase in album prices the public seems to think that the 45 is a better value than the LP. They may be correct, for it has been a practice in the industry to use the single as a loss leader. Some observers, especially those interested in rock music, believe the seven-inch single will soon go the way of the 78.[44] Although the newer configurations (CDs, cassette singles, and DATs) and the lack of space provided by record retailers for the vinyl singles are all threats, the death notice of the 45 as a means of delivering country music may be premature. Whatever its fate, the single is expected to continue to be an important format to the group who buys the most singles—the jukebox industry.[45]

"Anywhere There's a Jukebox"

Jukeboxes utilize a huge number of singles and those filled with country records seem to be increasing as fast as the number of radio stations. It was estimated that approximately 500,000 jukeboxes were operating in 1980, but the number is extremely difficult to document.[46] The recording industry does know their value, however, for jukeboxes use many of the singles and act as a means of advertising its products, and unlike most radio stations this outlet purchases the records.[47]

The jukebox industry acts on the country message in a different manner from the way radio does, but it serves as a gatekeeper in a similar manner. There is a playlist for a jukebox which (on most machines) is made of eighty to two hundred records (160–400 songs) and is prominently displayed on the front. It is a longer playlist than those of most radio stations and it usually contains more "oldies." Records commonly remain on a jukebox for years, while radio stations may play only a few "golden oldies." The recording companies lose part of the space where they could feature new releases, because a jukebox operator will leave a number of favorites on a machine. An operator may add only four to six new records at each service period, and this creates a tight selection process and provides another gatekeeper to the country music message.

"That's What Makes the Jukeboxes Play"

The jukebox is controlled by at least three gatekeepers. The first is the operator, who places the selection on the box and decides where the records will appear in the listings on the machine. The latter decision is important, for the first number is the one that receives the most attention, either because people will drop money into the machine and punch in the first numbers, or because the title will be the first one read by a potential customer. The second gatekeeper is the owner/manager of the place where the machine is located, who may or may not agree with the choices made by the operator. The primary concern for the operator is the income generated by the machine, and while the person at the box's location may be interested in the money, he or she must hear the music and therefore may request or demand that certain records be included or excluded from a machine. The patron with the coin acts as the third gatekeeper. It is the patron and the on-location gatekeeper who usually insist on keeping a record on the playlist. If one person runs the place for any period of time and if the patronage stays fairly constant, their favorites tend to consume more and more space on the jukebox, thereby restricting the number of slots open for the operator to add new material. When an operator makes a change, it is usually by a vote of the listeners. Each box is equipped with a counter (called a popularity meter) that indicates how many times a record has been played since the last service call. The meter will only indicate which record has been played, not which side, but this is all the information most operators need.

"Hello I'm a Jukebox"

The country music on a jukebox will vary from that played on radio in ways other that the number and tenure of the records in the rotation. Most records playing on jukeboxes are generally the same as those heard on radio (they both tend to select and create the popular choices), but some may be different. Jukeboxes located in bars and honky-tonks will usually contain loud, driving music that emphasizes heightened emotional feelings. For instance, songs that celebrate the lifestyle of the patrons ("Nightlife," "Swinging Doors," "From Barrooms to Bedrooms"), and those that contain "jukebox" in the title ("The Jukebox Argument"), drinking in the lyrics ("Here I Am Drunk Again"), defiant personal statements ("Hell Yes, I Cheated," "The Lord Knows I'm Drinkin'," "Mind Your Own Business"), or a dose of self-pity ("She Still Comes Around [to Love What's Left of Me]") stay a long time on many jukeboxes. Since the listener gives more immediate feedback in this part of the system, it takes only a short time before a jukebox will tell much about an establishment's steady customers and workers.

The country singer uses, or hopes to use, the jukebox in the same manner as radio to advertise personal appearances, and it is common for many patrons of a place where a particular singer is popular on a jukebox to show up as a group for his or her concert. These machines may be the best hope for the traditional performers whose records are still being played on them, but who are effectively closed off from modern radio playlists. The crossover is having an impact on the boxes, as is demonstrated when the Oak Ridge Boys' version of "Elvira" was selected as the most popular song for all types of music played on jukeboxes in 1981.[48] The message disseminated through the jukeboxes is more traditional and more tightly controlled by the real audience than what is heard on radio, but it does serve—with the qualifications noted above—the purposes of both the performer and the recording companies.

"On the Road Again"

The satisfaction of having a best-selling record playing on the radio and jukeboxes is surely great, but few can deny the importance of the personal appearance. No one can suggest that all those concerts performed in school houses, dance halls, fairgrounds, rodeo arenas, college fieldhouses, and honky-tonks (some with chicken-wire barriers between the bandstand and the audience to keep bottles and other debris away from the performers) are satisfying. However, by playing these and other places, professional performers generate their steadiest income. Most live audiences for country music concerts are relatively small in comparison to those for rock concerts, and the country troupers attempt to compensate for this by the large number of dates they schedule. The desire to attract a large audience and to be booked on more lucrative tours is one of the prime reasons why entertainers work so hard at making and promoting records. The performers and the recording companies pull together at this point when the release of a recording and the start of a tour coincide (which they usually do) because it benefits both parties.

"Big in Vegas"

The increased commercialization of country music altered the overall message by developing certain expectations in the audience. Before the recording industry encouraged the star system, a country music show might consist of the songs the performers liked or wished to sing, but recordings program the audience to expect performers to sing their hits. The listeners will allow some leeway on the "live playlist," but they do expect the performers to follow a rather definite agenda. Thus, the performers' use of recordings, radio, and jukeboxes to get a message to the people serves as a gatekeeper for live performances by restricting them to certain songs. Many concerts turn out to be little more than another live album: *The Best of X*. This causes a number of concerts to be rather dull for the singer, and the band gets bored with songs they have played many times and for which they can no longer generate much enthusiasm.

The second problem with live concerts is the practice of recording singers with session musicians and back-up singers, which creates a sound that can be manufactured in the studio but cannot be economically reproduced on the road. A few performers on tour use "pick-up" bands that rarely sound like the session pickers. The road bands used by other performers may sound better, but if they are not the ones used at the recording sessions, they will not sound the same.

The singer also has difficulty matching the sound he or she laid down on the master tape in the studio. Ironically, one of the more noticeable differences between the recorded message and the live one is the inability of the singer to establish the sincerity contract during the live performance. The listener hears a recorded version of a song under certain conditions that inspire a personal and unique relationship with the material. When the listener attends a concert and hears a singer do a song differently, either because he or she is tired of singing it, tired of traveling, tired of rodeo grounds, or has partaken of some substance that dilutes the concentration needed to sing with the sincerity and meaning that was originally generated in the studio, the listener is disappointed. It is nearly impossible to transfer the effort expended in making a record to the live performance. If there is a different group of pickers, no knowledgeable producer, or sound people who are unresponsive to the nuances in the music, there is little possibility that the song will be all the listeners have come to expect. (The person who controls the sound at many live concerts does much to destroy the listeners' perception of a song. They often spend a great amount of time adjusting the audio controls and then just slide them up to "pain" and let the power of the system determine the sound level.)

"My Heart Has a Mind of Its Own"

All these difficulties do not mean that the country audience is often disappointed at concerts, because in most cases they are not. Many listeners have developed their own expectations of the message, and no matter what the performer does, those views will remain, but in order to be increasingly successful the performers must attempt to reinforce—not destroy—those perceptions. Country singers (with a few exceptions) are known for treating their audience with respect and warmth by singing *to* them, not *at* them, and by spending as much time as possible talking to them after a performance. These professional characteristics together with the songs build a bond between the singer and the audience.

So, although the close personal relationship the audience *believes* it has with the source of a country message is usually developed from listening to recorded versions of songs, and even though some performers fail to live up to an audience's expectations, the special encounter at a live concert helps to solidify the interpersonal nature of the country music message.

"Coal Miner's Daughter"

Channeling the country music message through films and television is a rather recent development and has less impact on that message than the channels discussed above. One early film demonstrates how the message is sometimes altered. *Your Cheating Heart,* released in 1964, was a highly idealized description of the life of Hank Williams, and just as the singer's life was glossed

35

over, so was the music. Williams's renditions of his songs were considered too harsh ("hillbilly") for the mass audience, so Hank Williams, Jr., in his teens at the time, recorded them for the soundtrack.

A great step forward was made when a film about Loretta Lynn's life and music was released in 1980. Although Loretta did not sing her songs in *Coal Miner's Daughter,* Sissy Spacek did well in emulating Lynn's style and sound. The quality of the acting and of the story, as well as the music, did much for country music by exposing to it a great number of people who probably were not avid listeners before the movie received so much well-deserved publicity. *Urban Cowboy* carried the audience and the music a quicker step at about the same time. (The effects of this movie will be discussed in chapter 6.) Other films such as *Tender Mercies* and *Sweet Dreams* had less impact overall, but they did provide additional revenue and exposure for the performers and the owners of the songs used on the soundtracks. There is little difference between the messages distributed through these channels and those found in the recordings, and for good reason—they are generally using the same recordings.

A number of the television shows featuring country music follow the same procedure as the films by utilizing the recorded songs. The syndicated country shows serve as a platform for the entertainers, just as radio does; but unlike radio listeners, who can tune in a number of stations to hear the music, the audience for most country television shows must be more dedicated. They can be compared to the audience for early radio, when people had only a few hours a day when they could hear the music. The people who make up this modern audience have to search through the schedule and make an extra effort to view those programs which are usually presented on Saturday afternoons or early in the morning during the week. The message on many of these shows is also similar to radio, for they, like the films, often play a tape of the music while the performer mouths the words as if he or she were actually singing the song (this is called "lip-syncing"). Some more recent developments in the use of television allow the audience greater latitude in when and what they can watch.

The Nashville Network (TNN), for instance, has had a significant impact upon the industry. It was the most popular pay cable offering in 1986 and 1987, and is continuing to gain in subscribers.[49] Although the programming varies from concerts to another popular southern sport, auto racing, the music is given an important platform for display. The Country Music Television (CMT) network is another recent system (1983) and is a twenty-four hour a day outlet for videos. Whether the videos are a help or hindrance to the country scene is still open to debate; however, the videos surely provide another means to attract the younger audience that is the prime objective of the recording companies.

"The Lawrence Welk-Hee Haw Counter Revolution Polka"

"The Johnny Cash Show" and "The Glen Campbell Goodtime Hour" in 1969 ("Hee Haw" also began on CBS in the same year) served to spread the word, and just as "Barbara Mandrell and The Mandrell Sisters" found success in the early 1980s and the "Dolly" show struggled in the 1987–88 season, there is the increasing possibility that country will move on to larger audiences through this medium. The search for material to be transmitted by various cable television groups has stirred up interest in this music. The willingness of public television to broadcast "Austin City Limits," as well as a few Grand Ole Opry presentations and video clips, also signals a broader interest in the music.

The Receiver(s)

The fourth element in the country music process is the receiver or audience. Specific characteristics of the audience will be discussed in chapter 6, but a look at some general aspects of people who choose to be receivers of the country music message is appropriate here.

The dedication of some long-term listeners must be noted. Fans of country music have been unfairly labeled as uncultured, unintelligent, unsophisticated, uneducated, and unwashed. Those people who like the music but will not admit it—or decline to call attention to their preference—can be called "closet-country fans." The often-told story of the person who rolls up the window before stopping at a red light so no one will know he or she is listening to country music is more nearly accurate than the characterizations listed above. The closet country group is becoming more assertive, and those who do not care what others think of their musical tastes are enjoying the music and themselves as always. The negative perceptions of the music and the belittling of those who listen appear to be less noticeable as the music attracts larger audiences. Still, sterotyped descriptions, seemingly supported by superficial information, can be formed easily by an outsider.

One method of obtaining more accurate information about the country audience is to examine the messages that the members of that audience choose to hear. There is evidence for the theory that people select the messages that support their attitudes, beliefs, and behaviors and shun those that challenge or conflict with them.[50] Certainly, a person might be attracted to a song for reasons other than the verbal content, but—as previously noted—the lyrics are the key element in country music.[51] This theory provides additional support to Bill C. Malone's observation, made in the first edition of his landmark work on country music, that the music "has been consistently reflective and representative of the society which nourished it and of the changes in that society."[52] It is likely that the subgenres in the music, such as rockabilly and pop-country, have emerged because of changes in the audience, for as John Grissin said, "it is this kind of responsiveness to the changing needs and tastes of a people that gives Country music (as a generic term) its vitality."[53]

The messages may tell us little about the physical characteristics of the audience, but they should provide some indication of the topics acceptable to them. Within those approved subjects we should be able to identify aspects such as the audience's views of roles, behaviors, attitudes, and the language used to describe them.

Too many decisions about the music and the audience are made after examining a small number of songs and inferring that they are representative of all the music. It is just as unfair to examine only the songs one likes or dislikes, and to project from them to the remainder of the music. We will look at the songs the audience has made the most popular by buying records, requesting them on radio, and playing them on jukeboxes to determine the messages that more people are choosing to attend. The popularity of a song is determined by the fifth element in the country music process—feedback.

Feedback

Feedback takes place at all junctures of the country music process. A songwriter may rely on friends, spouse, co-workers, publisher, or a singer for opinions about an idea or song. A singer may decide to record a song and have the record producer or even a member of the band suggest some changes. The recording company provides feedback to the singer by deciding to release a single and then to promote it and the album. Radio stations supply feedback to the recording companies by choosing or refusing to program the release. Negative feedback at this stage will sometimes cause the company to store the album rather than ship it. If the jukebox operators buy the single, they inform the company by their subsequent actions of whether the recording has the power to stay on the machine for any length of time. When and if the album is released to the record outlets, the public will give their feedback by purchasing or not purchasing the recording.

The feedback that is supposed to reflect the audience's acceptance of a song comes from the charts found in trade publications such as *Billboard* and *Cashbox*. The hazard inherent in relying on a number of people to report radio play, record sales, and jukebox play for an individual recording is that the charts will contain incorrect or distorted information. Errors creep in and some deception takes place when data are collected for these popularity scales. A person reporting what is popular on a certain radio station may praise a friend's record and ignore one by a person he or she dislikes. The number of records sold on the retail level is often as misleading as the numbers issued by the companies. Jukebox operators may be harried or careless and may make up numbers for their reports. No doubt some of these problems occur, but the trade charts *are* the major feedback affecting the source and the channels in the country music process.

"Pick of the Week"

The country music industry relies heavily on the charts carried in *Billboard*,[54] although performers and companies will rely mostly on the chart giving them the highest ranking at any particular moment. Country recordings have been tabulated in *Billboard* since 1944, when the list was called "Most Played Juke Box Folk Records." In 1948 the chart was renamed "Best Selling Retail Folk Records," and the next year it was billed as "Country and Western." The title was shortened in 1956 to "C&W," and in 1963 it was labeled "Hot Country Singles."

The inability of the magazine to categorize the music may still suggest a problem. Undoubtedly, the recording companies have much to say about where an artist's product is listed by the way they promote it. The labels usually issue a record to stations that program country if it has the possibility of being played on those stations. If stations report the recording as country it will probably appear on that chart, but at times the people who compile the lists seem to make their own decisions. Part of the problem may be related to the number of charts. For instance, in late 1987 *Bill-*

board had eleven Hot Singles Charts (for Country, Country Singles Action, Adult Contemporary, Black, Black Singles Action, Crossover 30, Dance, Hits of the World, Hot 100, Hot 100 Singles Action, and Latin 50), nine Top Albums charts, and six Video Charts. This magazine also presents two charts for the most popular country singles of each year. The oldest is the year-end chart and the other is published to coincide with the CMA awards in October. Between 1967 (the first year of the October chart) and 1980 an average of six of the top ten recordings appearing on the October list are found on the top ten December lists. That means that approximately four of the songs that appear in October will not make the December list and four different ones will.

The variety of reporting stations and tabulation techniques may explain how a record will do well on a chart in one publication when one calls it country and the other does not. Whatever the problems with the charts, they are used, abused, and heeded as the source of feedback that greatly affects radio, recording companies, and most other elements of the country music process.

"Keep Those Cards and Letters Coming"

When radio stations rely on the charts to generate their playlists, the charts serve to perpetuate themselves. When a chart predicts that a recording has an excellent opportunity to move up, it is usually right, because the prediction alerts the programmers to the recording and many will play it for that reason. But the stations use a form of audience analysis to select their material. Some stations conduct telephone polls to determine the interests of their listeners. (This technique also serves as advertising by calling the people's attention to a station.) Others depend on requests from listeners and some react to those requests. This type of research varies from a wealthy station's sophisticated audience research to some small stations asking their advertisers if they wish to hear any songs.

41

Whether the stations use the charts or their own methods to design playlists, there is another form of feedback that affects them. In the larger markets the listenership of the station is judged by the Arbitron ratings. This organization conducts surveys of listeners and ranks stations according to the age, sex, and number of people listening at different times of the day. Since the amount and rate of advertising are often determined by these ratings, each station tries to pull in the largest possible share of the audience. Low ratings also encourage shifts in format and personnel. Whatever the biases or inexperience of the programmers, presenting the music an audience wishes to hear is a primary concern because their professional existence depends upon satisfactory ratings. To obtain those ratings they must appeal to as many people as possible.

Another form of feedback, which gives information to the system about the success of a particular song and is especially important to the songwriters and publishers, comes from services that tabulate the various uses of the music. BMI (Broadcast Music, Inc.), ASCAP (American Society of Composers, Authors, and Publishers) and SESAC (initial name only) are the major performance-rights societies that license country songs and collect fees for their use.[55] These organizations monitor the use of songs and collect fees from radio stations, jukebox owners, concert halls, and other places that use the music and distribute those fees to the publishers.

"To Make a Long Story Short"

The various parts of the country music system have been briefly noted as they make up the process through which most messages must travel in order to become successful. If we consider the stages and possible pitfalls in the process, we should be more sensitive to a message by understanding how it originates from a source (the songwriter or the singer), how it is sent through and is affected by the channels, why a receiver chooses to attend it, and how the audience's actions determine its fate.

42

A successful country song is a special form of communication: first, the source must select a topic of interest that can be communicated in approximately three minutes; second, the attitudes, beliefs, and behaviors contained in the message will not deviate far from those of the audience in order to encourage establishment of the "sincerity contract"; third, the message must be encoded in words that are easily understood and will get the audience's immediate attention; fourth, the message must be transmitted in a manner that will not hinder the reception of the message; and fifth, a desire must be instilled in the listeners to expose themselves to the message over and over.

We will now turn to those country songs that are assumed to contain successful messages.

PART II

The Message:

What the Folks Have to Say

Chapter 2

Hurtin' Love:

Most of the Folks Are Hurtin' Most of the Time

Many people seem to think they are good conversationalists, excellent drivers, and superior lovers. Many of those same persons feel they are more than capable of describing the content of a typical country song. David Allan Coe (who has more credentials than most people to speak about the music) suggested to songwriter Steve Goodman how to improve a song Goodman had written and considered perfect. Coe said the song was not perfect, for Goodman had failed to mention several important elements. With no reference to mama, trains, trucks, or getting drunk, the original version of "You Never Even Called Me by My Name" could not fulfill Coe's criteria for a perfect country song.

Coe and Goodman were having fun with the music and with the audience, but their joking is not far removed from some people's serious—if naive—perceptions of a typical country song. It is difficult to write and send a message through the country music process, and even though a few strange messages make their way through the system, most songs that achieve the greatest acceptance are those that deal with relationships between adult men and women. Approximately three of every four popular country songs relate to some facet of love, and most of the love songs depict a relationship that is unhappy or, to use the vernacular, "hurtin'." Songs with hurtin' love messages usually contain descriptions of situations where there is a lost love or lover (the "faded" love song), a wronged lover (the "somebody done somebody wrong" song), a love affair in which one of the participants is uncertain about his or her status in the relationship (the "worried" love song), or a love that is obstructed by some barrier (the "frustrated" love song). Some songs display several of these characteristics, but ordinarily one of these themes can be selected as the predominant idea in most hurtin' songs.

"Faded Love"

A love that is lost with little likelihood of rediscovery was a staple long before commercial country music. One effect of commercialization was the requirement that the lost love must be explained in two or three minutes, whereas the traditional or "old folk song" might contain numerous verses allowing for a more intricate plot and more detailed character development. A commercial country song must tell a lost-love story quickly, and the "folks" have successfully adjusted to this necessity.

There are three types of situations in a "faded" love song that quickly indicate that a hurt is to occur. One is a situation where the love, or lover, is gone and the person telling the story relates a passive and hopeless tale of longing and despondency in highly emotional language. The second situation is one in which the source hurts while accepting the responsibility for the pain, but will continue hurting without any other kind of reaction. In the third type of situation, the one who is hurting *does* take or attempts to take some action to overcome or diminish the pain and strain. The attempts may be as fruitless as the love affairs, but at least the people are displaying some initiative, and they offer a number of models for overcoming, or adapting to, a universal problem.

"Empty Arms"

A song written by Willie Nelson and made popular by Faron Young in 1961 is an example of a situation in which the source is so despondent and disoriented that all he can do is talk about it. In "Hello Walls," a woman has left a man and, as an excuse to convey his sorrow, he talks to the walls, a window, and finally the ceiling of a room. The source, in language that is conversational yet highly expressive, speaks to the objects around him and reveals much about his anguished state. After transferring the hurt to the walls he turns to the window.

Hello, window, well, I see that you're still here,
Aren't you lonely since our darlin' disappeared,
Well, look here, is that a teardrop in the corner of your pane.
Now, don't you try to tell me that it's rain.

From the window, the lonesome man averts his attention to the ceiling and finally admits the problem is really his and wishes the parts of the room to bear with him.

We must all pull together or else I'll lose my mind,
Cause I've got a feelin'
She'll be gone a long, long time.

"Hello Walls" is both typical and atypical of the lost-love song. It is atypical in its approach to the topic (direction of the message) and typical in that the source is alone, lonely, sad, disheartened, depressed, and generally unable to function in a rational way to overcome the problem (if there is a rational way to overcome such a problem).

There is no evidence in this set of lyrics that the woman had a reason for leaving (perhaps the man always carried on conversations with walls) or any indication of what event precipitated the departure. Vagueness is common in this type of hurtin' song. Patsy Cline released a song that was popular in the same year as "Hello Walls" in which this lack of detail is also found. The title of Cline's song describes the emotional state of the source and the lack of energy or ability to continue with a normal life. In "I Fall to Pieces" the woman, when she meets her former lover and his new friend, regresses to a state of helplessness. She repeats the lost lover's assertion that she would be able to get over him, but indicates by her actions that her lover was mistaken in his judgment.

Cline also recorded "She's Got You," another fine song of this type. One woman (the source) laments having a lost lover's old class ring, photograph, and memories while another woman has the man. The source infers that she is the loser in this exchange, but there is no indication that the other woman "took" the man or whether the man left on his own, leaving the mementos behind. Loretta Lynn also recorded this song ("covered" it) and it became popular once again in 1977. As we will see, this is an unusual message for Loretta Lynn to offer in her hurtin' songs, for she is not known for quiet acceptance of pain.

When the source does accept the pain, there are some rather novel ways to express the magnitude of the hurt. Dickie Lee quantified sadness by saying that since his woman has gone he would shed an additional "9,999,999 Tears." That pain returns "The First Thing Every Morning" to one person while another can say exactly when the love left—"(Lost Her/His Love) On Our Last Date." One singer insists that the hurt is unique in "Some Broken Hearts Never Mend," whereas another is more eclectic in his grief by noting that "Only the Lonely" know how he feels.

Some songs in this group take a different approach to the impact of a lost love or lover. One is famous for its so-called morbid lyrics. The song, popular in 1968, described a permanent loss when a woman died, leaving the man with memories. "Honey" was an interesting song and was not as depressing as some seem to think. A harsh and tragic end to a love affair is not unknown in this music ("Rocky" is another popular example), and death is not given ghoulish attention in these lyrics. In fact, the emphasis is on the enjoyable life the couple had during their time together. Although the man is hurting, little attention is given to the reason for the separation, and having the angels come and take the woman away allows pleasant memories to moderate the tragedy. Even though the mention of an "empty stage" and "small dark clouds" indicates loneliness, the image of death is softened considerably by recalling the happy life they had.

Other songs use death as an end to the pain caused by hurtin' love. George Jones's version of "He Stopped Loving Her Today" was given in chapter 1 as an example of how a singer's unique rendition of a song can permanently stamp a set of lyrics with an individual interpretation. This 1980 song is also an example of the "lost love and docile reaction" category. The man does little except read his lover's letters after underlining the "I love you's" in red after the woman leaves. The woman told him he would get over her in time, but he does not believe her and dies about twenty years later, proving his claim.

A variation of the "hurt and inert" theme is found in several faded love songs popular in the eighties. In these situations, the love they knew is gone, but the couple is still together and the one who did not initiate the loss is hurtin'. Contemplating leaving an unhappy love relationship is highlighted in these messages; however, the listener realizes from the way the song is interpreted that these people are not going to depart voluntarily. George Jones is certain he will walk away from an unhappy relationship in a song written by Tom T. Hall, but qualifies his plan by saying "I'm Not Ready Yet." This song failed to make the year-end charts, although it was on the weekly lists for seventeen weeks in 1980–1981 and peaked at number two. John Schneider made basically the same claim in "I'm Gonna Leave You Tomorrow," another recording that reached the top ten on the weekly lists in 1985–1986. The sources are hurting in both of these songs and the ones inflicting the pain do not care if the indecisive ones stay or go. Jones said that he would leave when his heart told him it was ready after admitting he had left a hundred times before. Schneider also confesses that yesterday he said he was going to leave tomorrow, but obviously he is still here today.

Merle Haggard had a song displaying these sentiments on the yearly charts in 1984 entitled "Someday When Things Are Good." In this song he selects a point in the future when he plans to leave and we know his claim is as flawed as those in the other two songs. He will go when things improve in the relationship— an event that is as unlikely to occur as George's heart telling him "it's time." The men in these songs know they are unhappy, know their states are unlikely to improve, and know the condition is caused by remaining in a relationship where they are unloved. Although they are aware of all these factors, they are still unable to act to erase the pain.

"I'm Sorry"

The second type of faded love song provides more specific information about how the love dissipated or why the absent lover decided to end the relationship. A song written by Mel Tillis and Wayne Walker is typical of the approach found in most lyrics in this group. The source is talking to the world in general and no one in particular, and the title tells much about the situation and the source. In "Thoughts of a Fool," a bit of detail is offered about the disintegration of the love because the source says he saw it fade "a kiss at a time." The source is helpless and admits it, but also indicates that the hurt is his fault. Accepting the responsibility for the hurt is quite common in a lost-love song, and this second group provides a small step from those in which the person is lost and floating to those where the people are partially analyzing the situation.

Another song suggests a rather drastic act as punishment for a hurt. "Statue of a Fool" describes a man who has lost his lover because of his behavior and realizes he had made a terrible mistake. The destroyed love is recalled as being so wonderful only a fool would have allowed it to die. The frozen statue is an appropriate description of the type of person this man seems to be. No attempt is made to regain the love, to think about a new lover, or even to continue with life, for the man is transfixed in space and time by his problem. The man wants to be on permanent display as a statue of stone garnished with a golden tear in order

> To honor the million tears he's cried
> And the hurt in his eyes would show
> So everyone would know.

Most people would not wish to be singled out for allowing a love to slip away, much less to be a monument for "all the world to see."

Waylon Jennings presented a song in 1978 containing a message that emphasized a less obvious tribute to lost love but did seem to show a man searching for continuing punishment. "The Wurlitzer Prize (I Don't Want to Get Over You)" uses country music as a trigger for a hurt because the man is feeding a jukebox in order to hear songs reminding him of the pain and suffering he created. Although this is an action taken in response to a hurt, it is not a plan for decreasing it—only for feeling it. This plan, however, might have more impact upon the people within listening distance of a jukebox than a statue with a golden tear would have on the world.

A number of songs that highlight the responsibility for causing the hurtin' love supply few attempts to rectify the situation and usually offer pathetic and weak appeals for recreating the lost love. Sometimes the people in the songs wish to have their lovers back simply because they have come to realize they miss them and, of course, they regret their actions. "Need You" takes this

"Statue of a Fool" by Jan Crutchfield. Copyright 1962. Used with permission of Sure-Fire Music Co., Inc.

approach while offering no incentive for the absent lover to return. The source's self-centered approach to resolving the situation may explain more clearly why someone left rather than indicate if anyone is apt to return.

Some of the songs in which the hurting person is assuming some responsibility for the situation offer interesting consequences of these interrupted relationships. In "The Most Beautiful Girl," the source tells us that his extremely attractive woman left him and asks if anyone has seen her. He recognizes that it is his fault she is gone, but he wants her back—or at least wants to know where she is. Once again, the source's pain is used as the rationale for wanting the lost one to return. Two of the most interesting songs of this type are a little more specific in their descriptions of why the sources are hurting. "Image of Me" tells of a man converting a sweet, innocent, country girl into a woman who drinks, talks too loudly, and tries to be the life of the party. It seems that the source knows (or hopes) that this is not the "real" person she is and that it is his fault she has gone through this metamorphosis. Again, no effort is made to modify or rectify the situation—only to suffer with it. Barbara Mandrell tells us that a woman made a mistake by allowing her lover to leave in the song "Sleeping Single in a Double Bed." The woman feels that she may have erred in what she said and did to cause her lover to leave, and she is unhappy over the loss of her "sleeping" companion.

"Walking the Floor over You"

The hurtin' song where some action is taken—or at least contemplated—offers some of the more complex messages in the lost-love category. There are many songs in which the one who is hurting reacts in a tentative, if not entirely appropriate, manner to do something about the pain caused by the absent love or lover and the situation created by that absence. Some may just walk the floor, others beg for forgiveness (whether they have done anything wrong or not), some threaten to retaliate, others try to hide the pain with lies, and some take to drink.

Many efforts to overcome a hurt are similar in that they are probably doomed to fail, yet they take varied approaches to failure. An attempt to keep in touch with the departed lover—regardless of the discomfort generated by the rekindling of memories—is a common reaction to the situation. Two songs using the telephone line as an umbilical cord to maintain contact are examples of this type of approach. "Wrong Number" describes a pathetic effort. The woman is obviously living with another person and the man calls her number just to hear her voice. After the woman answers, the caller remains silent so the woman turns to her unidentified companion, says it is just a wrong number, and hangs up the phone. This man will do whatever is necessary to hear the voice of his former lover and the song certainly suggests the unrealistic patience of both parties as well as a sense of hopelessness on the loser's part. A second song of this type has a classic title and is an example of begging for mercy without directly stating the plea. The man calls his former partner to tell her that it is upsetting to answer the telephone when her friends call to inquire about her. These reminders are more than he can stand so he has the telephone company change his number. The new telephone number is one of the best known in country music: "Lonesome 7–7203." Of course, the intent of the call is to let the woman know how to get in touch, if she so desires, and the message is filled with feeble attempts to create sympathy for the lonely man. A call from an old lover reverses the direction of the source in a song popular in 1987. The man in Ricky Van Shelton's recording answers the phone and is questioned about what "somebody" said that indicates he's mourning over a lost love. He attempts to deny a report that he was showing her picture and crying in public. The title, "Somebody Lied," suggests that the one who told the former lover about these acts was not telling the truth. The audience is certainly aware of who is lying and Shelton does it in classic style. We might also wonder about the motives of a person who has walked away from a relationship and then calls to question the one left behind. The source asks essentially the same question and uses it as a plea for sympathy when he asks if all she heard were true would it make any difference to her. He probably knows the answer, because such a call is obviously not intended to offer any comfort to the injured party.

At least the men in the above songs are direct, if unimaginative, in their appeals. Contrast these with others in the "lost and still trying" group of songs where the source is putting up a false front. The fake feelings are thinly veiled for the benefit of the audience and the person receiving the plea. One song written by Dickie Lee has been made popular three different times by three different singers. George Jones had the first popular version of "She Thinks I Still Care" in 1961, the second one appeared in 1974 when Anne Murray modified the lyrics, and in 1977 Elvis Presley returned it to the charts. This song deserves its periodic revivals, for it is a fine hurtin' song. The male source describes his behavior and then expresses wonder that the woman believes these actions indicate his love for her still exists. A key element in these lyrics is the ironical inference that the former lover may be enjoying the fact that the man is missing her.

> But if she's happy thinking I still need her
> Then let that silly notion bring her cheer
> But how could she be so foolish
> Oh, where could she get such an idea.
>
> Just because I asked a friend about her
> Just because I spoke her name somewhere
> Just because I saw her, then went all to pieces
> She thinks I still care.

Conway Twitty expressed a similar sentiment in "Hello Darlin'" when another of those chance encounters places the source face to face with his lost lover. He asks how she is progressing with her new love and expresses the hope that she is fine. When she asks, courteously but thoughtlessly, how he is faring, he responds, "Guess I'm doin' all right except I can't sleep and I cry all night 'til dawn." The Statler Brothers had another "wall" song displaying the same idea when they attempted to explain what a wonderful time a man was having since his love disappeared. In "Flowers on the Wall" they describe a man who found more detail in his room than the person in Nelson's song and offers a basic appeal to the lost lover—guilt.

A small step from the attempt to make an absent lover feel pangs of regret is taken in a group of songs that emphasizes that the one who left will eventually hurt as a result of this act. In "I Love You More Today" the source assures a woman that his love is still strong, but does suggest that someday she may miss him. Another song that contains one of those infamous accidental encounters with the departed lover provides some of the guilt-trip characteristics outlined above and also the subtle warning that she, too, will hurt in the future. "Funny How Time Slips Away" includes the contradiction that although time has moved slowly for the man since the woman went away, it seems like she left only yesterday. The time factor, as well as a timid warning, are also highlighted in "It's Just a Matter of Time." This song suggests the possibility that the source will be needed in the future and then the other person will understand how it feels to want someone and be rejected.

In a song recorded by Tammy Wynette a more lively threat is offered by a woman who is hurting because of the wayward desires of a man and decides to adopt the qualities that he finds so fascinating in other women. In "Your Good Girl's Gonna Go Bad" the woman describes how she is going to dress up, powder up, and go out partying because that seems to be what her man likes. She says she will be the swingingest swinger he has ever seen, but she implies that it will not be an entirely pleasing role for her to perform. It is a warning for the man to get his act together. No indication is given about whether or not the tactic is successful, but the proposed scheme is depicted in such negative terms that it is obvious the woman does not wish to swing so freely—she actually wants the man to settle down and love her for what she really is. The woman may turn out to be the person the man wants and then he can sing a modified version of "Image of Me" to convey his appreciation.

"There Stands the Glass"

The people in country songs are often accused of taking advantage of every opportunity to drink alcoholic beverages. Although this is not a characteristic found in a large number of the most popular songs (see chapter 5), some of the hurtin' songs do identify drinking as a reaction to pain. A title of one song sums this up rather well: "Sorrow on the Rocks." Merle Haggard wrote and recorded two fine songs of this type. In "Swinging Doors," the man calls his old lover to tell her that he feels more welcome in a bar than in their former home, and also to let her know he is still miserable. "The Bottle Let Me Down" clearly tells of the man's attempts to overcome the hurt of the power of the woman's memory, and of his failure to escape it.

> Each night I leave the barroom when it's over
> Not feeling any pain at closing time
> But tonight your memory found me much too sober
> Couldn't drink enough to keep you off my mind.
>
> Tonight the bottle let me down
> And let your memory come around

"The Bottle Let Me Down" by Merle Haggard. © 1966 by Tree Publishing Company, Inc. International Copyright Secured. All Rights Reserved. Used by permission of the publisher.

The one true friend I thought I'd found
Tonight the bottle let me down.

I've always had a bottle that I could turn to
And lately I've been turning every day
But the wine don't take effect like it used to
And I'm hurtin' in an old familiar way.

One of the most interesting traits of these drinking songs is the kind of beverage chosen to drown the pain. Wine is mentioned more than anything else, even though slightly more English words rhyme with "beer" than "wine." Not only is beer a more accurate word, but it is also the most popular drink served in those places where country music is most often played. "Wine Me Up" is a plea to have a bartender keep pouring to dilute a misery. "Red Wine and Blue Memories" explains the liquid's visual attractiveness and mental effects, while Emmylou Harris's version of "Two More Bottles of Wine" tells how much support a woman needs in order to get through a bad night.

"What Happened to Our Love"

There are several other special reactions to the lost or losing love situation. Hank Williams Jr. describes a special tactic in "The Last Love Song" when the man discovers the woman is leaving and wants to sing her a song. The song he sings contains some explicit physical details of the type that began to reappear in the 1970s:

And tomorrow night, what do you suggest
To take the place of your breast
Pressed against my chest
Oh, how I'll miss your tenderness.

A few songs that offer some reaction to the hurtin' situation are less than sincere in their approach. Buck Owens offered a series of questions for the lost lover in a song that appears to be a variation of an old military metaphor when he presented "Who's Gonna Mow Your Grass." Aside from an obvious lack of faith in the woman's abilities to take care of her needs and desires the song gives a light touch to a delicate situation but ignores the possibility that the man did not "mow her grass" very well in the first place. Roy Clark's song of lost love is a celebration of a woman leaving in "Thank God and Greyhound," but for the most part the subject is treated with great seriousness.

One of the most fascinating messages is found in the "Teddy Bear Song." Personification is frequently used in country music. A wooden Indian is the key character in a Hank Williams song that was made popular by him and again in 1969 by Charley Pride. "Kaw-Liga" stands in front of a store and falls in love with a statue of an Indian maiden that is removed from his presence. The source describes Kaw-Liga's feeling of loss. The "Teddy Bear Song," however, presents the opposite view. The woman is hurting and cannot cope so she wishes to be an inanimate object (a cuddly stuffed animal) that experiences no pain.

The solution to the hurting situation is seldom found in the songs in this "lost" group. There are a few examples where the loss is made permanent or the passage of time does indicate some progress toward a solution, or at least outlines more definite steps for making the separation a permanent state. "D-I-V-O-R-C-E" is a song where the word is spelled out so little "J-o-e" (the child of the parting couple) will not understand that his mother is discussing the dissolution of her marriage. The hurting woman is not looking forward to being divorced. This song also contains one of the few profane words found in popular country songs during this period, and it ("hell") is spelled out for the same reason the title is (perhaps this is done so the radio programmers as well as the four-year-old boy will not catch the word). Loretta Lynn has a message that is more specific concerning the problems that the woman depicted in Wynette's song may be about to experience. Lynn's version of "Rated X" does not refer to a movie rating, nor does it refer to an inferior brand in a television advertisement, though it does say that the divorced woman may be seen in the same negative light as an off-brand product. The woman in the song faces an unpleasant life after a divorce for at least two reasons: "The women all look at you like you're bad/ The men all hope you are." Janie Fricke reinforced the image of a divorced woman on the prowl in "She's Single Again" with descriptions of characteristics that others saw in the woman in Lynn's song.

Most of the remedial actions taken by the losers in love are futile attempts to get their lost lovers to return. Conway Twitty recorded a popular song in which the man lost a love "Fifteen Years Ago." Since that time he has married another woman, but when someone mentions the name of his former love he goes to pieces, as if the loss had occurred only a few weeks before. Time has slipped away, but it has not alleviated the pain. The man *was* able to continue functioning, and this is something that is not certain in many of the songs where the source is hurting and taking some tentative action to overcome the hurt. The actions taken in other songs in this group are most often designed to encourage the absent lover to return. The desire to just hear a voice, the too-frequent unplanned encounters with the old love (sometimes meetings can be more painful than expected, as in "I've Enjoyed As Much of This As I Can Stand"), begging to have the lover return, the false front that is obviously geared to generate guilt, and such other moves are unsuccessful—and for good reason. They display inherent weaknesses that may be understandable, but are taking a definite action by leaving the passive one with the pain.

Within the lost-love area there is little difference between women and men in the way they react. More women have left more men in these songs for the obvious reason that more men are singing them. Women made tremendous inroads into popular country music during the 1970s and certainly have recorded many lost-love songs, but it will take several more years for them to catch up. (Of the top fifty singles for each year from 1960 to 1969, there were sixty women identified as solo artists and fifteen members of male-female duets. For 1970 to 1979, 125 women were named as the primary artist and thirty-one appeared as members of duos. Seventy-seven women had singles on the year-end charts for 1980 to 1987, and twenty-four duos were identified on the lists.) Since men are more often the victims in this situation, we might ask why an audience that is supposed to be composed of people who have conservative social attitudes would accept this type of behavior from male sources. Some suggest that the answer lies in the character of the Southerner who at one time made up such a large part of the audience.[1] The rationale for this suggestion is usually a variation of the "Born to Lose" syndrome that is built up from the hard and often unsuccessful lives these listeners must endure. Programmed to accept failure, they do not expect to be successful in their love lives. There is probably some truth in this, especially when we consider the earlier periods of the music, but some doubt emerges when we look at the other types of hurtin' love that also receive wide attention.

"Another Somebody Done Somebody Wrong Song"

Many of the faded love songs offer vague reasons for the lost or diminished love. The justifications are often found in statements such as "I hurt her" or "It's my fault" or "Why did she do this to me?" and sparse information is supplied for determining the merits of these opinions. The sources are most concerned with the effects of the hurting act, not the act itself. When the act that creates the pain and instigates the loss of a lover, or the lover, receives the primary interest of the source, then it can be described as a "somebody done somebody wrong" song. There is little doubt that the most frequent reason for someone to feel wronged in a country song is when one person is untrue in a relationship. The situation in which there is an unfaithful lover is given much prominence in such a large number of songs that we will examine these separately in chapter 4. At this time we can note some of the other reasons given for causing, or receiving, hurt in "wronged" songs.

Conway Twitty recorded a song that explains the critical point in a dissolving relationship and describes the problem the man created. "This Time I've Hurt Her More Than She Loves Me" tells what a man did to hurt a woman, but does not say why it was this particular time that made the difference. While the man was spending his time drinking, the woman used hers to consider what she needed to make her happy. After admitting that he had done more than enough drinking to justify her leaving, he realizes that the accumulated pain finally outweighed all the love the woman brought to the relationship.

Drinking is named as the cause rather than the reaction to a hurt in many of these songs. Jerry Lee Lewis describes a weak man who refuses to turn down a free drink, and although he has been warned by his lover about spending too much time in a bar, he cannot get away from the locale and the beverage. He admits that drinking has made a fool of him, and then he also discovers it did more in "What Made Milwaukee Famous (Made a Loser Out of Me)." At least one man was more sensitive to what he was doing to the injured woman in "She's Got to Be a Saint." The man in Ray Price's song gives the impression that it will be better to leave her than have her continue suffering while he wastes money on drink and other activities. He knows she has been crying in her sleep, and after praying for her he answers that prayer by leaving. A song which speaks from the viewpoint of a woman who has been wronged by a man who leaves her alone and crying while he drinks is certainly different from those we have just seen. The wronged one describes the situation and tries to divert attention from the weakness of the man to the object of his infatuation. In "Whiskey, If You Were a Woman," the lead singer (Paulette Carlson of Highway 101) states that she could fight and conceivably win if the man were attracted to another woman, but has little faith she can compete with the magnetism of strong drink. It is obvious the man is doing the woman wrong by his behavior, but the woman refuses to place the blame on the man although she does admit he has a "tangled mind." This is also an example of one of the few recordings by a group that was able to establish a sincerity contract with a hurtin' song in the mid-eighties.

Some interesting behaviors are found in songs where the source places the blame squarely on the other partner. A few people display great pain, but do little more. Ernest Ashworth had a popular song with a great title that demonstrates pain and also indicates that the man is suffering because he loves the woman. The song contains what could be a model case for mental cruelty when it describes the arguments and pain the man is enduring. He is afraid to tell the woman that he loves her or that she is hurting his feelings since she would use that information to hurt him more. He would like to fight back with the truth, but he cannot—so he just keeps lying to her and telling himself, "Talk Back Trembling Lips." Another hurting source simply asks, "Don't You Ever Get Tired of Hurting Me?"

"Good Hearted Woman"

Several songs display much more assertive actions toward the one who is "doing the wrong." It is also in this area where some of the stereotyped sex-role behaviors are challenged. Women have often been described as serving the "doormat" function for the men in country songs as exemplified by Tammy Wynette's "Stand by Your Man."[2] Although this song is not a "reacting to a wrong" song, it does prepare a woman for that possibility. The source indicates that a man will behave in ways a woman will not understand and will do it because he is a man, and the woman should forgive and welcome him home—if she loves him. Wynette and her record producer Billy Sherrill took advantage of their success with this theme. In fact, all except one of the ten follow-up releases featuring various twists on the basic idea secured higher rankings than the number thirty-nine for "Stand by Your Man" on the 1968 year-end chart. Nine of the ten songs were written or co-written by Sherrill and contained basically the same message.[3] Loretta Lynn has often expressed disagreement with this philosophy. A study that analyzed 137 of Lynn's songs describing love relationships between men and women found 99 that did not support the stereotypical woman's role.[4] The study, however, included songs that were not released as singles and some that were singles but did not appear on the most-popular lists here.

Enough of Lynn's material did appear on the year-end lists to establish a strong portrait of a woman who does more standing "up to" than "by" a man. One of her early popular recordings was "Success," in which the woman complains about a man who spends more time trying to be successful at work than at home. In "Don't Come Home A-Drinkin' (with Lovin' on Your Mind)" a man is warned that "Liquor and love, they just don't mix/Leave the bottle or me behind." The woman in "Wine, Women and Song" threatens the man after describing actions she suggests are wrong and are *not* his inherent traits. Another song describes a man returning home to find a hostile and unforgiving woman. Loretta Lynn is part Cherokee and extremely proud of it; however, in "Your Squaw Is on the Warpath," the term "squaw" is just a nickname and a launching place for some fine metaphors.[5] She states in these lyrics that the woman is fighting mad about

"Don't Come Home A-Drinkin' (with Lovin' On Your Mind)" by Loretta Lynn and Peggy Sue Wells. Copyright 1966. Used with permission of Sure-Fire Music Co., Inc.

the man's drinking and running around and tells him about it in symbols that can be decoded in several ways:

That firewater that you've been drinking
Makes you feel bigger
But, Chief, you're shrinking
Since you've been on that love-making diet.

When a man "steps out" in "Happy Birthday," the woman is somewhat considerate when she tells him she is leaving:

Tonight I'll step out, too
And since I won't be here
Happy Birthday, Merry Christmas, and Happy New Year.

These songs, for the most part, describe specific actions the woman is planning to take, the indication that she expects the actions to cause the man to suffer, and that all the pain is going to be the man's fault. In one song, the woman is neither planning to leave nor threatening to if the man does not change his ways. She changes her behavior instead and tells the man he will no longer be able to cause her pain. This song, "The Pill," was mentioned in chapter 1 in the discussion of the problem of securing airplay for a recording that programmers feel might be offensive to listeners. Several programmers did refuse to play this song, but Lynn suggested that if more women were making decisions about which messages might offend an audience there would have been less of a problem.[6] The song is an attack on the double standard and even though the language makes the threat seem less ominous (one writer said the song was filled with "chicken-yard metaphors"[7]) there is no doubt that the woman is *not* playing the role of the dependent, long-suffering wife often attributed to women in country songs.[8] Lynn starts each of the following

"Your Squaw Is On the Warpath" by Loretta Lynn. Copyright 1968. Used with permission of Sure-Fire Music Co., Inc.
"Happy Birthday" by Ron Kitson. Copyright 1964. Used with permission of Sure-Fire Music Co., Inc.

verses from "The Pill" with a statement outlining what the man has done to offend her and proceeds to tell him what she has done to solve the problem, leaving him with little room to object.

I'm tired of all your crowin' 'bout how you and your hens play;
While holdin' a couple in my arms and another on the way;
This chicken done tore up her nest, and I'm ready to make
   a deal;
And you can't afford to turn it down, 'cause you know I've
   got the pill.

This incubator is overused, because you kept it filled;
But the feeling comes easy now, since I've got the pill;
It's gettin' dark, it's roosting time, tonight's too good to be real;
And daddy don't you worry none, 'cause Mama's got the pill.

A fine hurtin' love and happy leaving song was written by Shel Silverstein. Lynn was reluctant to record it because her name appeared in the lyrics.[9] Fortunately, Silverstein was able to overcome Lynn's objections to "Hey Loretta," for the song beautifully depicts a spirited woman's behavior toward an ungrateful man.

Lynn does sing some songs that support the stereotype of the dependent woman acquiescing to a man and to a hurt. For instance, she also recorded a version of "Stand by Your Man," although it was not released as a single. On the same album (*Woman of the World/To Make a Man*) where she covered Wynette's song, there are two other popular singles that used the stereotype of a weak woman who is encouraged to support a man no matter what he does. "To Make a Man (Feel Like a Man)" is very similar in philosophy to "Stand by Your Man" for it says that a man may be untrue or inconsiderate, but a woman must strive in every way to encourage and protect him. The man is absolved from upholding his share of responsibility in the relationship and all the duties are left to the woman. She must remain constantly vigilant and ever aware of how to love and satisfy the man. Mention is made of "wifely work" and outside forces that may turn the man away from the woman, and nothing is mentioned about a man being able to control his own actions or destiny.

Another popular single from this 1969 album also contained a message Lynn has expressed in several other songs. In "Woman of the World (Leave My World Alone)" the woman is concerned with an outside influence that is causing the wrong and its effects on her susceptible man. The woman is described as one who will lure the man and then drop him, and the source will have to console him over the loss. The negative statements about the other woman are less harsh and assertive than some found in Lynn's "cheatin'" songs, but she does describe her as a "devil woman" and also finds fault with her dressing habits when she says, "I wear more in swimming than you wear to parties where you go."

Both of these songs do support the role of the acquiescing, forgiving, and every-wary woman who coddles and is overly considerate of a man who is weak and likely to capitulate to outside attention (especially if the other woman is sparsely dressed). However, most of Lynn's songs are not of this type, for those in the "wronged" group usually depict a woman who is taking, or at least attempting to take, some action in retaliation for the wrong done her by a man.

"You'll Lose a Good Thing"

Some other songs in this group present atypical reactions by a person who has suffered a wrong. Bobby Bare's version of "Marie Laveau" is an example of one unique reaction. This "legend" song is a story about a witch and a good-looking man who attempts to trick her by promising marriage if she will make him rich. The witch fulfills her part of the bargain and then the man refuses to carry out his part, so Marie just does away with the

"Woman Of The World (Leave My World Alone)" by Sharon Higgins. Copyright 1968. Used with permission of Sure-Fire Music Co., Inc.

68

handsome liar. Johnny Duncan recorded a song where the source observes a man mistreating a woman. The source advises the man that if he does not change his behavior the woman will leave him, and he tells the philanderer that she will not have far to go for "She Can Put Her Shoes Under My Bed (Anytime)." We will find many more "wronged" songs when we examine those in which the wrong is specified as "cheatin'," but now let us look at some hurtin' songs where the person is uncertain or insecure in a relationship—the "worried" love song.

"Suspicious Minds"

When a person has lost a love or is suffering because of an insensitive or uncaring lover, there is some comfort in knowing the cause of the problem. If unhappiness is caused by uncertainty in a relationship there is little opportunity to solve the problem. The hazard in clearing up the uncertainty, of course, is the discovery that the fear is justified. Some of the worried songs suggest that it is better to remain uninformed than to confront a partner and discover that what is suspected is true. "Talking in Your Sleep" is an example of a song where the woman is unsure about whether she has a problem, but is staying awake trying to hear if her lover tips his hand as he sleeps. He has provided no specific reasons to support her apprehensions and, more importantly, she does not ask him when he is awake.

Waylon Jennings and Jessi Colter summarize the problem when they note how uncomfortable it is to maintain a relationship when both parties have "Suspicious Minds." Colter sings another song in which she is trying to overcome her lover's suspicious and untrusting nature. In "I'm Not Lisa," a woman attempts to assure a man who is unable to adjust to a new romance because he has experienced an unhappy one with a woman named Lisa. The woman in the song keeps telling the wounded man that he has nothing to worry about this time for, among other things, her name is Julie.

Even though a few of the people in these songs make slight efforts to overcome their uncertainties, most are as passive as the people in the faded love songs. One song describes a situation where the source is fairly sure the woman is attempting to pick up men in a bar, but he does not want to know for certain. This song is another one with a great title: "She's Acting Single (I'm Drinking Doubles)." Drinking is better than knowing he cannot stop her actions, if that is what she really wants to do. Therefore, his fear of losing her overcomes his desire to know the truth.

When tentative steps are taken they are often prefaced with open regret and uneasiness. A song by Ray Price involves a man who approaches his lover and requests clarification of his status in the relationship, but promises her "I Won't Mention It Again." Some people are more persistent in "mentioning" the problem, but less than rational in processing the information they receive. In 1965, Eddy Arnold made a recording whose central character is a man who used the word "world" to symbolize his environment and his lover. After asking his lover why another man was holding and kissing her in "What's He Doing in My World," the man wanted more than the woman's casual answer that the new man is an old friend.

When a person can say he or she is unloved there is no guarantee that the relationship will be free of uncertainties. The man in Sonny James's "Don't Keep Me Hangin' On" says he is a fool for accepting the woman's mistreatment and that she just wants him hanging around. He does not indicate when she would want him around, but the inconsistency of both of their acts makes for a rather bizarre and uneasy relationship. After saying he has been ill-treated and unloved, he describes a problem appearing in many of these songs: the inability to take decisive action.

Times when I say I'm leaving
You keep beggin' me to stay

70

When I try to go, you put on a show
And somehow I can't get away.

"Feelings"

Some of the worried songs contain situations in which at least one person is uncertain about his or her status in a relationship and does not face the cause of the anxiety. An individual's ability or willingness to focus on the root of the problem does not necessarily mean that the degree of worry is lessened; however, it gives a different perspective to the situation. A few of the persons in these messages foresee potential difficulties in a relationship and attempt to take advantage of what they have at the moment. In the early 1970s, songs appeared that expressed uncertainty about possible future unhappiness and told of people deciding to take possible advantage of what joy they could find.

Kris Kristofferson wrote several of the more popular songs in this group, which were made popular by other artists. "I've Got to Have You" is an example of a possibly happy love intermingled with potential pain and enough melancholy to place it in the worried category. Sammi Smith recorded the popular version in 1972, a year after her success with another Kristofferson song that was a landmark in commercial country music and which we will examine later. In "I've Got to Have You," Smith speaks for a woman who is concerned about the possibility that a man will leave or that the love will fade and decides that whatever the possible consequences she must have the man at this moment. Worry is overcome by passion; however, the uncertainty over the situation does not allow it to be a song of happy love.

Another Kristofferson song, made popular by Ray Price, has a man making a similar choice for a different reason. In "I'd Rather Be Sorry," the man, unsure of the ultimate outcome of the relationship, discusses with himself the possible pitfalls of falling in

"Don't Keep Me Hangin' On" by Carole Smith and Sonny James. Copyright 1970 by Marson Incorporated. Used by permission.

love. The title tells the outcome of the discussion although what the man says seems to indicate a lack of self-confidence and a belief that the relationship will not be a lasting one. The enjoyment of the interlude is considered to be paramount, and even if the final result turns out to be less than satisfactory, the effort is considered worthwhile. The approach to the topic and the use of language make this an interesting example of this type of song.

> If you hurt me you won't be the first or the last in a lifetime of many mistakes;
> But I won't spend tomorrow regretting the past for the chance I didn't take;
>
> Cause I'll never know 'til it's over
> If I'm right or I'm wrong loving you
> But I'd rather be sorry for something I've done than for something that I didn't do.
>
> When you touch me it's easy to make believe tomorrow won't take you away;
> But I'd gamble whatever tomorrow might bring for the love that I'm living today;
>
> Cause I'll never know 'til it's over
> If I'm right or I'm wrong loving you
> But I'd rather be sorry for something I've done than for something that I didn't do.

The messages of these two songs indicate that the people are actually considering the consequences of a relationship with the understanding that they may not turn out to be successful. The difference between these and other worried songs is that the decisions are made before the love begins to fade or, in some cases, before the affair is past the panting stage; a decision is made after the consideration of options instead of refusing to face the problem.

A few of the worried songs take approaches other than having the source of the messages express concern for possible or actual uncertainties in a relationship. A song that appears to add substance to the claim made in some messages that a man is weak and susceptible to another woman is found in Mickey Gilley's "She's Pulling Me Back Again." This man is asking his present lover to restrain him from returning to an earlier lover who is exerting pressure to get him back again. The man is obviously unable to fight off this temptation without assistance. Whether this type of appeal will be effective probably depends on his current lover's acceptance of the argument.

Another atypical worried song is Lynn Anderson's "Rose Garden." The unstated message here is that a lover is not particularly satisfied with the relationship. The source tells him that she could lie and say everything would be all right and that they would face no problems or anxieties in their romance, but she cannot and will not make this claim. She is quite clear when she says she did not promise him an easy time, she is not going to mislead him, and this explanation is the best she will offer. This is one of the few songs where the source is responding to one who is worrying, rather than giving the thoughts of one who is having the problem.

A song that demonstrates the sexual relationships described in popular commercial country music in the 1970s contains an element of worry or uneasiness that is caused by this type of behavior. In "Love in the Hot Afternoon," a man meets a woman on the streets of New Orleans and after a short time they are lying in a bed. He seems to be concerned about the casual encounter and not quite able to accept the warm interlude for what it is. He begins to talk about how pleasant the sex was (using euphemisms as blatant as those in the last sentence), but cannot keep from wondering about what the woman will be doing later that day and in the future. There is no mention of romantic love, or a continuing relationship, but he is worrying about her future behavior and cannot accept the philosophy offered in Kristofferson's songs

73

described earlier. No specific reason is offered for his lack of satisfaction and why he is so concerned with the future, but there is the feeling that the man is uncomfortable with this type of relationship and his uneasiness makes it a worried love song.

Another song that displays a situation where uncertainty is expressed by the one to whom the message is addressed, and little help is offered by the source, uses an old cliché to identify the catalyst for discussing a problem that can occur in "modern" sexual relationships. Larry Gatlin and the Gatlin Brothers presented a song in which the worried or uncertain woman has offered a reason for a response from the man. The source admits that he was, at the beginning, sure that she would be all he ever wanted (when her dress hit the floor), but he no longer feels this excitement; therefore, when "push comes to shove," he says "I Just Wish You Were Someone I Loved." The message lets the wronged one know that the worry was justified and provides support for the reticence most sources display in the worried songs when it appears they might be safer to remain silent and worry than to speak up and lose a love. In fact, the worried ones in "Rose Garden" and "I Just Wish You Were Someone I Loved" now have to develop other options from information they might not have wanted.

Perhaps the changes from traditional relationship patterns identified in the three examples just cited are a major reason for the new "worries" appearing in unhappy love songs popular since 1975. In a study of dissolving relationships the reasons for concern were fairly consistent during the ten years prior to 1975.[10] Men, during that period, offered three reasons more often than others for their fears: (1) losing a woman to another man (the "she's lookin' good" song); (2) another more exciting way of life will lure the woman away (the "wild side of life" song); and (3) his insensitive behavior will force a woman to terminate the relationship (the "ironing and crying" song). The three most prevalent reasons given by the women during the earlier period are closely related to those offered by the men. They were: (1) the woman fears another more exciting and satisfying woman will entice the man to leave (the "woman of the world" song); (2) the woman fears she will lose a man to a lifestyle (the "honky-tonk man" song); and (3) the woman fears the prospect of being alone (the "a bad love is better than no love" song).

Since 1975 there have been some important changes in the "worried" songs. The two major reasons given by both the men and women are still noted in the lyrics, but they no longer receive the emphasis they once did. The men still feel that women can be lured away and continue to believe it is the woman who will likely be "looking good" for another man. The women are still concerned about the men shopping around, but are placing more blame for the shopping on the man rather than on a designing woman. For instance, Rosanne Cash describes a man with his own ideas of love in "Seven Year Ache." A man expresses similar sentiments about a partner in a relationship who, he fears, is doing more than "looking" and confronts his lover in a song with a wonderful title: "You're Out Doing What I'm Here Doing Without." The worry over the intrusion of a third party in a relationship is no longer centered on the weak man and the "devil" woman. More emphasis is given to the partner (either male or female) who is looking rather than being pursued, as it was in the earlier songs.

The "Wild Side Of Life" rationale is still being used. The frequency and direction of this concern is the important shift during the later period. Women have objected considerably less, and men considerably more. The third reason given by both the men and the women in songs of the earlier period have changed in several important ways. The man in the earlier songs was concerned that his behavior was hurting the woman and she would ultimately leave him for that reason. Either the mistreated women did leave making the expression of worry unnecessary or the men are modifying their behaviors. Whatever the reason, few of these songs have appeared since the mid-seventies.

The third reason women gave in the earlier period seldom appears in the newer songs. It was the fear of the unknown or the inability to find a better love that caused a number of women in country songs to believe they should remain in a dissolving or unsatisfactory relationship. Other songs often added reinforcement to this view by suggesting that one hurtin' love relationship was usually followed by another. The use and the support for that reason decreased considerably during the late seventies and seldom appeared in the eighties. One reason the women may not be as "worried" as they were in the past can be found in the songs describing the fate of women who have lost loves. Women are now hearing of how a woman's life can be much improved in a new relationship. In some songs men admit that the women may have improved their lot by leaving rather than staying in an unrewarding relationship. A man in a George Strait song tells how a woman appears to have improved her situation by leaving in "You Look So Good in Love." The uncertainty in starting over is understandable and received much notice in the earlier songs. The unpleasant consequences that often occur if one does begin again are also highlighted. In the recent songs the dread is not completely erased, but women are deciding that future problems may not be any more unpleasant than those found in current relationships.

Whatever the direction of future love relationships, country songwriters and singers will identify the parts that create the most compelling uncertainties for either women or men and, if it is possible to explain them in three minutes, they will be described in a country song. The sources of the music have had little difficulty providing information in those songs where the hurt is caused by some type of barrier between a person and his, or her, love or lover.

"Do You Know What It's Like to Be Lonesome"

The lyrics in "frustrated" love songs relate situations where one or more persons are without love, or where accessibility to a lover is denied by some barrier. Frustration appears in the other types of hurtin' love songs (certainly in the cheatin' songs), but the primary emphasis is on the dissonance caused and displayed by the individuals rather than on the barrier. The faded love songs contain situations where the love relationship is deteriorating or over, and the message usually comes from the one experiencing the pain or loss. The "wronged" and "worried" messages are similar in that the problems are caused by a person in a relationship and are related to particular events. In the frustrated songs the problem is usually created by the inability to establish or further a relationship and the force which is hindering one is emphasized. Some of the messages are characterized by even more desperation than the earlier hurting messages, and perhaps this is related to the magnitude of the problem creating the barrier. The obstructions may be as real as a "raging river," as universal as a cultural difference, as individual as a personal value, or it may even be obscure, but just as significant to the people who are articulating a message of absent love in the lonely songs.

One of the few popular songs describing the separation of lovers because of a conflict between different cultures is Buck Owens's version of "Made in Japan," which was popular in 1972 and describes an American military man who is in Japan and falls in love with a Japanese woman. The couple is not allowed to form a permanent relationship because the woman's parents do not approve of their daughter marrying a man from outside their culture.

The man in Glen Campbell's "Galveston" is in an active war zone and believes he will never be able to return to the city where his lover lives. This song does not generate much sadness because Campbell's interpretation gives a lift to the lyrics and slides over the deep emotions embedded in the song. In these lyrics the message is not as clear as in most country songs, for it contains several ideas rather than one primary theme embellished with specific supporting details, and, in addition, the secondary ideas are emphasized at the expense of the principal one in the story. Also in contrast to this approach is a song by Loretta Lynn that did not make the top fifty on the year-end chart but did make the weekly top ten during 1966. In "Dear Uncle Sam" a woman is writing a letter to Uncle Sam expressing loneliness for her lover and asking that he be allowed to return home. Lynn's song focuses on the pain of an interrupted relationship caused by the man's service in the armed forces. The woman says she understands the necessity for people to defend their country, but suggests that her personal needs are also important. The song concludes with the woman reading the first line of the well-known telegram used by the government to inform the next of kin when a serviceman dies.

Several barriers are mentioned in "Running Bear," Sonny James's popular song that describes the obstacles facing an Indian man (Running Bear) and woman (White Dove). Running Bear is on one bank of a raging river and White Dove is on the other side. Their attempts to develop a relationship are further frustrated because their two tribes are in conflict. Their desire to be together overcomes their ability to reason (and swim), and when they meet in the middle of the river they embrace and kiss before drowning. These lyrics are accompanied by the tom-tom beat that media mythology dictates for songs with Indian characters.

Another man who displays great passion when separated from his future bride by a "raging river" is found in Warner Mack's "The Bridge Washed Out." The man is being delayed from marrying a girl on the opposite bank because the bridge over the river was carried downstream by a flood, the boats are floating away, and he cannot swim. He considers trying to ford the river even after admitting that he cannot swim but instead takes out his frustration by lamenting his bad fortune. Perhaps common sense is displayed in this song because there is a single barrier, or an obstacle that will recede faster than his passion, and that ensures the man will not suffer the fate of Running Bear and White Dove.

"What Kind of Girl Do You Think I Am?"

Conflicts between personal desires and social and moral values create barriers for some people. These barriers are just as formidable as, although easier to overcome than, the geographic ones and may be encountered when a person feels compelled to retaliate against an untrue or ungrateful lover. At times they are used as a reason for refusing to perform an act, and are often found in songs with references to premarital sex. Tammy Wynette describes this situation very well in "Womanhood," where a woman named Patricia is having great difficulty remaining the "good" girl her mother wanted her to be. The woman is encountering the conflict between potential physical pleasures and religious principles or, as she relates it: "I am a Christian, Lord, but I'm a woman, too." We must decide for ourselves about the outcome of the conflict, for shortly after midnight Patricia returns home and prays: "Tonight I've been through hell, Lord/Wondering if I did right or wrong." It is not clear what she actually did, but it is certain that the barrier is causing much unhappiness.

We will see a few people expressing happiness about finding their way into womanhood in some love songs in the next chapter, but the situation in "Another Lonely Song" is particularly indicative of this present group because the barrier is created by an internal conflict. The intent and construction of the message is similar to that in "Womanhood." A woman is offering an informal prayer asking for forgiveness or understanding for her desire to be in the arms of a man. She is, or may soon be, in his arms because she thinks her lover is with someone else. What is certain is that the woman's hurt is created by her belief that what she is doing is wrong though she does not want to be alone.

"Ain't Had No Lovin'"

The songs in which individuals express a desire *not* to be alone contain some of the most divergent approaches to removing the pain from a hurtin' situation. Included in the lonely group are songs of lust, flirtation, and desperation, and most are aiming to overcome the frustration and unhappiness of being without love. Sometimes there is only the fear of potential loneliness, at other times the message is about a search for love or a lover, and in a few cases there's the fever or jangled nerves that can occur when one is without a lover.

The major difference between these songs and the other hurtin' songs is the absence of a special relationship. In fact, it is the absence itself that creates the problem. A barrier is not always specified, although its existence can usually be inferred. In this group of songs other barriers such as moral and personal values become less of a force and are often overridden or ignored. Some of these songs created controversy among a few listeners and critics, some created amusement through the tactics displayed, some aroused pity by the descriptions of inept techniques, and some were appreciated simply for their portrayal of a universal problem.

"A Certain Kinda Hurtin'"

The song that created the most comment was written by Kris Kristofferson and recorded by Sammi Smith and it gained popularity in 1971. It has been credited with opening the way for the expression of more realistic attitudes toward short-term relationships. A woman is facing the prospect of loneliness and is attempting to alleviate the problem by asking a man to "Help Me Make It through the Night." She admits that her actions may be wrong, but she does not care if they are, for her wish to be with someone now is greater than her concern over what she may feel tomorrow. No regrets, no promise of potential love, no insistence on a future relationship, and no further obligations are mentioned. The message is a significant step from many of the early hurtin' songs and even more effective when sung by a woman.

Kristofferson telegraphed this same message earlier in a song made popular by Ray Price. "For the Good Times" describes a situation in which a man is losing his lover and approaching loneliness with trepidation. The source suggests a possible action that might lessen the magnitude of the future pain. The song is one of hurtin' love that is probably closer to the category of faded love except that the emphasis is on the sadness that he will feel when the woman leaves and the effort to postpone the unhappiness he will surely know by offering an interesting and novel proposal:

> Don't look so sad I know it's over
> But life goes on and this old world will keep on turning
> Let's just be glad we had some time to spend together
> There's no need to watch the bridges that we're burning
>
> Lay your head upon my pillow
> Hold your warm and tender body close to mine
> Hear the whisper of the raindrops blowing soft against the
>   window
> And make believe you love me one more time
> For the good times.

In 1972, a song found favor with a large audience by emphasizing a combination of the one-for-the road rationale and a faltering relationship. This message is given from the viewpoint of the person who is attempting to break off an affair rather than the one who is facing the possibility of being without a lover. "Four in the Morning," as recorded by Faron Young, describes an additional malady that has always affected people without companionship and was beginning to be openly mentioned in popular commercial country songs. Warner Mack describes it in "The Bridge Washed Out" as a case of nerves that caused him to be overwrought by his inability to cross the raging river to get to his lover. Some describe it as fire burning inside them and others do not even put a euphemistic label on it, but whether it is named or unnamed the lack of love or loving is alluded to in many sets of lyrics. Stepping outside the music to select a vernacularism from the vocabulary of the audience, the condition can be called "horny." Loretta Lynn almost named it in a song that was popular on the weekly charts about a woman losing her virginity to a silver-tongued devil who ushered her into womanhood after promising marriage in "Wings Upon Your Horns." Faron Young explains the problem while admitting that a woman would be better off without him because he has changed his mind for the tenth time about giving her up. Besides proving that he is a "morning" person and that it does not take long for the problem to develop, the source tells why he cannot relinquish his hold on the woman: "It's four in the morning and once more the dawning just woke up the wanting in me."

"All the Lonely Women in the World"

A variation on the immediate gratification theme is present in songs about loneliness due to the absence of a companion. This is in contrast to the two Kristofferson songs cited above where loneliness is *expected* to occur and sex is intended to be used as a last act to buffer the source from the initial hurt. When someone is lonely and without any companionship, there is usually an effort to overcome this barrier. The person who is unhappy about being alone faces multiple obstacles that are often vague and unexplained. The listener does not know why the person is lonely and whether that condition was created by another person or by the source; however, the very fact that a desire for love is expressed indicates that the state itself is a barrier to happiness. Once again the various techniques used to overcome the obstacle occupy the primary attention in the lyrics.

A common tactic for overcoming loneliness in an unhappy relationship is the threat of a sexual adventure as a form of retaliation by a woman who feels wronged. Though a threat of retaliation by "powdering up" and going out in search of another man is often mentioned, it occurs infrequently. A description of women made lonely by men is found in a song sung by Bob Luman, which might be considered both a warning to some men and a possible set of alternatives for others. "Lonely Women Make Good Lovers" is filled with stereotypical ideas and concepts. The sexual needs of a woman are recognized instead of being ignored as they are in most country songs, but the lack of control over those needs is also highlighted. While the lyrics may contain a warning to a man to ensure that he treats a woman "right," there is also the image of a man capable of manipulating a woman. The women are depicted as being hesitant to participate in this type of loving, but when weakened by wine and encouraged by a man they will be fairly easy prey. No consideration is given to the idea that a woman might *not* require this type of justification, that she could be as much of a predator as a man, or that who is using whom is debatable.

Some songs describe the search for someone to love as a happy event, but a few seem to have so much difficulty in accomplishing their objectives that they must be placed in the hurtin' group. One song, which is difficult to categorize because of its discrepant themes and strange sound (especially when heard for the first time), is an oddity in country music. Bill Anderson's "I Can't Wait Any Longer" was recorded with a disco sound that creates problems for a first-time listener because it is so unlike the melodies found on most country recordings. The song barely made the top country singles for 1978 at number 50, but it was there containing a message of unrequited longing. Perhaps it is just an example of lust, for the man described in the lyrics can hardly restrain his wild attraction to and intense desire for a woman. Since there is no evidence that the man is able to satisfy his desires, it can be assumed that the condition is semi-permanent, and if any emotion is as great as that expressed by this man, the frustration of his goal would have to be considered painful.

More typical of the lonely genre is another song written by

Kristofferson in which the source attempts to find temporary relief. "Stranger," as interpreted by Johnny Duncan, describes a man sitting in a bar where he is stoned and listening to sad songs on the jukebox that compound his loneliness. In search of some companionship, he propositions a woman who appears to be equally miserable. She agrees to his proposal but wants "to believe in him" while he pretends he is in love with her. This type of song exemplifies the effort, or need, to obtain companionship for both a man and a woman, for there is no mention of either person's sexual attractiveness. The setting where the lonely people meet, the music that intensifies the feeling of being alone, and the use of sex to provide the semblance of a relationship are quite common in the "lonely and deprived" songs.

"A Lonely Woman (In the Arms of a Man with a One-Track Mind)"

So far we have heard about loneliness from the view of male sources. Admittedly, the lonely women seem to be on fairly equal terms with the men in most of the above examples (other than Luman's song) for they display many of the same characteristics as the men and do not resist the effort to overcome the problem with typical arguments or reluctance. Since the pain of being alone is universal and no blame is allocated to anyone, there is little opportunity to find stereotypical behavior in these lyrics. A feeling created in most of the songs indicates that lonely women are more passive, or at least willing to wait to be sought out by men. In fact, Waylon Jennings's "Come with Me" is an invitation for a lonely woman to let a man help her get over her difficulty. The song further emphasizes the man's role as a predator who may seek to take advantage of the woman who is lonely. Perhaps the most common trait of a lonely woman is that she may be the victim (often a willing one) of a man who takes advantage of her need for a relationship—a situation that can be used by a man to satisfy his sexual desires.

84

One song clearly contradicts this view of the vulnerable woman suppressing her personal desires and participating in sexual episodes out of a need for any type of companionship. The first few lines of the lyrics sound like the traditional lost or "faded" love songs. Near the end of the first verse, however, we can see how different the song is from earlier ones with that theme. The woman in this song may be passive in that she is not actively pursuing a solution to her problem, but she is not hesitant to express when she feels a certain type of loneliness or to describe what would be required to solve her problem. A typical woman in the faded love songs wishes to have a man return and wants a wonderful man with a pure heart and a one-woman philosophy. This woman is lonely, but her situation can be alleviated by a man, any man. She does not want, as many of the earlier faded songs indicate, a long-term relationship; she wants someone to love her, and more importantly, to leave her. Once again, it is Loretta Lynn who offers the atypical view of a frustrated woman in "Somebody Somewhere (Don't Know What He's Missin' Tonight)."

It must have all started with that darn'd old late show
It made me so lonely and sad
And to make it all better I kept getting bluer
With each little drink that I had
Then I tuned in a D.J. who played ev'ry sad song he owned
Lord I need someone so
But ev'ry one I know is away being needed at home.

Somebody somewhere don't know what he's missin' tonight
Lord here sits a woman just lonesome enough to be right
For lovin' and leavin' how I need someone to hold tight
Somebody somewhere don't know what he's missin' tonight.

This song is one of the few which honestly discusses the needs and desires of a woman in the way that men's have been dis-

"Somebody Somewhere (Don't Know What He's Missin' Tonight)" by Lola Jean Dillon. Copyright 1976 Coal Miners Music, Inc. Used by permission.

cussed for years. However, the song depicts a lonely woman wishing for a man—not actively searching for one. Few women have moved this far in country music and when they do refer to the search it is found in the happy love songs or in the songs celebrating a certain lifestyle (these songs will be discussed later). What is important at this point, is how men react to women who are actively seeking casual sexual encounters. Men's descriptions of the effects of these brief interludes are similar to those women gave after an experience with a silver-tongued devil. Rather than celebrating the appearance of these "new" women, many men are frustrated by them.

Quick love has always been described either directly or indirectly in country music. Instant intimacy is the more appropriate way to describe this type of relationship, but in the music it is usually called a one-night stand. One man believed it could be even less time consuming in "If You've Got Ten Minutes (Let's Fall in Love)." Traditionally, men have been the predators in the happy and/or desperate search for these brief encounters. The objects of their hunt were most often the women who frequented bars and honky-tonks. The women who choose to attend such haunts were either the "bad" ones seeking a "wild side of life" or the lonely ones desperate for any type of male companionship.

We have seen a man take advantage of a lonely woman in "Lonely Women Make Good Lovers" and to a lesser extent in "Stranger." In both these songs women are plied with drinks to reduce their inhibitions and little is said about their needs. A second type of woman is not necessarily lonely; however, she is the object of many hunts for the simple reason she is a conspicuous quarry in the lyrical preserve. The honky-tonk queen (or angel) has a well-documented, if unclear, image in the music. To men she can be a welcome haven, to women she can be an unwelcome port of call; to both she has an inordinate amount of power to influence relationships. She can be the answer to a man's dream and the unknown in a woman's nightmare. The primary reason for such a vacillating image is that we seldom hear directly from her. Men usually sing about her in a positive way—unless it is their mother, sister, lover, or wife who has taken up residence in such a place. Women usually sing about her as a rival to lure away or destroy the weak-willed and susceptible man. If more women singers were to take up the challenge offered by Kitty Wells in "It Wasn't God Who Made Honky Tonk Angels," we might hear more from the perspective of the "queen" of the smoky kingdom.

It is obvious that these groups of women are being joined by another. There is no label for these women as yet, but they are making their presence known. A few in this group of women may be lonely, but they do not dwell on it or use it as an excuse for their behavior. A woman from this group may frequent bars and honky-tonks, but does not yet seem to be an artifact or as difficult to understand as the "queen" or "angel." She is using the locales for the same reason many of the men are—for a playground or a hunting preserve. She is honest about her motives for visiting such a place; she is not always there attempting to drown the troubles caused by a man, nor is she there because she has no other options. She is where she wants to be, doing what she wants to do. If we really believed all those male hunters, we would expect these women to be the answer to their dreams. They are not.

The prototype of these women was outlined beautifully by Loretta Lynn in "Somebody Somewhere." It was not the first song to mention the sexual desires of a woman, but those needs usually were to be satisfied in a more socially acceptable manner.[11] Traditionally the "good" woman in the music was to be content with whatever pleasure she might receive in a marriage or at least within the context of romantic love. These new women are displaying the traits of the men out in search of quick and unencumbered love. They reflect the attitude of a man described in a happy love song by Kenny Rogers. The man, in "Love or Something Like It," says he has love (or something similar) on the brain and is almost certain that he will be successful in the pursuit if he continues asking the "wrong" question of enough women. What the man in Rogers's song did not know is that the answer to his question may create other more perplexing questions.

The man who encounters one of these women uninterested in

long-term relationships and gets past the questioning stage often finds the effects of his efforts troubling. There were clues to this potential source of frustration at about the time Lynn's song was popular. For instance, the man in "Love in the Hot Afternoon" described his uneasiness after a brief encounter with a woman who was not hindered by traditional roles. A similar concern is expressed in another song released during the period and appropriately titled "Overnight Sensation." Mickey Gilley's recording did not make the year-end charts, but it did rise to number seven on the weekly lists. In that song, a woman warmly loves and abruptly leaves a man, and it is the man who remains in bed troubled over the realization that she will be with someone else that very night with no thought of him cluttering her mind.

In the 1980s, the frustration over this role reversal was expressed more often. In Conway Twitty's song "Tight Fittin' Jeans," a woman shows up in the bar and catches a man's eye. He somehow knows she is not a typical patron, and although certainly impressed, he is slow to act. He can hardly believe his good fortune after discovering she is a rich, sophisticated, and married woman who is interested in discovering how it would be to spend an evening with a "cowboy." She obviously impressed him very much. Disappointed over the absence of a continuing relationship, he is sitting in the bar reminiscing about a wonderful night of love. A man pining over a woman who has used him for her own gratification is a novel experience for a man in country music.

Some of these men may not know what they really want. These men have long said they were searching for a woman who wanted to make love as much as they did and afterwards leave them alone, but when they find these women they seem to be less than thrilled. These men are assuming the passive role that has been assigned to the woman in the music. Michael Martin Murphy released a song (reached number seven on the weekly charts in 1984) in which the man wonders if he spends the night with a woman "Will It Be Love by Morning." This is a switch from the old question whether he will respect her the next day. It is the man who feels uneasy about the situation when the woman indicates that not only will she have trouble respecting him, she may not even remember him the next morning.

Conway Twitty had another song on the charts in 1987 (written by two women) which increases the turn away from the image of the typical sexual predator toward that of men who are more interested in developing a foundation for a long-term relationship. The title explains the point very well: "I Want to Know You Before We Make Love." The reason for such a statement is best summarized in a song popular in 1986 that describes the reason for the frustration in many of these men. The Nitty Gritty Dirt Band (another group capable of establishing the sincerity contract in a serious song) released a song appropriately called "Modern Day Romance." The man in this song stopped to help a woman whose Corvette had broken down. He repaired the car and she offered him a ride. He left his truck and went along for the trip of his life—a spectacular weekend in Reno where they did not leave the room to gamble and wasted little time eating. At the end of the brief stay, the woman disappeared leaving a note to thank him for the good times. Near the end of the song the man is walking down the highway reminiscing about the weekend and how he tried to love the woman without any strings but fell in love anyway. The conclusion of the song summarizes the problem for those men having difficulty adjusting to the new women. The man says that his modern day romance has caused him some "old fashioned pain."

"Hurtin' for Certain"

If there is one type of song that exemplifies the special interpersonal relationship that exists between the singer and the listener in country music, it is the song of hurtin' love. When a source admits a deep personal loss and confesses his or her inability to maintain a romantic relationship while withholding few intimate details from the receiver, it demonstrates the type of self-disclosing statements that are ordinarily part of the communication between close friends. However, the admission of pain resulting from an action or inaction by someone relating a tale of hurtin' love is insufficient to guarantee that a song will achieve wide acceptance. Most of us have been exposed to a friend's story of a fractured romance and know it takes more than deep personal concern to maintain an active and continuing interest in the message. In order for a story to be of great interest, it must be filled with fascinating details in clear language that calls for more than empathic response. In addition, the story must be told exceptionally well. These elements are present in most of the hurtin' songs that were popular from 1960 to 1987.

The singers of lost or faded love songs portray people who, for the most part, are so overwhelmed by their emotions that they may be unable to function in any rational way. These people display depression, self-pity, despair, anger, and fear, with little hope for ever achieving emotional stability. When an audience is asked to accept these attitudes and behaviors from any source, a severe strain would seem to be placed on the establishment of the sincerity contract, but this is not the case. While there are qualitative differences between the language and images in the lyrics, the most important factor in developing the sincerity contract in these songs is the credibility of the singer interpreting the lyrics. Although the songs from the early 1960s lack the flavor of the hurtin' songs of the 1940s and early 1950s because of their smoother instrumentation, the lyrics did not change as much as the background. Realistic lyrics continued throughout the period, and even though the slicker productions and crooning vocalists may restrict the impact of some of these lyrics, there is still more emotion in the music than in most other musical genres. The hurtin' love songs were modified even less than some other types of country songs and will always strike a sympathetic response in the true country audience. When it was suggested to Willie Nelson that hurtin' songs have varied little over the years, he agreed and noted that he expected little change in the future, for they "seem to be the medicine that people need when they are going through those [unhappy] times. It's a period when they need someone to relate to, and they can relate to the hillbilly singing the song."[12]

The main reason why we have so many songs that stress unhappy love is that people wish, or need, to "relate to the hillbilly" who is expressing pain that may not be the same pain they feel, but is not altogether unlike the pain most listeners know. Most people have lost a love or a lover, have had someone "do them wrong," or have been otherwise worried or frustrated in the pursuit of love. Since most of the audience is composed of adults who have lived or observed many of these types of traumas ("Backside of Thirty" by John Conlee may really hit home for those not wishing to face single life after divorce), there is much in these heartbreaking stories with which to identify. To encourage identification with the message, the most successful country singers are willing and able to submerge themselves in a story and become part of it. Songs by Lefty Frizzell in the early part of the period, Conway Twitty in the 1970s, Randy Travis in the mid-eighties, and George Jones all through the period are excellent sources of the views of a man who truly sounds as if he is hurtin' in a song. Songs by Kitty Wells and Patsy Cline popular in the early 1960s and Loretta Lynn's songs through most of the period are fine examples of hurtin' songs from the woman's view. Unlike many pop and rock singers who attempt to create a two-part message by calling attention to vocal and instrumental techniques, most country singers expend great effort in creating a unified message. Certainly, a few popular country songs offer less than a completely straightforward message (we have examined a few of them), a few country singers and/or record producers employ techniques that may distract the listener from the message ("The Door" by George Jones has the sound of a closing door, but that does not weaken the sentiments in the song), and a few songs become popular when the approach is humorous rather than heartbreaking. However, most of the songs are as honest as the singer can make them by articulating the intensely personal statement with none of the embarrassment that some sources might feel and show if they were faking such feelings.

During the early 1970s the hurtin' songs may have carried more honesty than some listeners wished to hear, but most of the audience heartily approved. Especially significant in this group of songs was the work of Kris Kristofferson. The former Rhodes scholar has described the message contained in many of his songs as "echoes of the going ups and coming downs, walking pneumonia and run-of-the-mill madness, colored with guilt, pride, and a vague sense of despair."[13] They are also songs that had a major impact on commercial country music because of their articulate descriptions of absent love, which adds support to those who feel that many country songs are wonderful examples of modern poetry. While most hurtin' songs localize the pain by specifying a particular love relationship and the problems of two people that can be generalized by a listener, the song that deals with loneliness in general without any particular relationships are more indicative of hurtin' in the 1970s. Kristofferson's suggestions that people use sex to hinder the prospect of being lonely and to overcome the barrier of real loneliness serve to dilute some of the flippancy in many country songs that depict a wild and erratic search for casual sex.

One more item must be mentioned before we leave these sad, but magnetic, songs. Country lyrics are recognized for being "direct and honest stuff."[14] Loretta Lynn's version of "Somebody Somewhere" certainly presents a direct and honest statement of a woman's needs and places them on a level with those of any man. Admittedly, this is the most popular of the hurtin' songs with this approach by a woman and did not signal a trend. To imply that any one song is an indication of a change leaves one open to criticism that can be leveled at many observers of country music. Those casual observers, just like the people who think they are good conversationalists, excellent drivers, and superior lovers, often substantiate their claims by offering isolated and insufficient examples. Perhaps we can find more examples to support Lynn's approach in the "happy" love songs and in those where the people are often both happy and hurtin' in the cheatin' songs.

Chapter
3

Happy Love:

Some of the Folks
Are Happy Some of the Time

Donna Fargo, a former schoolteacher who found contentment outside the classroom, wrote and recorded a song entitled "The Happiest Girl in the Whole U.S.A." This song, which was popular in 1972, may typify "happy" love for many observers of country music.

Good morning, morning
Hello, sunshine, wakeup sleepy head
Why'd we move that bojangle clock so far away from the bed
Just one more minute that's why we moved it
One more hug or two
Do you love waking up next to me as much as I love waking up
    next to you
You make the coffee, I'll make the bed
Now tell the truth
Do these old shoes look funny, honey, it's almost time
Now you be careful, gotta go
I love you, have a beautiful day
And kiss the happiest girl in the whole U.S.A.

Skip-a-dee-doo-dah
Thank you, Lord, for making him for me

And thank you for letting life turn out the way that I always
   thought it could be
There once was a time when I could not imagine
How it would feel to say I'm the happiest girl in the whole
   U.S.A.

Reading these lyrics, we may believe we have discovered the
reason why more hurtin' than happy songs attain widespread
popularity. Nevertheless, we can find in Fargo's lines the characteristics generally found in happy love songs—songs in which a
singer is satisfied, secure, pleased, and, in some cases, exuberant
about a love relationship. Although the happy love songs are
more difficult to categorize than those with a hurtin' love message, many can be grouped by their approach to the subject. A
happy love song is likely to describe one of the following situations: a breach is healed (the "together again" song), a lover is
praised (the "somebody special" song), a love relationship fulfills
a personal goal or dream (the "behind closed doors" song), a
lover is lost in euphoria (the "pretty world" song), a search for
love has ended in some degree of satisfaction (the "love or something like it" song), or a lover is thrilled over the physical aspects
of love (the "trip to heaven" song).

"Together Again"

Happy love songs, unlike hurtin' ones, fail to maintain strong
and consistent positions on the year-end charts, and they tend to
cluster together according to type and artist when they appear. In
1964, Buck Owens had four very popular songs celebrating happy

love, and two of these were answers to wishes found in the hurtin' songs in which an unhappy person wanted the loved one to come back. "Together Again" was written, recorded, and made popular by Owens in 1964 (Emmylou Harris also recorded a popular version in the mid-1970s). The lyrics tell about a lover's return, when the sky is no longer gray and love is alive again. Although the song is presented in a rather subdued vocal style, the message does support the belief many hurting folks have in a cure for the pain caused by an absent love. Owens sounded more excited in "Love's Gonna Live Here," which was also popular in 1964. This time the man hears bells ringing, birds singing, and bees humming.

"Say it Again"

Several songs of this type offer mild twists to the happiness generated by born-again love. Dolly Parton's version of "You're the Only One" is a message from the wayward lover who admits that she has been unkind and insensitive but now realizes that she really loves the man she mistreated and abandoned. She promises the man that if he will take her back she will not break his heart again. She tells him she had to go away to appreciate what she left behind—a suggestion, perhaps, that she was unable to find anything better, rather than that he was so splendid in the first place. Whatever the merits of her case, she is back and filled with promises of future happiness.

Jeanne Black was happy in an "answer" song in 1960. Answer songs are responses to a message found in other popular recordings, and they occur frequently in country music. "Please Help Me I'm Falling," for instance, was answered by "(I Can't Help You) I'm Falling Too." "He'll Have to Go," a fine hurtin' song, was answered by Black with "He'll Have to Stay." The authors of the hurtin' song, Joe and Audrey Allison, are two of the three coauthors of the response (another common practice with these songs). In the first song a man is calling a former lover from a bar, saying that he knows she has a man there with her, and asking her to send the man away. The woman in the happy song admits that another man is with her and tells the caller she is satisfied with this arrangement. Her answer indicates that she is in the process of overcoming a hurt and is happier with someone else. We do not know the extent of the hurt, but we know that she reacted quickly to overcome it, for she located the new man in one day.

"Love's the Answer"

As new love or returned love can cure the pain of love lost, good and constant love can offer respite from the other pains the world gives us. Ronnie Milsap explains this in a fairly specific song called "What Goes On When the Sun Goes Down." The man explains the tribulations of life and then describes the way good love or loving helps people make it through the day.

> Every day with love renewed, we face another day
> Screen doors bangin', the boss complaining, and bills to pay
> Through it all, we wear love's smile from the happiness we
> found
> And only lovers know what goes on when the sun goes down.

"Somebody Special"

As we noted in the previous songs, the message in happy songs is often presented to the one who has made the singer happy. Unlike the hurtin' songs, when the other person is usually absent and no direct communication is possible (except for accidental meetings and telephone calls), in the happy songs the other person is present. At times a singer's gratitude is expressed about a few personal qualities or peculiar circumstances that may appear nonsensical to some people. It is important to remember that for all we know *both* parties in the relationship are happy, that happiness must be a privilege (in this music), and that perhaps one of the annoyances a person must endure to share this privilege is a certain amount of irrationality.

"My Love"

Buck Owens might have created some confusion for a rational lover (it could be a different lover, of course) when another of his happy love songs reached the charts in 1964. "I Don't Care" seemed to refute what he had insisted was important in another song popular the same year. In "Love's Gonna Live Here," he was pleased that he could hear the sounds of bells ringing, birds singing, and bees humming, and attributed his more acute perception to the presence of his lover. In "I Don't Care," on the other hand, he says:

> Well, I don't care if the birds don't sing
> I don't care if the bells don't ring
> Just as long as you love me.

This is typical of many lyrics in which the environment, and almost everything else, becomes unimportant in comparison to the feeling created by a loved one.

Charley Pride shows his approval and satisfaction when he compares a lover to an island. In "You're My Jamaica," the man is glowing in his description of a place where the "bikinied ladies" and "sweet rum drinks" are certainly attractive, but he has a recording of calypso music at home and tells his love "You're where I want to be" because she is his "heavenly haven." Freddie Hart believes his lover has angel wings on her pretty shoulders, but this does not seem to get in the way of her "Easy Loving." A number of such songs celebrate the woman's physical qualities while taking pleasure in the fact that her love is special because "it comes from the heart." Hart repeats the "easy loving" idea in a 1973 song that is a little more to the point. "Super Kind of Woman" is an expression of happiness for the wonderful and enthusiastic way a woman loves a man and tells why this is so important: "With her I am no longer half, but whole."

"I Love You Best of All"

A fairly risky way to assure a lover is found in a few of these songs. Some sources compare the quality of a present love or lover to those of the past to show that the new one is the best. At least two problems could be created by such a practice. Ignoring the hazards of a faulty memory and sampling size, we might expect the person being evaluated either to resent the comparison or to ask for further substantiation. Additional evidence could lead to the hurting found in the last chapter or the cheating in the next, but in the happy songs the literal comparison is presented in a style that suggests the source's pride and is intended to instill the same pride in the lover.

In Charlie Rich's version of "Every Time You Touch Me (I Get High)," a man tells a woman how it feels each time her fingers caress his skin. She has the miraculous power to blot out pain and cause him to live again. This is not an uncommon thing for a lover to say, but when he explains how he knows she is special, he develops the argument from comparison.

And I've been kissed by the very best
And I've been loved by quite a few
But after you I forget the rest.

He may have forgotten who the "rest" are, but he does not seem to have forgotten what they were able to do.

Freddie Hart's popular recording "My Woman's Man" tells of a man who is pleased for the same reason as the man in "What Goes On When the Sun Goes Down." The love and understanding he receives each night from his woman carries him through every day, and the ultimate compliment is that "She's the best I've ever had." It is left to a woman to be more specific about what it means to be the best of a long list of lovers. Tammy Wynette recorded a song co-written by Billy Sherrill (he was also a coauthor of "Every Time You Touch Me") that mixes several themes contained in "happy" love songs in the 1970s. The 1975 song tells how a woman toyed with a number of men, enjoyed deceiving them, and left them in tears. She admits that "love was just a game" and brags that she was a skilled and experienced player, but the present lover has accomplished something no other has been able to do. "(You Make Me Want to Be) A Mother" explains quite clearly that the woman did not expect this romance to be serious, much less to stir maternal thoughts. Not only does the song contain a fascinating description of a free-spirited woman, but in the first few lines it also offers an interesting rationale for the development of her unexpected thoughts.

You make me want to be a mother
I never thought I would
'Cause you got close
To what I cherish most.

"Every Time You Touch Me (I Get High)" by Charlie Rich and Billy Sherrill. Copyright 1975 by Algee Music Corp. and Double R. Music Corp. Used by permission.

"(You Make Me Want to Be) A Mother" by Norris Wilson and Billy Sherrill. Copyright 1975 by Algee Music Corp. Used by permission.

Some appreciative lovers combine their appreciation with a concern for the partner's well-being. Instead of emphasizing their own personal satisfaction, they mention the needs and desires of the lover. Since we are given inadequate information about the object of the love in most of the songs, we assume that both parties are happy, and it stands to reason that a better opportunity for happiness exists if less self-centeredness and more caring is expressed. Some of the songs offer assurance to the partner that everything will work out right. Anne Murray's "Shadows in the Moonlight," for example, explains that all a man need bring to a hideaway is his love, for the woman will meet him anywhere and they will make love from midnight until dawn. Since the time span is highlighted, perhaps it is necessary to add the following information.

> The night is young
> And, baby, so are we
> And I'm gonna make you glad you came.

Sharing and assuring are also featured in another song where the source wants his partner to experience the same intense emotion as he is. "Hope You're Feeling Me (Like I'm Feeling You)," sung by Charley Pride, tells of a man who is satisfied but is also occupied with a woman's feelings. Her love has changed him from a rather independent and out-of-control person, and he would be unhappy without her. Recognizing the uncertainty of a one-sided love affair, he hopes she has the same amount of love for him. Certainly, his concern for her happiness is as self-centered as that found in many of the other songs, but at least he expresses a need for sharing not found in all these songs.

A more distinctive message appears in Ronnie Milsap's "(I'm a) Stand by My Woman Man." This is not really an answer song; it might be considered an assurance song—one that assures a woman she will not have to put up with a man's "instinctive" behavior that can hurt her. The man is quite specific:

> At five o'clock she knows I'll soon be home
> She don't worry about me runnin' around
> 'Cause all of my good times are waiting right there for me
> And she knows where I'll be when the sun goes down.

A few of these appreciative songs emphasize sharing a good thing and are different in their approach. The Bellamy Brothers certainly consider a woman's needs in "Sugar Daddy." Suggesting that the woman deserves "little" things such as diamond rings, satin pillows, or a new Cadillac, they outline the desires of both the man and the woman.

> You're the kind of woman that likes to be on her own
> Except for those times you need a man all night long
> You like the finer things
> All my money can buy
> I like the way your body sings
> I love the fire in your eyes.

Bill Anderson had a prescription for dual happiness in a song that could be interpreted as a cheating song until late in the lyrics. A man is telling his lover that they should plan on leaving for a few days of loving without letting anyone know their whereabouts. The lines unfold in such a way as to suggest an illicit rendezvous, but with a twist in the lyrics he tells her he wants a "Wild Weekend" with his wife. Such a flattering maneuver is an expression of thanks and a need to share good feelings.

"She's No Ordinary Woman (Ordinarily)"

Another appreciative song serves as a positive response to those who need love and can be construed as support for the stereotypical view of women in country music. However, as we noted in "You're the Only One" and "Shadows in the Moonlight," a woman can be either one who has deserted a lover or one who arranges a schedule for lovemaking. The roles of men and women are not as specifically delineated in happy love songs as in hurting songs, and this makes it more difficult to distinguish the behavior of and attitudes toward men and women. "I Know How" was recorded by Loretta Lynn, but it could have been performed as appropriately by a man.

> Yea, I love him like he wants me to and I know how
> And it's my duty to know his moods when he gets moody
> Yea, I give him what he needs and that's why I'm his right now
> Yes, I know I love him right 'cause I know how.
>
> Yes, I know how to hold him when he needs holding
> And I know how to kiss him when he needs kissing
> I understand his every wish and his every wish is mine
> Yes, he knows I love to love him and I know how.

Two other songs provide rather drab pictures of married women who still generate appreciative notices from their husbands. Marty Robbins's "My Woman, My Woman, My Wife" describes a woman with wrinkled hands, graying hair, and a gingham dress. The trials of bearing and raising children while serving as a pillar for a husband who needs encouragement are recognized, and she is applauded for the quiet strength and inner warmth she has shown through a difficult life. The man proclaims great love for

"I Know How" by Loretta Lynn. Copyright 1970. Used with permission of Sure-Fire Music Co. Inc.

the woman and feels certain that she will be rewarded in her next life. Conway Twitty is more specific when he offers an earthly reward in a song that describes a woman as a homemaker and mother, but one who still turns him on. The singer mulls over several ways to express his love (a song, a poem, or just some promises), but decides the most effective way is to tell her that "I'd Just Love to Lay You Down."

It is not unusual to hear an appreciation for a wonderful love relationship expressed along with the assurance that the appreciation will not lessen over time. One of the most often stated assumptions in these appreciation songs (and in real life) is that the brightly burning love will remain at that level forever. Twitty just made that assertion and the claim was repeated through the 1980s. Randy Travis made essentially the same claim in "Forever and Ever, Amen." The man in Travis's song says he realizes that the color of a woman's hair will fade over the years, but insists that her hair is not what he loves. He knows the hazards of time and what it can do to a relationship and insists she is special enough to overcome the problem. He says time has erased his memories of other women and she has changed him from a happy hunter to a contented and satisfied lover. Although the reasoning in the song is flawed by a lack of evidence, Travis's interpretation of the lyrics overcomes the innate fallacies and this 1987 recording continues the tradition of fine happy love songs. Another song, popular in the same year, uses a rather interesting method to assure a lover of the permanency of a happy love. Michael Martin Murphy uses an argument from genetics when he tells a woman about the success of his ancestors' love relationships and promises he will be hers forever because he is a product of "A Long Line of Love."

"Only One Love in My Life"

Some of the poignant love songs are those expressing the simple idea that a partner is not only a lover, but also a friend. It is a rare and valuable person who cares enough to help another without offering value judgments, to forget as well as to forgive, and to give love without keeping score. Just as this type of person is difficult to find, it is also difficult to express one's feelings for them, but several songs in this group make splendid efforts to do that. Anne Murray's "You Needed Me" expresses a woman's thanks to a person who is concerned for her and tells of the many things that were done to help her through difficult times. When the woman needed comfort, strength, dignity, hope, and the truth, she says her lover gave it and "even called me friend." The woman knows how special this type of person is and says she will never leave "Because I've finally found someone who really cares."

Don Williams, who has recorded a number of love songs that depict this type of caring, did the popular version of a song illustrating how a love can be expressed by magnifying some of the virtues of friendship. Although "You're My Best Friend," written by Wayland Holyfield, refers to some of the elements noted in earlier songs (life given to his children, love such as he has never known, one reason for his existence), what matters most here is the fact that his wife is his best friend. This simple statement highlights a close, shared love, and Holyfield's lyrics present this warm message with no distractions from the central thought. Williams's interpretation of the lyrics allows the message to be tender and sincere with none of the syrupy sentiments that can result when a source overstates a feeling of gratitude.

"Behind Closed Doors"

The primary intent of many songs is to state that the joy generated by a lover is one that satisfies the achievement of a personal goal. The sources relate the pride and glory the lover has provided, and even though some incredibility seeps into a few of the messages and while some do not flout the feeling, they are not hesitant to express it. Charlie Rich's "Behind Closed Doors" gives an excellent picture of a man whose woman demonstrates her love in private. While he says that they have nothing to hide from anyone, he is concerned with the tendency people have to "talk." Perhaps it is the people's knowledge of specific detail that concerns him—not the fact of her love. He takes great pride in that she makes him feel like a man, and that is all he says about what goes on in the privacy behind that closed door.

Pride turns to amazement in Conway Twitty's "(I Can't Believe) She Gives It All to Me." The man in the song wonders about his good fortune in the very love that brings him such pleasure. He certainly is not suggesting that the love should be shared or restricted in any way, but the fact that it is not is nearly too good to be believed. His astonishment is demonstrated in the first verse.

> I pinch myself when I wake up each mornin'
> 'Cause I'm constantly amazed when I see
> Exactly everything I've always wanted,
> But I can't believe she gives it all to me.

There is some mention of the woman's feelings in the last verse, but no indication that he tells her these things that amaze and satisfy him. She sees his love in his actions or, as he says, "Somehow she knows I need her desperately." It is this overlooking or deemphasizing of a lover's feelings that make such songs of personal fulfillment different from those that state gratitude toward the lover.

"It's Such a Pretty World Today"

Tom T. Hall can put life and love into better perspective than most. In "I Love," a song he wrote, recorded, and made popular, Hall places his lover in a list of objects, items, and behaviors that might at first appear nonsensical and understated. After naming sixteen things he loves (in addition to his loved one), he adds eight more:

> I love honest smiles, kisses from a child
> Tomatoes on a vine and onions
> I love winners when they cry, losers when try
> Music when it's good and life
> And I love you, too.

If this does not clarify a person's status in a relationship, then it probably cannot be done. Where a person stands in a love relationship, the perception of his or her environment, and the effect of love upon those perceptions are important parts of the experiences of love. A large number of happy love songs nevertheless take an approach that gives little to the audience except a description of euphoria. Sometimes we are told about certain qualities of the lover or a few aspects of the love that create this personal glow, but in most cases this material is secondary to the general sense of buoyancy. Many people conveying this type of message seem to be afflicted with an irrationality equal to that displayed by those who have lost a love, and the heightened emotion created by happiness appears to be as difficult to cope with as the depression suffered by one who cannot function after a love has disappeared. These songs usually deal with a magnitude of a feeling rather than with the individuals or situations. Perhaps the feeling is so great that the source has difficulty expressing it in simple words. Anyone who has been in love feels that the experience is unique, but trying to verbalize it may tend to prove the universality of the condition rather that its uniqueness. Some songs deserve special notice for their attempts.

"It Must Be Love"

Buck Owens discusses a physiological ramification of happy love in "My Heart Skips a Beat," but for the most part it is an all-encompassing and pervasive love that is the center of attention in such songs. Wynne Stewart exemplifies this in a song that was popular in 1976. "It's Such a Pretty World Today" tells how the source's perception of the world has changed since he met his lover. He mentions blue skies and sunshine first of all. He is specific only in saying that she is "his" and that it makes him happy to be close to her; what she is doing, has done, or will continue to do is not mentioned. Only the love that has changed his ability to know his surroundings is spoken of further.

"World" is a key word in these songs. In the same year as "Pretty World" was popular, George Jones offered an invitation to "Walk through This World with Me." Jim Reeves was past the invitation stage in "Welcome to My World." Sonny James used the term to identify his lover when he told her "You're the Only World I Know," and David Houston did the same with "You Mean the World to Me." (Houston was so happy he included a semi-yodel in the chorus.) An interesting limitation on the "world" concept is found in a song made popular by the group Alabama in 1986. A view of the world is not the central theme in the happy love song "She and I," however, the use of it as a set of self-imposed parameters is different. For instance, the source describes the lovers' world as small and self-sufficient. Not only is this view contrary to the limitless view described in the songs just mentioned, the source also observes that some friends think the couple's views and the behavior used to maintain them are a little strange. Some sources extend their analogies even beyond this planet. Sonny James identifies his lover as heaven—even when all she does is speak—in "Heaven Says Hello." Lynn Anderson carried the "world" and "heaven" images further than most of the others. Her version of "Top of the World" describes a woman who has been elevated to such a high plane that she is able to view the entire universe.

Referring to the lover as "heaven" and "the world" is an ordinary device in these songs, but in one of the more interesting sets of lyrics a lover is identified by the event that was occurring when they met. The song is called "Snowflake," which is also what the source (Jim Reeves) calls his new lover. (She should feel lucky that he did not meet her in a hail storm.)

"Timber I'm Falling"

Some songs about euphoric love are concerned with the greatness and endurance of a love that seems too good to be true. Conway Twitty and Loretta Lynn, in one of their many successful joint efforts, recorded a version of "I Can't Love You Enough." They are unable to place restrictions on the amount and quality of their love, but both are equally sure that they are getting more than they can give. This song would have been placed in the "appreciative" group, but here the fact of love itself is emphasized over credit for the love. The sources get quite specific in telling what they would do for love. For instance, Lynn suggests that if she were starving she would refuse food if given the choice between a steak or his loving. Twitty is more mercenary when he says he wouldn't sell her love for a million dollars.

Another male and female duo who made several popular recordings during the period were Jim Ed Brown and Helen Cornelius. They recorded a song suggesting that their love was special for its abundance. "If the World Ran Out of Love Tonight" used "world" in the more literal sense, but the man and woman in the song are interested in the amount of love they could replace if the need arose. The song takes an approach that is seldom used

108

in this type of love song although it is sometimes found in songs celebrating sexual attraction. This approach makes love a goal; the lovers will pretend that they must make enough love in one night to supply the world in case the love outside their bedroom were to disappear. They have great faith in their abilities and capabilities, or little understanding of how much love the world needs. They have set for themselves, in any case, an enjoyable if tiring task.

The specificity found in the last two examples is not indicative of most songs that are primarily concerned with all-consuming love. The persons describing the euphoric love tend to be slightly confused about their reasons for being in such a joyous state but they are certain that their experience is unique. They feel an expansiveness and a heightened perception of their environment. That environment is primarily one of their own making, one that appears slightly self-centered and must be similar to the atmosphere created by the lost loves in the last chapter. The fall to earth after the loss of love can be especially hard for those who have felt that they transcended this world in their happiness. The songs in this group must be dealing with a new or fairly fresh love—one that flashes and burns brightly but seldom maintains the intensity generated at the start and therefore cannot keep the lovers isolated from the real world for very long.

"Love or Something Like It"

Some of the people who are looking for the "starfire" love described above are having fun hunting for it. A song (mentioned briefly in chapter 2) that typifies the "hot pursuit" of love by describing the scene, the techniques employed to entice the object of the search, and the reaction to success is found in Kenny Rogers's version of "Love or Something Like It."

Show me a bar with a good-looking woman then just get out of
my way
Turn on the jukebox, I'll show you a song you should play
Sooner or later, a few shots of bourbon, I'll think of something
to say
Whoa, I can take or leave her, I'd like to take her away.

Liquor and music, a good combination, if you've got love on the
brain
I never knew two women who acted the same
Some want to drink first and some want to just sit and talk
Whoa, it's two in the morning, I'm running and she wants to
walk.

Something's got a hold on me
It's cheap but it ain't free
Love or something like it
Got a hold on me.

That's when I asked her, my place or your place, I hope I'm not
out of line
I asked the wrong thing to just the right woman this time
She knew a hotel, she even had a name we could sign
Whoa, the cheaper the grapes are the sweeter the taste of the
wine.

Some of the characteristics of the hurtin' songs, where the
hunt is more desperate and the source expresses little joy, are
also found here. The source finds a good-looking woman pre-
sumably alone in a bar and is the predator in the hunt. The man
uses music and liquor to get into the proper mood for his less-
than-original proposition, but he is perceptive enough to know
that women require different approaches. Although he seems to
adhere to the philosophy that if you approach enough people
with the same question you may finally get the answer you want,

he recognizes the essential irony of the game he plays when he tells us, "the cheaper the grapes are the sweeter the taste of the wine." There is a hint of cheating in the lyrics when the woman suggests that instead of going to his or her place they should check into a hotel under assumed names.

Another song in this group depicts a man who also has something like love on his brain and is filled with an even greater sense of urgency. The Bellamy Brothers display both a novel use of language and a straightforward hunting technique, used by a man with a disdain for small talk. "If I Said You Have a Beautiful Body Would You Hold It against Me" describes a hunter who is not worried that a woman might want a drink or conversation before she is pressed into making a decision. This song comes to the point rather quickly. There is a reference to nature—sunshine—that is common in the "pretty world" songs, but it is mentioned only as an example of the small talk the man's daddy told him to disregard. There is no indication that his approach was successful for this man or for his father, but he seems to be enjoying the attempt.

The Bellamy Brothers rejected their daddy's advice in a song popular in 1986. In "Lie to You for Your Love," the source tells a woman he would say anything to get her love and he proves it. This approach may be no more successful than the one described earlier, but once again the Bellamy Brothers are in hot pursuit and taking a different tact. Conway Twitty takes a similar approach in "Desperado Love," popular during the same year. The man in this song will not only lie, he threatens to steal her love if necessary. The urgency displayed in this type of hunt has not disappeared from the music even though we have seen earlier how a successful hunt can lead to a number of problems.

"Do You Want to Go to Heaven"

Conway Twitty uses a different tactic when he describes a man's thoughts in "I've Already Loved You in My Mind." The song describes a man's fantasy and the technique he uses to convince a woman that she need not worry about the lack of a formal introduction. She hesitates to dance with him because he is a stranger (although she has noticed him), and even though we might wonder about this type of approach, it turns out to be as successful as it is daring.

> I thought I'd never seen a girl like her in here before,
> And I could see her watchin' me as I walked across the floor,
> I asked her if she'd like to dance when the band starts up again,
> She said, "I never dance alone with strangers, I don't even know
>   your name."
> I said, "We're not exactly strangers, you and I;
> My thoughts were runnin' wild and free as I watched you
>   tonight,
> Just think about it and you'll find
> We're not exactly strangers,
> I've already loved you in my mind."

When the band starts playing, either the music or the desire to get closer to someone who would use such a line causes her to move into his arms. The second fantasy occurs while they are dancing, for at the end of the set she repeats the sentiment stated in the chorus—that they are not strangers anymore. Whether two fantasies make one encounter, or the scene is continued later, is unknown, but Twitty's interpretation of his own lyrics seems to indicate that hope and happiness abound.

At least one song offers a counterpoint to the successful hunting songs in which a willing woman is finally located. Loretta Lynn recorded a song that responds to a man whose approach does not meet with acceptance. The song is similar to some of those hurtin' songs where a woman objects to a man's interest in sexual gratification and little else. In the hurtin' songs, the woman is often fighting a man who is putting his hands all over her, or attempting to trick her, or already has tricked her, and the woman is feeling anger, resentment, or pain. "You Wanna Give Me a Lift" displays no pain or discomfort, and in fact indicates that the woman is satisfied or secure in her stand. Most would agree that it is unnecessary to be absolutely overjoyed in a relationship in order to feel satisfied or secure. Being free of hurt and willing to declare exactly where a person wants to be in a relationship suggests that the person is not overly concerned with the problems facing people in the hurtin' songs. Lynn describes a woman who says she is "game for just about anything/But the game you've named I ain't gonna play." After relating how the man offers a drink and his "friendly hands," the woman admits her feelings but then tells what she plans to do about his desires. He may turn out to be the one who hurts.

> I'm a little warm, but that don't mean I'm on fire
> You want to take me for a ride in the back of your car
> You wanna give me a lift, but this ole gal ain't going that far.

In five of the six examples of searching-for-love songs, we find a man who successfully hunts for a willing woman. The fortunate men do not appear to be looking for women who will let them whisper sweet words in their ears, for then there would be no need for the privacy of cars or hotel rooms. The men leave little doubt that they are not in the mood for conversation or a drinking companion. Kenny Rogers talks of "love on the brain" and this is not the kind of love that sharpens someone's perception of nature.

"Old Fashioned Country Love"

One of the most fascinating characteristics of country love is the great variety of ways in which sexual love is described. Eu-

113

phemisms abound. The art of telling these stories without using specific terms and having the audience comprehend the real message is a key element of country music. We discover how effective the sources are when a nonbeliever is exposed to the music and is startled by the lyrics. Even an "outsider" is capable of understanding the true meaning of some of the love songs (a meaning they might not wish to know) without having the message spelled out in language that is offensive (although the meaning itself may be). As noted in the opening chapter, there was a time when some of the songs were quite explicit in describing sexual drives, qualities, and behaviors. When the language became less explicit, the key to detailing sexual love was to delicately choose terms that could be decoded in several ways by an audience. The terms and phrases that the audience understands were put to work in describing situations and qualities that both the source and the receive can visualize but for various reasons do not wish to spell out. Success in telling such a story without using concrete or precise language is similar to the way shortcut techniques or understatements are effective among a group of people who have common backgrounds and experiences and are capable of communicating with very few words. The use of the "inside story" depends upon the source's ability to employ key words and phrases (or even technical jargon) that have both common and extra meanings for certain people. The perceived close-knit relationship that exists between songwriters and/or singers and the audience for the music permits the transferring of meaning and extra meanings without the precise and specific language that would be required in order to communicate to an "outside" audience.

Since the beginning of commercial country music, the sources and audiences have sustained a common vocabulary that allows them to communicate meaning without stating things in specific terms. The happy search songs demonstrate this ability, but in the early 1970s there was a definite step toward the use of more explicit language to describe sexual love—a love that was never absent, only cloaked in "inside" terms. When the sources, with the approval of the channels over which the message was disseminated, were allowed to send these sentiments, not only the original audience but almost anyone could understand what the songs were always about.

"Trip to Heaven"

The woman in Loretta Lynn's song "You Wanna Give Me a Lift" describes her condition as a "little bit warm" but not "on fire." The women and men in the songs that feature the sexual love theme have passed through the warm stage and are burning brightly. Even though the trend toward a greater and more direct description of the physical became more prevalent in the early 1970s, we should keep in mind that the language in the most popular songs did not change drastically.[1] What did become more noticeable in the most successful songs was the specific rather than the general reference and the lack of references to a romantic or lasting love that seemed so necessary in the earlier love songs. There were fewer attempts to disguise the sexual appetite by implying that it was love in general, and not someone's body in particular, that was creating the titillation in an encounter.

The narrowing of the theme to focus on sexual excitement seemed to increase the clever use of euphemisms—terms that might be overused but are always understandable to the audience. For instance, being transported to heaven by love was not an original way to describe the effect of a new and exciting love affair, but Freddie Hart did it extremely well with a song that is more narrowly centered on the commonly understood cause for the transport. "Trip to Heaven" has some of the characteristics of the appreciative songs, for the man is concerned with his partner's welfare and feelings. (The "hope you are feeling me the way I'm feeling you" concern does not necessarily express an in-

115

terest in another's welfare; it could also betray a fear that the speaker is not an equally good love partner.) The appreciation in this song, however, is secondary to the exuberance experienced and expressed; since it seems that the feeling is a sudden sensation rather than something that might be felt over an extended time, one must conclude that it relates to a feeling experienced by a sudden burst of love. Since the common cause for this type of reaction is generally understood by most listeners, they would have little difficulty in decoding the true meaning of the message. Hart presented the song with the excitement anyone must feel on such an occasion:

> How does this grab you, baby?
> Can you believe what's going on?
> Did you get that so good feeling?
> It's coming on so strong:
> Ain't this loving really something?
> I think my heart just touched the sky.
>
> I just took a trip to Heaven:
> I didn't even have to die.

The anticipation of the sexual encounter is another common element in this group of songs. In 1973, the same year in which "Trip to Heaven" was popular, Conway Twitty had one that carried as much excitement and was more specific than Hart's song. There is a little confusion about the circumstances under which the man and the woman get together, but there is no confusion about the nature of her previous loves or of this one. Twitty's song is entitled "You've Never Been This Far Before." While noting the dissonance the woman is feeling (he says he can hear the echoes of her thoughts), he is also able to tell that she is a novice at love, and he mentions how patient he has been while waiting for this moment.

116

> I don't know what I'm saying as my trembling fingers touch
> forbidden places
> I only know I've waited for so long for the chance we are
> taking.

He doesn't appear to be very experienced himself, even though he seems able to read her mind, and he is assuring either her or himself about another concern he believes might be troubling the woman.

> And as I take the love you're giving I can feel tension building
> in your mind
> And you're wondering if tomorrow I'll love you like I'm loving
> you tonight.

It is difficult to get more specific than this and still have a record played on country radio stations. There is no reference to a lasting love. (He may, sometime in the future, feel like the man in the Gatlin Brothers' song "I Just Wish You Were Someone I Loved," who said he no longer feels the way he did when the woman's red gingham dress hit the floor.) There is no illusion that the love itself is greater than loving. There is no suggestion that this is just another silver-tongued devil lying to a woman in order to make love to her, like the man in Loretta Lynn's "Wings Upon Your Horns." In Twitty's song there is a celebration of sexual love, what it does to a man and what he thinks it can do to a woman who is being ushered into womanhood. The man is caring, tender, a little shaky, and free of guilt.

Guilt is not completely absent from some of these songs. We have noted that this type of reaction is prevalent in the hurtin' songs, where a woman (in most cases) was tricked or encouraged to participate in sex and then had second thoughts about it. If guilt is expressed in the messages, then the songs are found in the hurtin' category. One song in the happy group, however, does mention guilt, or at least makes it clear that the couple is sinning. The Kendalls refer to premarital sex (they mention how other people must remember a first love) and then say they have no negative feelings about making love. In "It Don't Feel Like Sinning to Me," they admit that some people would insist that what they are doing is wrong, but they use the modern rationalization that it couldn't be wrong because it feels too good. They decide that people will find some reason for speaking evil, so they might as well continue with their activities, especially since what they are doing "feels like love." The "if it feels good, do it" rationale is central to several of these songs, and Jeanne Kendall certainly makes the woman in Curly Putman and Michael Kosser's lyrics sound convincing.

The absence of information about the marital status of the lovers reduced the amount of guilt found in many of the happy love songs of the 1980s. If the couple is not identified as being married or unmarried, then a primary cause for uneasiness is removed from the narrative. Two songs having similar titles and expressing great happiness about sexual encounters lack any references to the marital status of the participants. Both of these sources are men, both are morning people like the man in Faron Young's "Four in the Morning," and both are thrilled. In 1986, Kenny Rogers had a popular recording entitled "Morning Desire." The man in this song tells how much he enjoys waking up beside a woman and talks himself into a situation that almost certainly will result in the woman's losing sleep. Lee Greenwood used more blatant language (even in the title) in "Morning Ride," a recording that achieved popularity in 1987. In Greenwood's song, the man is expressing his joy over an early morning sexual episode that provides a wonderful beginning to his day. Greenwood's song had one important element that was missing from Rogers's recording. The woman in Greenwood's song requests to ride for a second time. We do not know if the man wishes, or is able, to take this trip, but we do know the woman who speaks out about her desires is not causing the pain some do in a few of the hurtin' songs.

"I Really Got the Feeling"

Some of the happy love songs set forth the singers' feelings in much less precise terms. Freddie Hart describes what the man in "Trip to Heaven" was feeling in another song with a title more confusing than the lyrics. The man in "Got the All Overs for You (All Over Me)" uses some different terms to discover what could be a messy problem.

> Love's vibrations I can feel them when I hold you
> I just tremble and my passion rises high

Once again we see passion damaging a man's ability to control his physical behavior, while noting that the woman's sweet lips both satisfy and keep him hungry. He feels that only lovers have this problem and he is probably correct, but he goes on to state that the "blessing is heaven sent and meant to be."

T. G. Sheppard is much more precise about the source of the "blessing" in "You Feel Good All Over." The man is pleased and excited not only because she feels good all over but also because all of her is accessible to him. He shows no tendency to discriminate against any of her parts, for all sections set him off, and even though the intense emotion he is describing might be dangerous to his (and her) mental and physical well-being, he insists that he needs her for convenience and for her ability to trigger his passion. After telling her how good all of her parts are, he singles out the power of the simple act of holding hands.

> When you're holding my hand
> I'm one hell of a man
> When you kiss me, you set me on fire
> You're so easy to hold from your head to your toes
> You fill me up with desire.

119

Loretta Lynn and Conway Twitty join in on a song that sums up the messages whose primary interest is sexual desire. In "Feelin's" they describe both the desires and the ultimate solution to the sexual drives that bring a man and a woman together without guilt or other problems overshadowing their encounter. The man approaches the woman and suggests that he should take her to a cozier locale where he can take her into his arms, and the woman tells him that she would be lying if she did not admit she had the same inclination. In the last verse they are together where they can make love. The man says he has wanted her in this position for a long time and she tells him she can't say no.

It is once again left to women to describe the ultimate conditions affecting the people in these songs. They are not fighting the feelings; they are fueling them through a general lack of control or concern for possible future consequences. They are passionate and happy and they have found men in the same state who, if in a few cases might demonstrate slight tensions, let nothing distract them. Dolly Parton describes this in the lyrics of a song she wrote, recorded, and made popular in 1978. "Baby, I'm Burning" depicts a condition with no explicit language, or little else that could be considered offensive, but one full of intense feelings.

"A Love Song"

Although fewer happy love songs achieve widespread popularity than those emphasizing hurtin' love, country does have some that attract a large and grateful audience. The heyday of the "winning" love song was probably in the 1940s and 1950s; certainly that was a peak period for this type of music.[2] During the

1960s, 1970s, and 1980s, some exceptional happy love songs appeared, although unlike hurtin' songs, of which a large and steady number appear on all of the lists, the number and overall positions of happy love songs rise and fall for reasons that are difficult to explain. All of the elements in the country music process contribute to this erratic pattern, but certain influences affect the flow of this particular message more than others. The varying moods of the audience ultimately regulate the number of popular happy love messages, of course, but more important is how that message is perceived by the songwriters, singers, recording companies, song publishers, radio stations, and other elements involved in the creation and delivery of the message. These people who make the decisions that allow a song to move through the system are unlikely to buck any popular trend; by continuing to supply the types of songs that are most popular, they are improving their chances for success. Certainly, this encourages the song publishers to push for this type of material from the songwriters and plug this same type of material for the artist to record; so it is a fluke if a happy song gets into the hands of singers. If a singer is also a songwriter, there is a better opportunity for a deviant (i.e., different from anything popular at any point in time) message to get recorded. A singer can usually insist on selecting a few songs to include on an album although this does not guarantee a song's release as a single, or even if that occurs, that the single will be promoted by the record company.

The singer's preferences for certain types of material must also be considered. Just as most actors hope to obtain roles that are loaded with possibilities for displaying deep emotions, a singer is usually more capable of interjecting greater feeling into a song that calls for a serious interpretation, instead of the light and sometimes fluffy sentiments found in happy love songs. If we compare the artists who have popular happy love songs to those who are successful with the hurtin' ones, we find a few who are equally proficient with both types (Conway Twitty comes immediately to mind), but many singers seem to have problems establishing the sincerity contract with a happy message. Some listeners, for example, appear to have difficulty accepting a happy message from George Jones, because he has created such a strong image with the hurtin' and cheatin' messages that the audience feels he is not serious when interpreting a happy song. The believability he establishes with sad messages hampers his credibility with happy ones although he has made some popular recordings about happy love.

A flurry of happy love songs appearing from 1980 to 1987 may have been caused by the particular talents and types of singers that were being pushed by the recording companies. During this period, the industry was obviously impressed with the success of groups such as Alabama who had twelve songs on the year-end charts from 1980–1986. The recording companies did not go as far as to name any of the new groups South Carolina or Mississippi, but they did seem to think that by placing two or more people together a group might be created which would sell a large number of records. Some of the new groups could actually sing a country song; however, many of them could not—or would not—sing different types of music containing different messages. Rather than note the qualities that make a group successful in the country field most of the new people were allowed to perform in a self-indulgent manner like some groups in other fields of music. The typical new group concentrated on upbeat music whether the message was sad or happy, pushed the instrumentation to the front rather than allowing it to deliver the message, and competed with each other to send a message. The successful groups in country (for the most part) are those that allow one individual at a time to act as the primary source with the remainder providing harmony and support. When a group operates in this newer fashion, they may burn brightly for a brief period but quickly burn out because of their inability to adapt to the system. People who listen to country music are loyal, but the audience attracted to the newer groups is almost as fickle as the people who place the groups together.

After the new groups and new style were created, the recording companies faced one major problem. The companies became agitated because radio stations failed to play as much of this music as they produced and complained that radio would not accept new acts. In turn, the radio stations played more oldies and complained that companies were not producing the type of music their audiences wished to hear. The radio people were more accurate in their assessment because many of the new acts must record and release the type of material that never was a predominant part of popular country music. Groups were flooding the market with one type of music and were unable to send other types of messages with any sincerity. One reason an audience may hesitate to respond to this type of love song might be the inherent difficulty of accepting a happy love message from any group if all the members insist on sending it at the same time. When this happens in real life we begin to doubt the reason for the happiness. Several people telling about the same happiness derived from the same relationship with a particular woman or man is not the ordinary fare for most listeners. Happiness should be made as personal as unhappiness, and unless a group allows one person to be a single source and send a sincere happy message, they will generally be ignored after the novelty fades away. These groups provide evidence to indicate that it requires more talent and discipline to sing a variety of country messages than to sing a joyous one. It even requires more ability to send a quiet and intimate happy message than a frenzied out-of-control one. The new groups seem to forget, if they ever knew, that lyrics attract the dedicated and faithful country listener. When the lyrics only serve as an excuse for some people to perform aerobics on a new electric guitar, that group will end up enjoying the exercise in someone's enclosed garage.

A combination of the actions and reactions of the songwriters, singers, publishers, recording companies, and the audience, therefore, determines the availability of happy songs. If a relatively small number is available, then only a small number will be popular. When a few slip through and achieve success, then the funnel expands to allow more to become available, and this is probably the reason for sudden bursts of happy songs that appear in certain years. As they fade away, there is a return to the standard formula that restricts their access to the system.

Dorothy Horstman identifies another important characteristic to consider when looking at the happy song when she notes that this type of message is difficult to write, since the subject is not conducive to a compelling message. For instance, there is little opportunity to include conflict and tensions, two elements that make for interesting stories.[3] When writing without these key factors, one must rely on novel situations and clever language. Perhaps it is for this reason, among others, that in the 1970s the songs began to carry more explicit, concrete descriptions of sexual love. Country music has a well-deserved reputation for being realistic and not being addicted to the "Cocktails for Two" or "fantasy" syndrome that pervades "pop" music.[4] When in this tradition the songwriters began describing the more specific happiness springing from physical love rather than the general qualities of the environment, there was additional opportunity to make the songs interesting. Sexual qualities are more ear-catching than a new way to use the words "world" and "heaven" in a song.

There is one other factor that must be considered when discussing happy love songs. It is common in this type of song for the singer to speak directly to the love object. Even when the source is communicating a sense of happiness to the world, there is an overriding feeling that the most important person in the world is the partner, not the listener; the message is not directed to an outside audience. Although the message is, of course, intended for mass consumption and obviously meant to be overheard, it seems to be intended for a particular loved one. The hurtin' songs, on the other hand, are directed to the listener, and the listener is an integral part of the communication even if the source is speaking to the one causing the pain. In the hurtin' songs, we noted how the source often provides personal, self-disclosing statements to an audience. This practice signifies that the singer feels a close bond with the listeners, much like the relationship that exists between two close friends. We do not find this in most of the happy love songs.

An audience, as Willie Nelson said, can relate to the "hillbilly" who is singing a song of unhappy love.[5] Many in the audience have experienced the same feeling. Why is this not the case when one is singing a song of happy love? Perhaps we don't want to hear from someone who is happier than we are. Perhaps, since the message is not, on its face, very interesting, we turn our attention elsewhere. Perhaps it is more difficult to relate to someone who is happy and rather irrational than it is to someone who is full of pain and displaying the same quality. Perhaps happiness is more private than sorrow. Perhaps it requires a stronger interpersonal bond if it is to be shared. Whatever the reasons, the happy message is not the type that helps to build the sincerity contract between the singer and the listener. Even the "Nashville sound" with softer voices (crooning styles), smoother instrumentation (violins rather than fiddles), and background singers supplying smoother and softer bridges between and behind the lines (and occasionally adding information to the message) did little to help the happy love song to gain wider acceptance.

Chapter
4

Cheatin' Love:

Some of the Folks
Cheat Some of the Time

Jimmie Rodgers recorded the first in a series of Blue Yodels in 1928. Commonly called "T for Texas," this song describes a situation in which the singer believes a woman is unfaithful and threatens to get his gun and shoot the untrue Thelma just to see her jump and fall. The unfaithful lover or spouse had been depicted in country music since the early ballads, and it is not surprising that a hint of a type of song known as "cheatin'" should appear in the earliest period of commercial country music.

Songs that emphasize the unfaithful lover might be included with those in the chapters on happy or hurtin' love; however, this group of songs usually features the relationship itself. One, two, or any number of persons affected by the cheatin' fallout may be hurting, but the feeling created by the relationship usually receives the most attention. In the happy love song the source of the message may sing about being happy, but that happiness is usually created by the object of his or her love. Hurting songs are often similar in this sense because the hurt is generated either directly or indirectly by the other partner in the relationship. In most cheatin' songs the relationship itself becomes the prime consideration.

A number of old-time country songs spoke of the illicit love relationship, but the topic was generally ignored in early commercial country. People who believed the public would be offended by this subject in songs packaged for mass distribution stifled its development.[1] Whatever the merits of that opinion, it was 1948 before the cheating song became readily available to the buying public.

"Slipping Around"

It is generally agreed that Jimmy Wakely's and Margaret Whiting's version of "One Has My Name, and the Other Has My Heart" was the first of the popular commercial cheatin' songs.[2] Today this song might be considered a mild description of the lust-in-my-heart syndrome, but it was shocking enough at the time of its release to cause some unfavorable reactions from the guardians of the people's morality, although the song gives no indication that the cheating relationship was anything other than a simple statement of misplaced love. It is important to modern country music, for the song demonstrated that a large number of listeners wanted to hear about the situation.

Cheating songs gradually became more direct in describing illicit love relationships. Most contemporary popular cheating songs involve a situation in which a person is being tempted to cheat, is attempting to cheat, is cheating, or is reacting to cheating. The first type of song certainly is enjoyable to hear and to analyze. It is necessary to look at the situation in which the event occurs, the people involved in the situation, the reasons offered for the act, and the effect of the act to fully understand what commercial country music is saying about infidelity.

"Don't Let Me Cross Over"

When someone is being tempted to cheat and does not go through with it, the source seems to have greater latitude in expressing strange, interesting, and even slightly bizarre situations than in other country songs. "Almost Persuaded" depicts a rather common situation in which a person is being tempted.

> Last night all alone in a barroom
> Met a girl with a drink in her hand
> She had ruby red lips, coal black hair
> And eyes that would tempt any man.
>
> Then she came and sat down at my table
> And as she placed her soft hands in mine
> I found myself wanting to kiss her
> For temptation was flowing like wine.
>
> And I was almost persuaded
> To strip myself of my pride
> Almost persuaded
> To push my conscience aside.
>
> Then we danced and she whispered I need you
> Take me away from here and be my man
> Then I looked into her eyes and I saw it
> The reflection of my wedding band.
>
> And I was almost persuaded
> To let strange lips lead me on
> Almost persuaded
> But your sweet love made me stop and go home.

Note that this man is sitting all alone in a bar when he is approached by an attractive woman who touches his hand and probably encourages him to dance (and hold her in his arms). While he is dancing the source seems to be irresistibly drawn to the woman, and the temptation is so overwhelming that the conclusion to the song sounds unrealistic. Some might wonder why the man needs to see the reflection of a wedding band (visualize the location of his left hand in order to have a ring reflect in the woman's eyes) to remind him he is married. A poor rationalization allows the man to recapture a weakened resolve and offers a sop to a wife who surely would require more explanation than is offered in this song.

If one carefully examines this song (especially from the view of the wife) some important questions might be asked. Where was her sweet love when he went to this bar all alone? Where was her sweet love when he was being approached by a strange woman? Why did it take the reflection of a wedding ring to remind him he was married? Perhaps the logic does not have to be overwhelming when the result is socially correct. The man did not go with this beautiful, aggressive woman. He is weak, but not to the point of submission. The wife's reaction must be a variation of an old axiom: To forgive for almost erring may be more satisfactory to the forgiver than to forgive for erring all the way.

This song appealed to a large audience by describing a situation in which someone is sorely tempted but strong enough to turn away from the temptation at the last moment. A version recorded by Tammy Wynette has some intriguing modifications in the lyrics. The alterations allow a woman to sing the lyrics, but may demonstrate more than that simple maneuver. Wynette's version was not as popular as David Houston's (no other singer's version was as popular), but the changes in the gender-specific terms are interesting. Where Houston says that the woman had "ruby red lips," Wynette mentions "baby blue eyes." When he talks about a "smile that would tempt any man," she sings about the "smile that any woman understands." The dancing woman asks Houston to "Take me away from here and be my man," and the male dancer asks Wynette to "Let me take you away and be your man." Wynette says the man approached the table and "placed his hands over mine," but Houston said the woman approached his table and "placed her soft hands in mine." The non-verbal and verbal cues used to suggest the male tempter have more meaning than one might expect. The song was written by men, and perhaps it indicates the way they believed the language would be most acceptable to the public, or maybe it is the way they think a man or woman would act in the same situation. It must be noted that in country music it is rather common to mention blue eyes and black hair, and these two characteristics are often highlighted by both men and women referring to an attractive member of the opposite sex.

The hesitancy to succumb to a sweet temptation continues in the music. Reba McEntire offered two fine examples of this type of situation in 1983 and 1986. The problem is approached differently in each song and the audience does not really know if the women in her songs were "almost" or ever "persuaded." In the first song the woman is dangerously near the line of demarcation from the faithful to the fulfilled. The title of the 1983 recording tells us the new romantic interest is unique: "You're the First Time I've Thought about Leaving." We know her resolve is vacillating and the urge to leave is given more support than the desire to remain. In 1985, McEntire released a song she wrote entitled "Only in My Mind." This is one of her finest efforts and it cleverly leads the listener along an unclear path. The woman is sitting with her husband on a park bench (while the children play nearby) and for some reason the husband asks if she has ever cheated on him. The woman reacts beautifully (although she blushes) by telling her husband that she had only thought of cheating. Cheating in this instance is not clearly defined for all she admits in this song is a close interpersonal situation. No reference to sexual attraction is made. She is better able to communicate with the other man than with her husband about some things (perhaps the husband asks too many pointed questions) and the cerebral relationship falls far short of the cheatin' ones we normally hear about in these songs. This woman needs and cares for another man as a friend, and whether or not this is in the category of cheating must be left to the woman. In the first song, the woman is excited and happy with her predicament and in the second she remains articulate although slightly confused. Little thought is given to averting what may ultimately result from being tempted to cheat in either song.

Another song popular in 1987 describes a man deliberately seeking a situation in which he is tempted by a former lover to cheat. A man in Dan Seals's song tells a woman that he has not forgotten what attracted him to her and admits "You Still Move Me." The difference between this song and the two by McEntire is what the man does when he faces temptation. He wonders if the old lover would still excite him and after discovering that she does, decides to leave rather than allow the temptation to continue.

Randy Travis's first major hit was a recording in which a man resists the temptation to cheat. "On the Other Hand" was popular twenty-one years after "Almost Persuaded," but contains several features of the older song. The man in Travis's song admits that the new woman has some outstanding qualities, that he has a burning desire for her, that the woman at home is no longer very passionate, and that he has forgotten how "real" love feels. No matter how powerful the reasons are, he tells the new woman the ring on his finger will not allow him to get involved. Travis's fine interpretation of these lyrics establishes a strong sincerity contract and adds much to the tempted-but-true cheatin' songs.

"(I Can't Help You) I'm Falling Too"

There is an odd twist to the request for assistance in some of the songs where a person is being tempted to cheat. The source of the message is weak, but instead of seeing the reflection of a ring, the person wants the new object of affection to aid in resisting the affair. In "Don't Let Me Cross Over" a great desire for the new affair is clearly stated, but the source does not want the situation to develop past the panting stage. A similar message is found in a song made popular by Hank Locklin in 1960 and by Janie Fricke in 1978. "Please Help Me I'm Falling" is about falling in love and falling into an illicit relationship and it is one of many that indicates that an affair of the body is controlled by the heart.

Both of these songs are also examples of the "being tempted and being true" genre. Whether the participants remain true is left to the imagination of the listener, for verbalizing the fear of a possible event does not preclude the possibility that the event will occur. What makes these two songs special is the request for assistance, not to start, but to prevent an affair. The love offered as justification for the possible encounter is probably platonic, but there is the wish to modify that to a more physical relationship. Each listener has to provide an answer to the question of how long such a situation can or will exist.

In the six songs given as examples of the "being tempted to cheat" group, we find one person stopped by a burst of well-aimed light with no pain mentioned, and two sources enduring a double hurt from the lack of love at home and the inability to rectify the situation outside the home. Houston's, Seals's, and Travis's messages indicated that the sources were strong enough to resist the temptation, but in two songs the sources needed assistance. The most popular version of each of these songs was performed with a great deal of sincerity and the singers seemed to be actively involved in the situations. This is an important factor in the audience's acceptance of any message in a country song. Houston and McEntire do not indicate that the situation was painful (perhaps it was even exhilarating), but the successful versions of the other songs did express discomfort and pain.

A steady diet of being tempted and having to turn away surely makes for a frustrating love life. Anyone who has faced any type of great temptation knows that it is not easily turned away, and if temptation can create guilt, then perhaps the thoughts of Kris Kristofferson might be a more realistic course to follow. In one of Kristofferson's songs a person takes a chance on falling in love even though it might turn out to be an unpleasant experience, because "I'd rather be sorry for something I've done than for something that I didn't do."

"Heaven's Just a Sin Away"

The cheatin' songs in which the source is attempting to cheat appear to be leaning more toward Kristofferson's logic. Temptation has led these people one step closer to the cheating line. Planning can be even more frustrating than being tempted, and the help requested in these songs is quite different from that asked for in the songs above. While the song that emphasizes the temptation seems to end with resistance or an attempt to resist, the message in the next group of songs begins after the battle of resistance is lost.

Losing the battle with temptation and planning to engage in loving combat allows for intricate situations. One of the most fascinating planning phases comes when the potential affair is used as a threat to the legitimate partner. An affair that follows a warning to a person that if he or she does not change the person offering the threat will cheat might be labeled a retaliation affair. A common justification for a retaliation affair is the loss of love at home. In country songs the word "fire" is often used to describe the burning desire or passion that is supposed to exist in a relationship, but much time is expended in relating in general symbolic terms what it ought to be. The fire metaphor is used in every way possible, with banked fires for temperate relationships, dying fires for faltering relationships, roaring fires for intense relationships, and so on. Another reason offered by the individuals who are attempting to cheat is boredom or lack of excitement—a pilot light relationship. What many of the people planning to cheat seem to wish for is the inferno.

The situation most often found in this group of lyrics is a combination of the banked or doused fire and the retaliation rationale. Merle Haggard's "Carolyn" describes a situation in which the man has a warm-heart to cold-heart talk with the woman who is not fulfilling all of his wishes. The source describes some possible lovers who might be available in a large, distant city. The out-of-town women are pictured as wearing yellow and scarlet dresses and strange perfume. This information does not come first-hand to the source, but is a story he has heard and feels compelled to pass on to Carolyn. Haggard then offers several reasons for seeking love outside the home.

> Carolyn, a man will do that sometimes on his own
> And sometimes when he's lonely
> I believe a man might do that sometimes out of spite
> But, Carolyn, a man will do that always when he's treated bad
>   at home.

"Hearts on Fire"

The flickering flame at home can be another justification for an affair. When the possibility of an affair exists, the excitement of that encounter builds on the lack of interest at home and the situation can be both humorous and poignant. In one of the male-female duets, the unexpected word choices and plays on words are characteristic of many songs in the cheating genre. Bill Anderson (who has recorded a number of cheating songs) and Mary Lou Turner combined to provide one of the most realistic statements about potential cheating with a fine use of language in "Sometimes." The song is primarily a question-and-answer session between a man and a woman, which begins with a personal question and continues rather quickly about whether each is married, is happy, or has ever considered having an affair.

Although guilt is not present in Anderson and Turner's song, it has been a prominent feature of many cheating songs from the time they were introduced into commercial country music. As has been mentioned in the case of some of the earlier "being tempted" songs, guilt has sometimes overridden the temptation to have an affair. Perhaps it was necessary for the writers and performers to verbalize the guilt feelings in order to allow an illicit affair to be mentioned at all. Perhaps guilt is an inherent ingredient in such a relationship. But whatever the reason, guilt is an important part of many early cheating songs. One of the most popular ways to express guilt is to use terms derived from the vocabulary of religion. Since the heaven, hell, and sin terms are common tools to describe pleasure and pain, it is no wonder that they appear in country songs and almost eclipse the fire metaphor in the frequency of their use. Many listeners consider infidelity to be a sin and that is a natural way to treat it in a country song.

"Daytime Friends"

Twenty years after the initial appearance of cheating in commercial country music, the thesis (which most of us already knew) that pleasure overcomes the fear of sin surfaced in some of the more popular songs. Justification for sinning has always been the province of the dedicated sinner, and during the early period the justification for the affair was central to the message. Thirty years after the appearance of the genre, some songs appeared that treated the illicit affair as a sin worth the cost and offered no justification, other than pleasure, for the act. This is quite common in the cheating songs about affairs in progress, but it has also surfaced in songs where the potential participants are mulling over temptation or making plans to start an affair.

Another male-female duo offered a song in the late 1970s that exemplifies this "sinning can be fun" idea. No one is crediting country music with originating this philosophy, but earlier the sin of cheating was treated as a punishable offense. The Kendalls recorded a song in 1978 that set forth a new view in a way that made it quite palatable to a large listening audience. Their effect on the use of the "heaven" and "sin" terms may be substantial, for even a casual observation of the songs released in the year following the Kendalls' hit reveals a number of releases with these terms in the titles. It is the song that concerns us, and although it contains some traditional value-laden words, it does offer a philosophy that seems to fit in with the sentiment of a large number of people in the late 1970s—"Heaven's Just a Sin Away."

This song also contains the Devil-made-me-do-it rationale that is very common in songs where cheating is taking place.[3] The lack of will power and the sexual attraction are quite clear. The strength of the Devil and the weakness of the source are old standards, whereas the introduction of specific statements about the sexual attraction of the objects is a relatively late development in commercial country. What makes this song stand out is not the transference of blame but the fact that no one is said to be hurting. The sin, in this instance, does not seem to be a punishable offense. It is wrong, but it is not going to hurt anyone.

Another modern development is demonstrated in this song. It is the woman who is singing the "cheating for the fun of it" message. The woman's voice is the key source in the performance, and the image is that of a woman planning to cheat. Although women were an important part of the development of the cheating genre, they usually were members of male-female duos. Loretta Lynn has had the largest number of popular cheating songs in all types of cheating situations. She has several in the retaliation category where she is threatening a man who is running around with a little running around of her own. She is quite explicit in some of her songs when she threatens to find a man in order to deliver retribution to a trifling man. In "I'm Going to Put the Big Old Hurt on You" she tells the man that she is going to hurt him because she is going to cheat and plans to return home and tell him all about it. Most of her songs where this type of behavior is indicated are primarily hurtin' love songs with plans to meet the hurt with an alteration of the "eye for an eye" philosophy.[4] More women are singing all kinds of country songs, and it is only natural that they should start singing more cheating songs.

It was a woman singer who offered a unique reason for destroying most of the clichés found in songs where the source is attempting to cheat. Sammi Smith's version of "It Just Won't Feel

Like Cheating (with You)" is as close to cheating as any where the source is talking about the possibility of an affair. She covers the typical clichés in the first verse, sexual attraction in the second, and assures the man in the third this is the first time she's cheated.

I'm not the kind of woman
Who leans across the line
But I just let your eyes undo
All the ties that bind.
So now I'll let you touch me
I can't wait to touch you, too
It just won't feel like cheatin' with you.

I know it wasn't hard for you
To get behind my door
But believe me this is something
I've never done before

And tonight will be the first time
That I've ever been untrue
But it just won't feel like cheatin' with you.

In this song, no pain or punishment is mentioned. It is the feeling, not the guilt, that is the prominent feature.

"Borrowed Angel"

One of the best-selling of any "attempting to cheat" songs was recorded by Kenny Rogers. "Lucille" became a household word when she stepped into that bar in Toledo and pulled off her ring. After the drinks finally hit her, she tells the source that she is tired of her present life and is looking for whatever a new life has to offer. When her husband appears on the scene, the source is apprehensive; however, all the man does is beg Lucille to return to the farm. The case he presents is based on the unfortunate timing of her departure rather than the act of leaving. After the husband fails to convince Lucille to return to help care for the children and gather the crops, the source and the woman have a few more drinks and leave the bar and go to a hotel room. The song contains an unusual reason for the failure to consummate an affair of this type. After settling in the room the woman approaches the man; however, he is unable to make love to her because he keeps recalling the husband's desperate pleas.

Here we have a man who obviously wanted to pick up a woman in a bar. He saw her remove her ring, moved in rather smartly, and realized he could suffer the consequences when the husband made an appearance. After making such an effort to take advantage of the situation, he failed when it counted most. The song's basic appeal (aside from Rogers's fine interpretation) was that it showed one man's compassion for another. The source could not make love to a woman who had so mistreated her husband. This understanding of the problems of the husband obviously fell on many receptive ears. It is a fine story told with great sincerity, for Kenny Rogers makes an audience believe this situation could actually occur.

This song is another example of the sincerity contract gladly made between the source and the receivers of a message. The audience accepted Rogers's claim that he would be unable to make love to a woman because he felt compassion for her husband. As a counterpoint to the obvious acceptance of Rogers's message, we can look at Waylon Jennings's version of the same song. In fairness to Jennings, it must be noted that his version was not released as a single, a normal prerequisite for the success of a particular country song. It did not receive the promotion of a single, but it is doubtful that it would have enjoyed the same success as Rogers's version even with a major push by the recording company. It is difficult for many listeners to accept Jennings's claim that he would take a woman to a hotel room and be "unable to hold her" because he is thinking of her husband; his interpretation of the song does not lend credence to this, and the message is contradictory to many others Jennings has offered in the past.

There is another way to consider the situation described in "Lucille." If we were to look at the message from Lucille's perspective, then perhaps the man in the bar has a misplaced sense of compassion. Lucille was unhappy with her life on the farm, and when her husband explains why he wants her to return, it seems that she might have grounds for her feelings. The husband offers little reason, except for a sense of guilt disguised as responsibility to him and the children, for her to return. Her own feelings and desires are not mentioned by the husband, and this may be another reason why she is looking outside the home for whatever the other life has to give. Her misfortune is compounded when she finds a new man who is adept in the barroom and incompetent in a hotel room.

"Hell Yes, I Cheated"

In the cheating messages noted above, we have seen people who are facing temptation and those who are attempting to cheat meeting with various degrees of success; some fall to temptation and some resist it. The cheating situations these losers and winners encountered in the early days were rather vague; this lack of detail was found on the first commercial cheating record. Over the years, the messages were to become more specific and intricate.

Incidentally, when Jimmy Wakely and Margaret Whiting's "One Has My Name, the Other Has My Heart" forced its way into country music, Whiting's name was left off the record.[5] Just as the Capitol label was breaking precedent with the release of the recording, they were creating another precedent by leaving the woman's name out of the picture.

139

Wakely and Whiting followed their first successful cheating song with another written by Floyd Tillman called "Slipping Around." Three versions of this song appeared on *Billboard's* "Top Singles of 1949." The duet version was number four on the chart, Ernest Tubb's was number fourteen, and Tillman's version ended up number twenty-five. There were two other cheating songs in the top twenty-five songs of the year, and cheating was on its way to becoming a central theme for commercial country music.

"Slipping Around" was a little more specific about the situation than "One Has My Name, the Other Has My Heart," but it certainly was not graphic. Frustration and the desire to make the loving legal were the key elements. These elements became as central to the genre as the genre to the music. An excellent example of the impact of the lyrics is demonstrated by Floyd Tillman's experience in "Lucky Strike Hit Parade." Tillman was requested to modify two lines in the song because the censors thought them to be immoral.[6] The lines, fairly bland by today's standards, contained references to the man and woman in the song (each was tied to another person) and still found in many cheating songs.

Most popular cheating songs until the late 1950s were vague and general statements. "Back Street Affair" did contain an apology to the new woman who unknowingly became involved with a married man (the source of the message) and must suffer shame. There was some blame placed on the wife, who was untrue before the husband was, but the new affair is described simply as an example of romantic love—a love the source wants to bring out into the open. A few years later another song, "Release Me," was a plea to an unloving wife to allow the husband to go to his new love.

The messages in these songs are similar in that the blame is usually placed on the unloving wife because she had caused the man to stray in search of a new love, who is an answer to the man's dreams. The blame is usually not a severe condemnation, just an indication that the husband is unhappy at home. The husband, however, has shopped around without finding happiness in a new affair. The wife will not let him go, so the husband and his new friend must suffer society's disapproval. The incongruities in these messages are ignored. If the entire community knows about the affair between the man and his new love, why are the wife's extramarital affairs such a well-kept secret? Is the man so inept or his wife so clever? The source usually considers the affair to be wrong and wants to make it right (i.e., legal). The wife obviously lacks love in her heart, but wishes to continue the man's suffering by hanging on to him.

"Devil Woman"

Three of the top five songs in 1961 were about cheating and the situations had changed from those in the 1950s. The following year, however, one song introduced a new but enduring characteristic. Marty Robbins released a song about "sin" and a "bad" other woman. Since the time of the old ballads, the "bad" woman has been a source of temptation for a semi-weak man; but the detailed description of an evil, scheming woman did not appear in a popular cheatin' song until Robbins's song, "Devil Woman," which was number sixteen on *Billboard's* year-end chart for 1962. Both men and women have taken advantage of the "blame it on the other woman" rationale in cheating songs ever since. The "bad" woman was described quite often in the hurtin' love songs. When a woman was hurting she often refused to blame her man, but would shift the blame to a woman who was taking advantage of him. The wife in Robbins's song did not place blame; in fact, she is the classic forgiving woman. Here we have the strong, mean, devil woman and the loving, abused, forgiving wife—stereotypical roles for women in many country songs before women started singing more of them. The conclusion of the song suggests that the source will be able to break the spell cast by the "Devil Woman"—maybe. We are not told how this woman gained so much power over the man and whether the man ever

141

enjoyed being under her power. We do know that the man wants to end the relationship, which is unlike some of the earlier messages where the sources wanted to end the marriage and continue the new relationship.

"Walk On By"

This guilt suffered in a cheating situation seemed to receive less emphasis in the mid-1960s. A male and female duo gained the attention of a large audience with a song that exemplified this change. Their song, using some of the same rhetorical techniques found in "Sometimes," is a telephone conversation between a husband and the other woman, with the wife as a silent participant in half of the conversation. The man is pretending that the caller is his employer asking him to work late. Since the woman on the other end of the line reacts so well to whatever the man says, it is obvious that similar conversations have taken place in the past. This is one of the first popular cheating songs to outline specific devious behavior by the cheaters. Such behavior has certainly been occurring in the other messages, but this song delineates one particular type of lying. The title is another of the fine ones that appear on these songs. Country music has a number of excellent titles, and even though this one is not a "hook line" (the line that immediately secures the audience's attention and concisely describes the key concept in the lyric), its meaning is fairly obvious. Roy Drusky and Priscilla Martin introduced a slightly humorous aspect of cheating in their popular recording of "Yes Mr. Peters." The song is not intentionally humorous, but the blatant deception, the skillful lying, and the deliberately ambiguous wording bring some irreverence into the situation. When the telephone rings, the husband answers and pretends he is talking to his boss. The wife is obviously overhearing the husband's comments and he skillfully answers the caller's questions and does not let the wife know he is talking to a lover. The fear of being discovered is secondary to the anticipation of being together. No

142

information is given about the wife, but she is a person of some concern to the caller. The reference to not wanting to live a lie is the only hint of possible guilt in this song, and perhaps this is not really guilt. It might be that the "other" woman simply does not like the inconvenience of such an arrangement. The song does give some information about the other woman, a characteristic that begins to take on more and more importance in the songs. Robbins calls her a devil—someone evil and endowed with fantastic powers enabling her to wreck the man and the home—but some songs begin to take a kinder view of the other woman.

"The Other Woman"

A more compassionate view of the other woman and the art of lying is found in one of Conway Twitty's songs. Twitty, a master with a cheating song because he sounds so sincere, is putting someone on in his "Darling, You Know I Wouldn't Lie." The source has a great deal of faith in his ability to convince his women, and apparently he is attempting to persuade the person who has been the victim.

Here I am late again for the last time;
And like I promised I just told her goodbye;
Please believe me for this time, it's really over;
And darling, you know I wouldn't lie.

Didn't I come and tell you about her,
How temptation lured she and I;
Now I know it was only fascination;
And darling, you know I wouldn't lie.

I had to let her down easy; as slow as I could;
After all, she's got feelings, too;
But it took a little longer than I thought it would;
But this time she knows we're really through.

She wanted to hold me forever;
And this lipstick shows her final try;

143

And these tears on my shoulder are proof that she failed;
And darling, you know I wouldn't lie.

Tom T. Hall wrote a song about the power of the other woman by saying little about her. There is no guilt or sorrow expressed in his song other than a recognition of the man's hypocrisy. "Margie's at the Lincoln Park Inn" is a fine song, and Bobby Bare's interpretation presents the situation in just the right manner. The song makes an extremely important statement about the art of cheating. None of the earlier popular songs emphasize the hypocrisy found in many cheating relationships. This source is going about his everyday business of being an upstanding citizen, dutiful husband, and caring father—but his thoughts are on Margie and he is expressing no regrets for those thoughts.

This type of song may have more appeal to a cheater than to a noncheater. The cheater can point to the person who appears to be monogamous and think that perhaps it is a fake image. Those who do not cheat, and wish to condemn anyone who does, may think the source has no sense of morality. Some listeners might have preferred more suffering than what is found here, where the only suffering is in the waiting. It also may have caused consternation in some listeners because it suggests that cheating is not the isolated occurrence it appears to be in the other songs. The second verse reminds the listener that more people are involved in illicit relationships than is apparent in most other cheating songs.

My name's in the paper where I took the Boy Scouts to hike
My hands are all dirty from working on my little boy's bike
The preacher came by, and I talked for a minute with him
My wife's in the kitchen, and Margie's at the Lincoln Park Inn.

And I know why she's there, 'cause I've been there before
But I made a promise that I wouldn't cheat anymore
I tried to ignore it, but I know she's there, my friend
My mind's on a number, and Margie's at the Lincoln Park Inn.

144

Next Sunday, it's my turn to speak to the young people's class
They expect answers to all of the questions they ask
What would they say if I spoke on modern day sin
And all the Margies at all of the Lincoln Park Inns?

The bike is all fixed, and my little boy is in bed asleep
His little puppy is curled in a ball at my feet
My wife's baking cookies to feed to the bridge club again
I'm almost out of cigarettes, and Margie's at the Lincoln Park
    Inn.
And I know why she's there.

The other woman was gradually taking on a role of her own in these songs even though she still receives the blame for leading some men astray. The Devil, who tempted many to cheat, is also given credit for much cheating activity. In most messages where the Devil is successful, there is usually an expression of deep regret. There appears to be a correlation between the Devil's power and a stated desire to be a faithful husband. When a source is unable to maintain a family environment, there is assurance that the individual is not to blame—the fault lies outside the control of the source. An example of this situation is found in another song recorded by Conway Twitty. The message is exemplary in describing the role the source thinks he is supposed to emulate, the stereotypical role of the suffering wife, and the problem created by both roles. Twitty does an especially fine job of interpreting "How Much More Can She Stand" in the traditional mold of the source who is cheatin', suffering, and refusing to accept responsibility for either.

There's a devil in my body that I just can't satisfy
Other women haunt me even though I love my wife
It's because I really love her I try to save her heart with lies

But I know, she knows
I can see it in her eyes.

I try to stay at home, love only her, play with the kids, and
  watch TV
But then my mind becomes unsure about the kind of love I need
My reasons for cheating, they're as good as lies can be
How much more can she stand and still stand by me?

"After the Fire Is Gone"

The suffering wife, a common character found in early cheating songs also began to take on a greater variety of qualities during the 1970s. The woman at home was still blamed for some cheating activities. For instance, she is still credited with putting out the fire of love. A few songs that gained acceptance in the 1970s did not specifically name the wife, but under normal circumstances there would be no one else to blame. Often, the husband is lamenting this situation while searching for an inferno and, by implication, is blaming his wife for allowing the fire to dwindle. Conway Twitty and Loretta Lynn, one of the most popular duos in commercial country music, recorded a song that names some of the qualities needed to rekindle a flame. It was released in 1969 and, like Hall's song, it was an indication of more specific messages to come. A traditional situation (the home environment not being as warm as they would like) is described along with the specific qualities lacking in those who remain at home. "After the Fire Is Gone" is a title that sums up the cheating rationale rather well.

Your lips are warm and tender
Your arms hold me just right
Sweet words of love you remember
The one at home forgot.

146

Each time we say's the last time, then we keep hangin' on
For there's nothing cold as ashes
After the fire is gone.

"Back to Back"

Significant changes began to appear in the messages of cheatin'
songs receiving some measure of general acceptance. Many of
the traditional justifications are still found, but they are expressed
in more detail. There is no way to say whether the impetus for
these changes was the emergence of women singing their own
versions of the cheating songs (rather than as part of a duet with
a man) or a change in the attitudes of the listening audience. It
was probably a combination of both factors, along with the acquiescence of the record companies and radio stations in permit-
ting this message to be recorded and transmitted. In any case,
lost love at home and newly discovered love outside the home
began to be described more realistically.

Loretta Lynn, who has appeared on the popularity charts with
several "reacting to cheatin'" songs, began to tell what the lack
of love at home really meant. In "Another Man Loved Me Last
Night," the source may feel some remorse for the act, but we are
told that she enjoyed a warmer relationship at one time and has
found it again.

While he's sleeping well I'm crying here awake
Not being loved was more than I could take
Tho it was wrong there in his arms it seemed so right
When another man loved me last night.

Yes another man loved me last night
I'd almost forgotten what love was really like,

147

But I'm only human, only a woman,
I let another man love me last night.

The description of guilt and shame was becoming as vague as that of love in the earlier songs. The element of sexual attraction was beginning to be dealt with and judging by the popularity of these songs, it was being accepted by more and more people. Country songs are filled with euphemisms for sexual needs and attributes. In a song we examined earlier, Sammi Smith suggested that it was not difficult for the man to "get behind my door," a statement that can be translated in many ways. There is still less graphic language found in these songs than in some other musical genres, but the meaning is becoming less obscure. For instance, in "Ruby, Don't Take Your Love to Town," it is not difficult to realize that the love Ruby is transporting is not the kind of love discussed in a Gothic novel. The use of more specific references to sexual fulfillment in a cheating situation has allowed more exuberance to be expressed in the message. Earlier, we noted that little enthusiasm was expressed for the act of cheating, perhaps because the sources could not talk about what makes a cheating act worth all the effort some of them exert.

The woman in "Another Man Loved Me Last Night" says that she had forgotten what love was really like. When the source begins to talk about sexual excitement with a new person, perhaps we can see why all these people are enduring all this pain. The negative aspects of the relationship have received most of the emphasis in the popular cheating songs; however, some thirty years after the first one came on the market, the participants are expressing a few more positive feelings for the act of cheating.[7] When we examine the cheating songs that were popular after 1948, it is difficult to determine from the content of the messages why so many of the sources cheated, because few of them seemed to be enjoying it very much. When the sources began to enjoy it more, the guilt began to fade.

"Another Man Loved Me Last Night" by Lorene Allen and Peggy Sue Wells. Copyright 1970 by Coal Miners Music. Used by permission.

Even when explicit language is absent, a feeling of physical pleasure is created by the song. For instance, in the late 1970s, T. G. Sheppard recorded a song that expresses both his and the lover's excitement in terms that, while not as explicit as they might be, do make the meaning clear. The song contains a variable that has marked cheating songs from the very first, and that is the lover's frustration. Frustration is not the key element in most of these songs, but it is found in nearly all of them. In the later songs, the frustration is not to be overcome by the dissolution of a marriage—a more convenient schedule will do. Sheppard explains all this in "When Can We Do This Again."

> In a house in the suburbs
> Comes the end of one more working day
> Dinner's cooking in the kitchen
> And I just put one more beer away.
>
> I've just gotta see her
> Gotta find the way to slip away
> She's burning in my memory
> And even now I can hear her say:
>
> She said, "Now, when can we do this again?"

"Two-story House"

The mundane life at home is another situation that is taking on increasing significance in a few songs. Barbara Mandrell discusses this in one of her most popular songs in the early part of her career. The source in "The Midnight Oil" expresses shame and guilt, but not enough to end the relationship. The major difference between this message and many of the others is that the source is a woman—proving that the Devil does not practice sexual discrimination.

And tonight I'll cheat again
And tomorrow I'll be sorry
I'll feel kinda dirty 'cause I'll have the midnight oil all over me

God knows his dream would shatter
If he knew the Devil had me and won't set me free
While I'm puttin' on my make-up
I'm puttin' on the one that really loves me.

Although guilt is expressed here, it is not severe enough to cause her to take off the make-up and stay at home. In fact, fewer songs are talking about trying to stop cheating and more are speaking of continuing a relationship. Long-term relationships would seem to indicate that some persons are learning to cope with the problems created in the affair and appreciate the advantages. One song that describes a long-term relationship suggests that the obstacles of frustration and inconvenience can be overcome by careful planning. The message also points up another variable, seldom stated but running through most of these songs. One must be terribly energetic in order to participate in some of these affairs and lead double lives. The source and the other woman in Mel Street's "Shady Rest" describe a long and obviously enjoyable relationship, which must indicate a high energy level. The source of the message has been having an affair with the woman in the song since she was twenty-one years old. They found a cozy room in an underpopulated motel that had what appeared to be a pleasant environment. When the man read in the newspaper that the woman had married someone else, he felt that she must have it all, until she called him three weeks after the wedding to continue their relationship.

Now she's thirty-one
With three kids at home and husband waiting
And I've got kids of my own
But I spend my time at home anticipating.

"The Midnight Oil" by Joe Allen. © 1973 by Tree Publishing Company, Inc. International Copyright Secured. All Rights Reserved. Use by permission of the publisher.

And there beside the highway, underneath the trees
We spend two nights a week in good ole number three
   And winter nights are cold
We found a home away from home at Shady Rest.

The frustration created by the inability to be with the new love as much as one might wish, as described in the title of Faron Young's "Loving Here, Living There and Lying in Between," is a major complaint in some of the newer songs. Some people solve the problem in much the same way as the people in "Shady Rest." Conway Twitty and Loretta Lynn dealt with this when the couple in their song scheduled their illicit activities "From Seven to Ten."

"Married but Not to Each Other"

One aspect of many of the newer songs is the absence of a specific reference to marriage. It is obvious that someone in the song is being unfaithful, but not necessarily to a spouse. In addition, the family, although still mentioned, does not receive the emphasis it once did; such references are more likely to appear in the songs where cheating is being contemplated than in those where it is already taking place. When marital status and family members are mentioned, as we have noticed in some of the last songs cited, the spouse and children are referred to with little sadness or mention of pain. Perhaps the lack of overwhelming guilt, or the felt need to state that guilt, is one reason why the family is not receiving as much emphasis as before.

Some of the consequences of cheating are still found throughout the songs, but with minor rhetorical twists that make them unique. The expression of discomfort or the inability to justify the act to the participant's satisfaction are more sophisticated. What can be done with a problem such as that in one of Loretta

Lynn's songs when a source discovers a new love who has really created a feeling of excitement? Whether a sexual fantasy—an uncommon topic in country music—creates turmoil or provides a necessary diversion is debatable, but the source in this song appears to be leaning toward the side of discomfort. This message also contains a confusing sense of guilt.

> While he's making love, I'm making believe
> It's just a matter of time till I'll be with you
> So I'm making believe till you make it come true
> While he's making love, I'm making believe.
>
> I feel guilt in his arms, 'cause I'm not really his
> I pretend that I hold you, while I'm returning his kiss
> And if I close my eyes, he won't know he's deceived.

Several songs popular in the 1980s, identify what must be a realistic consequence of the cheating situation. In a 1980 recording there is little reference to the two women involved other than the adaptation of a line from the first commercial cheating song when the source says that "One's got my money, the other's got my heart." The Oak Ridge Boys put a lot of enthusiasm into their version of this song, but the message found in one verse of "Trying to Love Two Women" indicates what must be a common mental and physical problem faced in many cheating situations.

> When you try to please two women, you can't please yourself
> When you try to please two women, you can't please yourself
> The best is only half-good, a man can't stock two shelves
> It's a long old grind and it tires your mind.

Two women also recorded songs describing the frustration and other matters that "can tire the mind" in this type of relationship. The woman in Crystal Gayle's "Too Many Lovers" is not obsessed with her inability to satisfy two men, but is concerned about the hassle it creates in her normal activities. Tanya Tucker is more specific about why a monogamous relationship is more soothing and less complicated in "One Love at a Time." The woman in this 1986 song is more concerned about her inability to keep birthdays and other important details in the lives of two men straight. These songs illustrate the internal turmoil created by the relationships rather than the harm the situations cause for others.

Another song that illustrates the changes taking place was recorded by Barbara Mandrell. The source, the other woman, asks questions about the propriety of loving a married man. She tells how her family and friends insist that it is wrong to love such a man, but she answers her own questions and the others' suggestions in the title. "(If Loving You Is Wrong) I Don't Want to Be Right" is an adamant statement by the other woman to her family, friends, lovers, and listeners, showing that it is not necessary to apologize for an extramarital affair in order to have a large audience.

We have focused on cheating songs popular since 1960, in which the act of cheating has been portrayed as increasingly enjoyable. Shame and guilt remained as a consequence, but were not important enough to stop the affair. When women began recording cheating songs successfully, the women they described took on more character and were found at all points of the cheating triangle. The reasons for cheating came to be described more realistically and in more direct language. The consequences became more sophisticated, and some relationships began to take on a semblance of permanence while the sources started to settle down to overcome the frustrations that occur in any affair.

"I Got Caught"

Those who are cheating and worrying suffer a pain and strain quite similar to the pain of being cheated on. There are fewer popular cheating songs of this type, and the reason may be that this can be the most unpleasant aspect of an affair. Jimmy Wakely and Margaret Whiting were on the charts in 1949 with the carryover popularity of their first commercial cheating song. The strength of "One Has My Name, the Other Has My Heart" was still high (Jerry Lee Lewis returned the song to the charts in 1969) when Wakely and Whiting recorded "Slipping Around." That same year, they answered it with "I'll Never Slip Around Again," in which the man who was cheating in "Slipping Around" has married the woman with whom he was "slipping." The other woman has already started being unfaithful to the source, who now realizes the error of his ways. This is another modification of the "Eye for an Eye" punishment, and suffering abounds in the source, who is now reacting to the situation—just as his first wife did.

Hank Williams wrote and recorded "Your Cheating Heart," in which the source of the message is pointing out that the cheater will suffer for her transgressions. It is clear from the message that the one being cheated on—the source—is enduring much pain and hopes that the pain will be transferred to the one who is responsible. There is no way of knowing whether the woman ever does pay for her cheating heart, but after listening to Williams sing this song, most will side with him.

Few songs about reacting to cheating were popular in the 1950s; however, in the early 1960s George Jones wrote and recorded a song that describes a man who is reacting to a trifling woman. In this song the source is watching from his window as his wife and another man hold each other. The source thought his life was wonderful, and his desire to have it continue is a common reaction in popular country songs when a man discovers his wife cheating. The source describes the life he was living and how he happened to discover the unfaithful wife in "Window Up Above." The eavesdropping source is desolate, but he does not fight for the woman he loves. Acquiescence to the wishes of the cheating party is characteristic of the male source in this type of song. Some songs that do not gain a large audience's attention do mention the confrontation and the hint of possible violence, but few instances of injurious behavior occur in the popular reacting songs. Most of the injuries are inflicted on the one who discovers someone cheating.

Two other songs that were popular in the 1960s offer similar views of the injured and passive men. The title of Roy Druskey's "I'd Rather Loan You Out" says it all, and in Charley Pride's version of "Does My Ring Hurt Your Finger" we hear from a source who will not risk a confrontation by asking his wife if she is cheating. The man simply asks her if she takes off her wedding ring when she ventures out at night because it is too small. He was sure it fit when he was happier and wonders whether the happiness would return if the ring were stretched. Perhaps the source heard "Almost Persuaded" and hopes his wife will see the reflection of her wedding band and remember that she is married.

In 1982, two more songs followed this reacting-to-cheating line. One song adds to the "ring" lore, but turns it around. Lee Greenwood accepts the responsibility for his wife's straying in "Ring on Her Finger (Time on Her Hands)." The man in Greenwood's song believes his absences and inattentiveness caused the woman to go to strangers. Moe Bandy beautifully sums up the pay-back rationale in "She's Not Really Cheatin' (She's Just Getting Even)." The man in this song is observing his lover "painting up" and preparing to go out on the town. She's repeating all the lies he has told to her in the past. He is unhappy that he was such a good role model and that she was able to learn so rapidly and well. Although he admits he is going through hell knowing what she is doing, he does not confront her, try to modify her behavior, or suggest he is going to remove himself from the situation.

The women described in all of these songs are aggressive, assertive, and active in their illicit relationships. The men are marked by just the opposite qualities; they are being cheated on while staying at home looking out the window or worrying about a ring size. Except in Williams's message, in which he obviously wants the untrue woman to be hurt, there is little stated desire for revenge. Maybe in this case it is the man who cannot keep the fire lit at home. A woman displayed a similar passive mode in a song popular in 1986. After releasing the two popular cheating songs we examined earlier, Reba McEntire had one filled with the same type of agony and concern men expressed in the songs we have just seen. The woman is vague about the reasons for her concerns in "Whoever's in New England." She is apprehensive about a lover's repeated absences but promises that she will take him back when he is no longer interested or welcome in the northeast. This is one of the few recent recordings in which a woman reacts to a cheating situation by quietly accepting the pain.

"I Cheated Me Right Out of You"

It is left to a woman to lash out when she discovers that her husband is running around. Two of Loretta Lynn's most aggressive songs are those in which the source reacts to cheating. "Fist City" and "You Ain't Woman Enough" contain messages directed to the other women, women who make the mistake of telling the source personally or through others about their involvement in the affairs. "Fist City" offers one of the most graphic demonstrations of verbal abuse and threatened physical retribution.

> You've been making your brags around town
> That you've been a-loving my man
> But the man I love
> When he picks up trash
> He puts it in a garbage can
> And that's what you look like to me
> And what I see's a pity
> You'd better close your face

And stay out of my way
If you don't wanna go to fist city.

If you don't wanna go to fist city
You'd better detour around my town
'Cause I'll grab you by the hair of the head
And I'll lift you off the ground
I'm not saying my baby's a saint
'Cause he ain't
And that he won't cat around
With a kitty
I'm here to tell you, gal
To lay off my man
If you don't wanna go to fist city.

In neither of these songs is the source giving up her husband
without difficulty. She seems to understand her man rather well,
and he should feel fortunate indeed that hostility is not turned on
him. Lynn has made some other records in which the source
stands up to a man with language and threatens acts equal to
those described above. In fact, in the same year that "Fist City"
was so popular, Lynn sang a song entitled "You've Just Stepped
In (from Stepping Out on Me)," where the source discusses
cheating with a man who has been untrue. After she uses rather
mild and pleading terms in her criticism and suggests that his
conscience must be bothering him, she informs him in the last
line that she has just stepped in from cheating on him. Unlike
some of the songs about the retaliation affair, the source in this
message does not issue a warning and wait to observe its effect;
she cheats and tells.

The rarity of confrontations initiated by either a man or woman
in these songs may be due to the injured party's fear that he or
she might face the situation found in one of Willie Nelson's recent cheating songs. The song not only presents a dilemma for

157

the one being cheated on, it also highlights a modern occurrence found in cheatin' songs—the desire to continue rather than terminate an affair. The man in Nelson's "Why Do I Have to Choose" was challenged by one woman about his involvement with another woman and asked to decide which one he wanted. Using what can be called the "Dr. Zhivago rationale," the man explains that a good love is hard to find and refuses to change the status quo. The consequences of such an exchange could place a challenger or the challenged in a precarious situation. The listener does not know whether this particular two- or three-party relationship can be worked out to the satisfaction of all participants; however, we do know that the source is open and honest (after being confronted), and does not appear overly concerned about the possible results of his decision.

There is a great temptation to wander outside the popular recordings to select some songs in this category. There are many reacting-to-cheating messages that appear in songs on the weekly charts, but they seldom find their way onto the final chart for the year. Perhaps the audiences still do not want to hear some things about cheating. A song by Bill Phillips that peaked at number ninety on a weekly *Billboard* chart in the summer of 1978 outlines the modern-day problem associated with reacting to cheating. His song, "Divorce Suit (You Were Named Corespondent)," describes a modern solution to an old problem, and although audiences have accepted many descriptions of all facets of cheating, they still have not openly accepted several options open to one who has been cheated on. Conway Twitty (who also recorded "Divorce Suit") has a few cheatin' songs that either were not released as singles or did not achieve high ratings on the charts, but are fine examples of unique approaches to the problem. In one song, he offers a wonderful treatment of a word that has several meanings inside and outside the musical environment. The lyrics describe a man using a classic escape maneuver when reacting to a cheating women. He also expresses severe confusion and concern when attempting to solve the problem as he perceives it. A man tells how he went straight home after work to find his lover gone. She returns at three in the morning crying and refusing his attempts to comfort her. Before he leaves for work, the man decides not to wake her because he thinks she probably needs the rest. He wonders if he has done something to make her act in such a weird manner and in the last line of the chorus he makes an observation which could be interpreted in several ways. The line also serves as the title: "Something Strange Got into Her Last Night."

"It's a Cheating Situation"

Commercial country music was legally of age before it discovered that cheating was a topic the audience wanted to have represented in their songs. Although Jimmie Rodgers hinted at cheating in his 1928 song, it was twenty years later before a song emphasizing an illicit love relationship was released. The early sources took great pains to ensure that the attitudes and behaviors expressed in the songs were as close as possible to those the audience held. The messages were rather vague in their descriptions of the situations, the participants were usually apologetic for their acts, and they offered weak rationalizations for their behavior, which were probably not far from those being offered by many of those listening to the music. The protection of the home, especially the wife and children, supported what the sources thought the audience believed. The marital vows, although badly bent, were seldom broken. If they were broken, the one who applied the pressure would soon suffer and regret the decision.

The other woman was often depicted as out to get a weak-willed husband. She was, on many occasions, aided by the Devil, who took what appears to be an inordinate interest in the sex lives of a number of men. There was little enjoyment in the situation and the lack of happiness was often blamed on the woman at home.

The woman at home was normally characterized in two ways. She was pictured as the long-suffering, forgiving, and private person who would keep her pain to herself or, on the other hand, someone to be blamed as the reason for the man's extramarital behavior because she was the first to cheat.

The act of cheating was seldom mentioned in specific terms, for it was believed that the audience would be more receptive if the topic were described in vague terms. The channels through which a message had to be transmitted were perhaps over protective of the sensibilities of the audience. The recording companies and the radio stations acted as gatekeepers to protect the audience. If a writer or singer could not be specific or explicit in recording a message, or if the source succeeded in getting it recorded and the radio stations refused to program it, the song would not find its audience.

The language used in a song must be easily understandable; there can be few, if any, qualifying phrases. This means that the songs will often be filled with clichés, but a cliché can be effective. The beauty of the language in many country songs is found in the clever way in which well-known words and phrases are used to tell a story. If the words are isolated from the song, then they certainly may seem simplistic. Putting them together in an original and novel manner is an art, one that is difficult to achieve when dealing with a forbidden topic such as illicit love.

When the recording industry and the radio stations relaxed their control over the use of certain language (sometimes this was inadvertent when a source would slip deliberately ambiguous words into a song), the descriptions of the acts became more specific. When the language (or deliberate misuse of the language) in the late 1960s and 1970s became more explicit, it allowed more realistic reasons to be offered for cheating. The weak man continued to be a staple character, but even a weak man could admit the area of his weakness. The excitement of the situation, the sensual gratification, the desire for a new lover, and sometimes just the desire to alter a dull life began to be mentioned as reasons for cheating.

"Temporarily Yours"

When Loretta Lynn and some other women began writing and singing more songs, there was a better interpretation of the role of women and more realistic characterizations of men. The other woman took on some favorable qualities and the wife at home became indignant as well as sad. Women were described as having the same qualities as men. They cheated for the same reasons the men said they did. The Devil also tempted women— sometimes as a silver-tongued man rather than a vague force that controls a person's behavior.

Along with the greater freedom of language and the influence of the female sources, the cheating situation gradually began to take on more pleasant characteristics. When little enjoyment and much suffering were expressed in the early songs, this left much for the audience to assume. The fact that the audience was able to visualize what was occurring from so little information tells us much about the audience; it took only a few well-chosen words to key the audience to the source's thoughts. Perhaps the audience knew all along why people in the songs were cheating. Perhaps they knew that there was at least some temporary joy to be had in an affair. Certainly, those partaking—and probably those who were not—felt that there had to be some pleasure in order to make the situation worth the trouble.

Country music attempts to articulate the feelings and ideas of its listeners, since many are unable or unwilling to do so for themselves. When it was felt that an audience wished to hear cheating described in negative terms, only negative ones were offered. As the genre progressed, the songs set forth the positive and enjoyable aspects that certainly were present in a few such situations.

The rhetorical function is to adapt to the audience as the music has done; but at the same time the songs gradually attempt to modify the attitudes held by that audience. The persuasive technique is suggested by the theory that it is more effective to change an attitude in small bits rather than all at once, so the changes in the music were gradual. The more realistic descriptions, more specific use of language, more acceptable and rational descriptions, more specific use of language, more acceptable and rational descriptions of women, more logical consequences of an affair, and views from all sides of the cheating situation have gradually worked their way into the genre.

The choice of a topic is the first rhetorical decision to be made, and as the channels become more free-flowing the sources approach the topic according to their perceptions of the audience. That perception is either confirmed or denied by the audience's decision to expose themselves to a song. The fun a few sources are displaying in their descriptions of affairs is a good indication that they and the audience are feeling more comfortable with the genre. It appears certain that as long as members of the audience practice cheating, the sources will continue to describe it and sing about it.

Chapter 5

Livin':

Most of the Folks
Are Livin' When They Are Not Lovin'

Love themes so permeate country music that the people in the songs seem to adhere to the philosophy that "If You Ain't Lovin' (You Ain't Livin')." We certainly find much evidence to support, and few items to contradict, that action in the lyrics examined up to this point. One of the most interesting characteristics of the music, however, is the attention given to experiences of everyday life. Just as the descriptions of "country love" make it distinctive, the songs of "livin" are special, and just as love songs have always been a central part of the tradition of the music, so have songs about the daily lives of the people.

The tendency to write and sing about all facets of life, even the mundane subjects, and to make these topics palatable and in some cases fascinating, is another key to country music. This type of message adds support to the claim that the genre is primarily a lyric music—stories are told that the audience finds germane to their lives and interests. Country music holds no attraction for those who do not want to be reminded of where they come from, where they are, or where they are likely to be going.[1] Country music provides a view of life through all its cycles and occasionally speaks of what is in store after that life is over.

These songs describe the way a person has lived (the "good old days" songs), the way he or she is living (the "I'm just me" songs), or the way he or she wishes or plans to live (the "one day at a time" songs). In order to discover some reasons why the country audience finds these songs so compelling and some critics find them so difficult to understand and accept, let us examine some of the more popular ones that deal first with life in general, and then with one life in particular.

"It's My Life"

Many of these lyrics exemplify the art of songwriting at its best. They are examples of how a creative songwriter is able to describe a life or a moment in a life in such a way as to attract and hold a large audience. It helps if the listeners and sources share comparable backgrounds and if the audience has the ability to supply a few details in order to flesh out the word-pictures. A readiness to accept the message, the leeway given the source to present a different and sometimes unpleasant idea, the ability to laugh at themselves and even at some serious situations mark good listeners for these songs. The sincerity contract is put to a severe test in a few of the messages, but the wide popularity of the songs tells us that the contract is made and, in some instances, made gladly.

"In the Good Old Days (When Times Were Bad)"

Some country songs display a preoccupation with the past. We see individuals who are still pining for a faded love, regretting an act of cheating that has caused a love to deteriorate, or recalling other people and events that have affected their lives. Although the descriptions of current happenings greatly outnumber the songs about the good old days, the latter songs do provide a certain relationship with the past. Perhaps the best-known song of this type is one written and recorded by Loretta Lynn. Few writers have reached as many people through different media as Lynn has with the story of her life. "Coal Miner's Daughter" was originally the title of a song, then it was the title of an album, later it served as the title of her autobiography, and finally it was the title of a popular movie. There is probably no need to repeat the tale of Lynn's early life in a coal-mining community during an economically depressed time in rural Kentucky, the trials of a close-knit and loving family, and how they battled the environment and the economic elements to survive. A justifiable sense of pride in the strength of the family and their relationship to each other that fills the lyrics is a characteristic found in many of these songs.

Though most of them tell of a longing for the warmth of a united family, a few messages convey a strong desire not to return to an earlier way of life. Roy Clark's version of "I Never Picked Cotton," for instance, is a boast from a man who has committed a crime for which he must pay with his life, but never had to pick cotton as the rest of the family did. The man is to receive a harsh punishment (common in many of the early songs about crime), but the song is filled with a defiance and pride for never having toiled in the proverbial "cotton field back home."

This defiance is typical of the attitude found in other songs in the lifestyle group—the livin' songs—but is atypical of songs describing a source's early years. The sense of pride found in Lynn's song is also found in one of the most touching songs in the latter group. Dolly Parton's poignant story of a child receiving a coat sewn by a loving mother, her pride in its beauty, and the other children's laughter at a coat made from bits of scrap cloth is told in "Coat of Many Colors." Although the reaction of the small girl to the torment caused by her peers' ridicule is not fully explored, the pride expressed by the adult author for having a mother who could make such a lovingly crafted coat is the key to the lyrics. The message must be especially significant to those listeners who, as children, wore clothes designed and sewn by their mothers. It may be even more meaningful to those people who had to wear handmade garments and were ashamed of it. The song is capable of reproducing pride in some listeners and regret in others, who in later life feel that they were unappreciative of the love and kindness that their mothers lavished on them.

Songs that do show appreciation and perhaps a longing for the past are more numerous than those presenting a defiant, hostile, or negative view of an earlier time. Claude Gray's version of "Family Bible" depicts a family with few worldly goods, but with one thing the source wishes were more important in the present. The family worked hard and earned little, but they had abiding religious faith gained from reading the Bible. The source's desire for people to adopt the behavior of his family, and his observation that people are not reading—much less acting in accordance with—the scriptures, supports one of the images of the music.

Singers/songwriters often long for the past because they believe things were better then than they are in the present. The Judds used a unique approach in "Grandpa (Tell Me 'Bout the Good Old Days)," that was popular in 1986. They ask a member of another generation to recount memories of better days in this song. The source wishes men and women would stay together as they supposedly did in the past rather than separate quickly as they do in the present, for fathers to remain at home and accept their responsibilities rather than abandon them, and for life to be simple and relaxed rather than complex and hurried as it now is. Whether Grandpa can—or even if he will—answer the questions to the satisfaction of the source is not disclosed. A better past, mythic or real, is just a counterpoint for an indictment of the present in this particular recording.

"Wonder If I Could Live There Anymore"

The desire to turn back the clock is also a common theme in songs written from the viewpoint of someone who is no longer

166

free to control his or her own destiny. Prison songs are usually statements of life in the present or the recent past, but some emphasize a longing for what the source had long ago. "Green, Green Grass of Home" contains a message from a man who is in prison and dreaming of how wonderful it would be to go home again. He can imagine stepping from a train to be welcomed by his mother, father, and girlfriend. He recalls the places where he played as a child, and he thinks the only thing that will have changed is the paint on his house. The idyllic picture of how it would be to return home is an understandable dream for one who has no possibility of going back.

In one song, Charley Pride questioned the desirability of going home.[2] A touch of *Our Town*—the vision of the mother working in the kitchen while the father works overtime to pay the grocery bills, the smell of cooking, the roosters announcing the dawn—is tempered with the realization that, while the past is wonderful to recreate in the mind, the man is beginning to miss his home town and childhood less than he once did and perhaps a single visit would suffice. This modified version of the going home theme is probably more realistic than the belief that everything would be the same as it was before. The title sums up that feeling with the question, "Wonder If I Could Live There Anymore?"

"I Wanna Go Home"

Those who cannot live as they did in the past or, more specifically, in a place from the past, are exemplified in one of the most expressive songs in modern country music. The song depicts the plight of a southerner who left home to find work in a northern factory and now longs to return to the place where his family and friends still live. The feeling in the chorus of "Detroit City," by Mel Tillis and Danny Dill, is shared by many who left their homes in the South to find work before the Sun Belt states began to attract many of them—or their children—back. Perhaps in the future we will hear a lament from someone who has moved to Houston to earn a living and wishes to return to the cold winters of

East Lansing. The impact of the sentiment expressed in "Detroit City" was so potent that the first recording of this song by Billy Grammer had as its title "I Wanna Go Home." Although Grammer's version was moderately successful, it was left to Bobby Bare to turn it into a national anthem for many dislocated people. It is still recorded periodically (Dolly Parton included it on her *9 to 5* album in 1980) and is a classic of modern country music.

The man in Bare's version of the song has moved to Detroit and is dreaming of his home and family just like the man in Pride's song, but instead of wondering about his ability to adjust and be satisfied upon his return, the man in Detroit is in conflict with his ego. He has discovered that he is never going to be a success in Detroit but he has led his family to believe otherwise by writing that he is doing fine. He explains his true situation and ultimate hope when he tells of making cars during the day and bars at night and wishing the folks at home really knew how unhappy he is.

Several songs emphasize the past without restricting the images to a pleasant aspect of being poor or expressing a desire to return to a place. Merle Haggard, who is a master of these songs, wrote and recorded "Hungry Eyes," which tells how a family survived, why they were faced with continuing and crippling poverty, and the frustrations and unhappiness inherent in such a situation. The song describes people who are attempting to live under a depressing economic system with no way to escape. The father is a hard-working man who does all he can to provide for his wife and children (just like the father in "Coal Miner's Daughter"). The source tells us that there is another class of people holding his father down and controlling the family's existence. The mother wishes for more than the father is able to provide, and her desires are not unrealistic. The song must have a great impact on any individual who has suffered, or seen others suffer, from the same plight.

Mama never had the luxuries she wanted
But it wasn't 'cause my daddy didn't try

She only wanted things she really needed
One more reason for my mama's hungry eyes.

Songs about the past are often descriptions of life recalled by a
memory that filters out the most difficult and trying times and
selects only moments of pride or unhappiness. When the desire
to return is expressed we find little of Thomas Wolfe's realization
that it is impossible to go back home; there is no apparent aware-
ness that the place and people have probably changed as much as
the source. To find a more realistic appraisal of home, environment, and people, we can turn to songs that deal with life in the
present.

"I'm Just Me"

Songs about current livin' can be divided roughly into those
that describe a general lifestyle and those that deal with specific
social or economic conditions, personal behavior, and the peaks
and valleys experienced in everyday life. A song that displays
several of the most impressive qualities of both types was written
and made popular by Tom T. Hall. Hall's ability to compose this
kind of message has earned him the title of the "Storyteller" of
country music. No one tells a story any better than he does, and
"Ballad of Forty Dollars" is one of his most interesting songs.
Though the scene—a graveyard—might seem inappropriate for
relating how one lives, the story is told by a man who has helped
to dig a grave for an acquaintance. He observes the funeral from
his truck and comments on the people and artifacts as they relate
to his life. There is no trace of maudlin sentiment for the recently

departed—although a pickup truck, a shiny limousine, and the widow do receive some appreciative notice—and no great sorrow over the source's real loss. Note the sharp images and how the entire scene is brought into focus by the source's acute perception of the event, how the dead man is not the center of attraction, how the woman is depicted, and how the source's attitudes are carried throughout the narrative. Here is an honest set of observations, with no second thoughts about thinking them or making them public or any guilt about such free-flowing associations. The man telling the story is what he appears to be; the others may not be what they wish to appear.

The man who preached the funeral said it really was a simple
    way to die
He lay down to rest one afternoon and never opened his eyes
They hired me and Fred and Joe to dig the grave and carry up
    some chairs
It took us seven hours, and I guess we must've drunk a case of
    beer.

I guess I ought to go and watch them put him down, but I don't
    own a suit.
And anyway, when they start talking about fire and hell, well, I
    get spooked
So I'll sit here in my truck and act like I don't know him when
    they pass
Anyway, when they're all through, I've got to go to work and
    mow the grass.

Well, here they come and who's that riding in that big old shiny
    limousine?
Hm, look at all that chrome, I do believe that's the sharpest
    thing I've seen
That must belong to his great uncle, someone said he owned a
    big old farm
When they get parked, I'll mosey down and look it over, that
    won't do no harm.

Well, that must be the widow in the car, and would you take a
    look at that?

That sure is a pretty dress, you know some women do look
   good in black
Well, he's not even in the ground, and they say that his truck is
   up for sale
They say she took it pretty hard, but you can't tell too much
   behind a veil.

Well, listen, ain't that pretty when the bugler plays the military
   taps?
I think that when you're in the war, they're always hired to play
   a song like that
Well, here I am, and there they go, and I guess you could call it
   bad luck
I hope he rests in peace, the trouble is the devil owes me forty
   bucks.

We get enough information from the man who has lost the
forty dollars to make some generalizations about his economic
and social conditions, as well as a few of his personal attitudes
and behaviors. He worked for seven hours to help dig a grave; he
is a beer drinker; he drives a truck; he is partial to pickup trucks
and their special place in the lives of their owners; he admires
shiny automobiles, music, and pretty women; he does not care to
hear hellfire and brimstone messages; he does not own a suit (even
if he did own a suit it wouldn't be worth the trouble to put it on and
take it off for this occasion, for he has to cut the grass as soon as
the ceremony is over); he is not particularly concerned about the
personal financial loss caused by the death of a man who owes
him money; and finally, he is fond of rhetorical questions.

"What's the World Coming To"

A single set of lyrics can tell us much about an individual;
however, some country songs take a wider approach. They com-

ment on life in general. Even though they may be specific about the life of the person who is the catalyst and conveyor of the message, they can often be seen in much broader terms. Songs that concentrate on general lifestyles most often provide a particular view of society or a social issue. Certainly many that we will examine as specific lifestyles can be generalized to illustrate the society as a whole, but there are a few that seem to offer more far-reaching views. For instance, "Okie from Muskogee" describes the attitudes and behaviors of people in a small city in northeastern Oklahoma, but it surely deserves more than that narrow interpretation.

This song was co-written, recorded, and made popular by Merle Haggard, and it has probably been as overused, misused, and abused as any country song popular during the modern period. It has been used to demonstrate the ultraconservative nature of country music and its audience, the narrow and provincial attitudes of Merle Haggard, how the music and the audience hold dear the "traditional" (read "backward") values, how some people viewed the "hippies" who wore long hair and sandals, the lack of understanding for rebellious college students who were more interested in political activities than in football, how group and public sex were frowned upon, how drugs were to be shunned and drinking liquor was to be condoned. It does say most of these things, but it is also a song that was fun to write, sing, and hear. The people who could be considered the hated objects of these attitudes seemed to appreciate the song as much as those who were praised. Those under attack may have liked it because they really knew how much "truth" Haggard and Roy Burris wrote into the lyrics. On the other hand, they may have dismissed it by accepting what was written on a few restroom walls during the same period: "Reality is just an escape for those who can't face drugs." Whatever the reasons for its popularity, it hit the mark with a large audience and surely characterized the music, Haggard, and the audience in the view of many outsiders.

172

"Okie from Muskogee" did glorify the behaviors and attitudes of a conservative subgroup in our society and damned the attitudes and behaviors of those with opposite lifestyles, and although the song may have been written as a joke, it was taken seriously by many whose attitudes were reinforced by this articulation of their views. It supported the opinions of others who felt that the people represented by Haggard's view of Muskogee were accurately portrayed. Just as it is impossible to identify the real reasons for the appeal of television's Archie Bunker, it is also difficult to focus on an explanation for the success of "Okie." There is no problem, though, in saying that it portrayed the lifestyle of a certain group of people and became a hit with those who were complimented, those who were slandered, and those who simply enjoyed the irony, hypocrisy, and humor of the whole thing.

This song not only received great attention in the media; it was responded to by one country songwriter and singer, though the response did not achieve anywhere near the popularity of Haggard's song. It must be mentioned that the response did not have the opportunity to reach a wide audience, for it was not played on many radio stations nor was it covered by a popular recording artist. It did, however, have a significant following with an "underground" audience. Jerry Jeff Walker recorded "Up against the Wall Red Neck," which carried the original idea to its illogical conclusion. It suggests that the people in Haggard's song are beer-drinking, bullet-headed rednecks who drive pickup trucks and enjoy creating general havoc among the hippie population. Throwing in a little Freudian psychology and Phillip Wylie's theory of "Momism," the song implies that the rednecks are products of their environment and heritage (their mothers made them what they are), and Ray Wylie Hubbard's lyrics reduce the heroes of Muskogee to their lowest common denominator. They are more than provincial, less than unfeeling, and completely satisfied with views and behaviors that are not subject to change.

Once again, country music presents different sides of a question, and at least a few people who "seriously" accepted the comments of Haggard laughed at their descriptions in the song that is usually called "Redneck Mother."[3]

"Here in Topeka"

Another common perception of country music is that it is demeaning in its portrayal of women. We found some support for this opinion in several of the hurtin' songs recorded by Tammy Wynette, but we also discovered other examples from Loretta Lynn that offered conflicting views. However, one of the best descriptions of the stereotypical woman is found in a song recorded by Lynn. Written by Shel Silverstein, this song was originally called "Here in Topeka," but its better-known title is "One's on the Way." The woman in this song is being ill-treated by her husband, is suffering the problems and frustrations of caring for a couple of children while expecting another, and is married to a man who is inconsiderate of her problems and expects her to accomplish all her "wifely" duties for his convenience while he drinks with his buddies and invites them home with little warning. The song also tells us why some women who endure all these problems have little time or energy left to worry about what is going on outside their immediate surroundings. Lynn added a personal footnote to the lyrics when she said as the record fades out, "Oh, Lord, I hope it ain't twins again." She followed this song with "Hey Loretta," another song written by Silverstein, and "The Pill"; and they give different views of a woman facing the same problems outlined so effectively in "One's on the Way."

Some of the women causing problems for the "good old boys" in the hurtin' songs are very different from the one fighting for her existence in Topeka. "Jose Cuervo" was the number one song for the year 1983 and the woman described in Cindy Jordan's lyrics is not staying home ironing, crying, and expecting.

174

Shelly West's interpretation enhances the qualities of a woman who consumes too much alcohol, but is not contrite about her behavior. The woman also wakes the morning after in a happier mood than most individuals would be if they had consumed as much tequila as she did.

Women with some of the same characteristics as the one in West's recording are found in other songs. Two of them are described in a song by Mel McDaniels. The song appears to be a celebration of success and failure with women coupled with the desire to have other men identify with his experiences. Although the song is about love, it is not a love song. It is about how love relationships create a lifestyle for a man. In the first verse of "Stand Up," McDaniels tells of finding success with a woman in the back seat of a car. He then asks the listeners to stand up and testify if they have experienced this same joy. The remainder of the song tells as much about a woman as a man. The woman in the second verse lets the man buy her drinks in a bar and then goes home with the bartender. Again McDaniels wants the audience to speak out if this has ever happened to them. The last verse displays a more modern and aggressive woman. McDaniels relates another short story of success in the hunt for sexual gratification. However, when he is satisfied and believes that everything is wonderful the woman tells him, "Honey, you ain't through." An increasing number of men in the music are beginning to identify with the man in McDaniels's song and testify about their encounters with these new women.

"What We're Fighting For"

Along with the generally accepted conservative attitudes toward social, marital, and personal behavior there is also the opinion that country music offers similar views toward patriotism and serving the country in time of war. Again, a Merle Haggard song draws much of the attention. Because of his success with "Okie from Muskogee," his record company urged him to write another one along the same lines. Even though the singer/songwriter had other songs available, he recorded "Fightin' Side of Me." This song contained many of the same attitudes found in his earlier hit. The man in the second song insists that he does not want people to put down his country and what it stands for, and he especially dislikes those who refuse to fight for it. The fact that the song has not held as much continued interest as "Muskogee" is probably explained by the lack of interest in conscription and the relative lack of broad humor in the attitude behind the song. It seems to take itself much more seriously that did "Okie."

A few other songs focus on wartime situations. Sergeant Barry Sadler co-wrote and recorded "The Ballad of the Green Berets," and the World War II exploits of John Kennedy were eulogized in "P.T. 109," but for the most part war is not a topic for many popular country songs. There is no doubt that when patriotism is mentioned it is supported, but most songs tell instead of the heartache and sadness caused by war.[4] Merle Haggard recorded "Soldier's Last Letter," a song that was written in the mid-1940s and became popular in 1971. It tells of a mother receiving an unsigned last letter from her son. The boy died before finishing the letter, but not before telling her that the country must be kept free and that he believed he was helping to accomplish that end. Loretta Lynn's tale of loneliness in "Dear Uncle Sam," examined in chapter 2, describes the pain of being separated from a loved one. Her song also ends with the death of her lover, but the lyrics focus on the woman's loneliness, not on war.

One of the most popular songs that focused on the pain of war is also a cheatin' song. Mel Tillis's "Ruby, Don't Take Your Love to Town" describes the hurt an unfaithful woman dishes out to a man who has been severely injured in an "Asian" war. The paralyzed man is tormented by his wife when she goes downtown to find men who can satisfy her needs, something that he is no longer able to do. Although the song was written about a man who suffered his injury in Germany during World War II, Tillis updated the lyrics for the mid-1960s.[5]

> You have painted up your lips and rolled and curled your tinted hair

Ruby, are you contemplating going out somewhere?
The shadows on the wall tell me the sun is going down
Oh, Ruby, don't take your love to town.

For it wasn't me that started that old crazy Asian war
But I was proud to go and do my patriotic chore
Oh, I know, Ruby, that I'm not the man I used to be
But, Ruby, I still need your company.

It's hard to love a man whose legs are bent and paralyzed
And the wants and needs of a woman your age, Ruby, I realize
But it won't be long, I've heard them say, until I'm not around
Oh, Ruby, don't take your love to town.

She's leaving now, 'cause I just heard the slamming of the door
The way I know I've heard it slam one hundred times before
And if I could move, I'd get my gun and put her in the ground
Oh, Ruby, don't take your love to town.

"Thank God I'm a Country Boy"

Many of the songs celebrate small-town or rural life and are closely related to the songs about home. We noted that most going home songs contain messages from people who have moved from the country to the city; it is rare for anyone to express the desire to move back to the city from the country. Country music has paid little heed to the out-migration patterns created by the increasing number of people who are returning to the rural environment, and it still emphasizes the desire to get out of the cities, usually a move from the North to the South. One study of country lyrics found that the cities, states, and rural environments in the South are named more frequently than any others in the nation.[6]

The object of the heart's search is identified in one song that was popular in 1977. Waylon Jennings recorded a song about a specific lifestyle that began to draw increasing interest during the late 1970s. This type of song, examined in greater detail later, called attention to the tribulations encountered by performers of country music. Jennings's song is important at this point for its reference to a general style of living that is hectic, stressful, and, most of all, stifling. This is one of those situations where the source has selected a specific place for escaping an unhappy way of living. The place and the reason for going are told in the title and subtitle of "Luckenbach, Texas (Back to the Basics of Love)":

> So baby let's sell your diamond ring
> Buy some boots and faded jeans and go away
> This coat and tie is chokin' me
> In your high society you cry all day
> We've been so busy keeping up with the Jones'
> Four car garage and we're still buildin' on
> Maybe it's time we got back to the basics of love.

There is a sense of pride in songs that give a special luster to life in the country. At times, though, there is some recognition of the stereotypes often assigned to people from rural areas. Cal Smith's "Country Bumpkin" is a love song, but early in the lyrics a country boy is a victim of derogatory comments about his background and even the size and shape of his body, taken somehow as an indication that he is a "rube." However, the woman learns to love the bumpkin, with all his faults. This is an example where the country person wins over the odds and foils the city folk.

Hank Williams Jr. has recorded several songs in which he compares and contrasts the rural and urban environments and invariably finds the city a loser in the exchange. In 1982, he takes the approach that must strike home to a number of listeners when he emphasizes the fear of violence and crime reported to be a big part of city life and the ability of the boy from a rural setting

178

to cope with that violence. In "A Country Boy Can Survive," the source (a country boy) does not mind being labeled in a derogatory way by a friend from the city and is deeply upset that the city boy lost his life during a mugging. He thinks that his ability with a gun and aggressive nature would serve him well if confronted with this type of situation. Violence is not absent from other songs in the lifestyle group (e.g., "Coward of the County"); however, it is not as common in the most popular songs as some might think.

A more typical approach to the rural-urban theme is found in Merle Haggard's "Big City." In that song, the source just wants out of the city and into the peace of the country. The more laid-back lifestyle in the upbeat "Country Boy," by Ricky Skaggs, and the stereotypical images described in the calmer "Country State of Mind," by Hank Williams Jr., reinforce the views we normally encounter in the music. Williams is much less aggressive—in fact he is just the opposite—in this song popular in 1986. He describes a calm, serene state of mind that must be enticing to listeners who wish to return to such places as Luckenbach. Lying on a bank fishing while letting the world drift by makes those people residing in rural areas appear to be living the good days today.

Loretta Lynn shows pride in some of the qualities of a person from the country when she sings "You're Looking at Country." This reaction is common when a person wants to go home to the cotton fields, pastures, open spaces, warm climate, and away from the big, impersonal city with its bright lights and other distractions so alluring to some of the lovers in the hurting songs. Even some basic inconveniences of rural life are treated in a few songs. "Ode to the Little Brown Shack Out Back" is a song about outdoor toilets and all they represent in inconvenience and discomfort, but it suggests that they will be missed when progress (a city ordinance) moves them aside. The ability to laugh at or overlook many of the problems of the rural atmosphere is coupled with little favorable mention of what city life has to offer; these songs most often celebrate the good times even when they were bad.

"Po' Folks"

The "poor but proud" songs set forth the economic conditions and the attitudes toward them that receive the greatest attention. We have seen examples of this in Lynn's "Coal Miner's Daughter" and Parton's "Coat of Many Colors"; another song that highlights the theme is Bill Anderson's "Po' Folks," a description that contains an important difference. In the first line, the man indicates that he is still perceived in a certain way because of his past, thus indicating that he retains the taint of his background. Anderson presents the attitudes of those who see poor people as more than economically deprived, tells how the poor can survive, and, more importantly, shows us at least one positive aspect of such a situation.

There's a whole lotta people lookin' down their noses at me,
'Cause I didn't come from a wealthy family.
There was ten of us living in a two-room shack
On the banks of the river, by the railroad track,
And we kept chickens in a pen in the back
And everybody said we was po' folks.

My daddy was a farmer but all he ever raised was us,
Dug a forty-foot well, struck thirty-six gallons of dust.
The Salvation Army gave us clothes to wear,
A man from the county came to cut our hair.
We lived next door to a millionaire,
But we wasn't nothin' but po' folks.

We was po' folks livin' in a rich folks' world,
We sure was a hungry bunch.
If the wolf had ever come to our door,
He'd a had to brought a picnic lunch.

My grandaddy's pension was a dollar and thirty-three cents
That was ten dollars less than the landlord wanted for rent.
The landlord's letters got nasty indeed.
He wrote, "Git Out!" But paw couldn't read
And he was too broke to even pay heed,
But that's how it is when you're po' folks.

180

But we had something in our house money can't buy
Kept us warm in the winter, cool when the sun was high
For whenever we didn't have food enough
And the howling winds would get pretty rough
We patched the cracks and set the table with love
'Cause that's what you do when you're po' folks,
And we wasn't nothin' but po' folks.

The poor man in Anderson's song is the son of an unsuccessful farmer, the man in Detroit is making cars, and the father in Lynn's childhood is mining coal; these are typical jobs in country music. We will shortly look at two other occupations that figure prominently in the music of the 1970s, but we might look further at the general status of the working person. Earning a living was and still is an important topic for country songwriters/singers, and they usually describe the hardships, disappointments, and futility in the lives of people in blue-collar occupations. The sources do not call the workers or the jobs "blue-collar," of course; few blue collars appear on T-shirts and people working in jobs that might be categorized as "blue-collar" are unlikely to use the term (and so are those who write and sing popular country songs).

The inability to earn a living is highlighted in a classic country song. In 1982, John Conlee brought Harlan Howard's "Busted" back to the charts. This song beautifully describes the hardships, desperation, and hope for the future that often appear in songs about survival in a jobless world.

My bills are all due, and the baby needs shoes
But I'm busted
Cotton is down to a quarter a pound
And I'm busted
I got a cow that went dry and hen that won't lay
A big stack of bills that get bigger each day

"Po' Folks" by Bill Anderson. © 1961 by Tree Publishing Company, Inc. and Champion Music Corp. International Copyright Secured. All Rights Reserved. Used by permission of the publisher.

The county's gonna haul my belongings away
'Cause I'm busted.

I went to my brother to ask for a loan
'Cause I'm busted
I hate to beg like a dog for a bone
But I'm busted
My brother said, "There ain't a thing I can do
My wife and my kids are all down with the flu
And I was just thinking about callin' on you
'Cause I'm busted."

Well, I am no thief, but a man can go wrong
When he's busted
The food that we canned last summer is gone
And I'm busted
The fields are all bare, and the cotton won't grow
Me and my family got to pack up and go
But I'll make a living, just where I don't know
'Cause I'm busted.

Merle Haggard furnishes an excellent way to describe those who are wage-earners in a song he wrote and recorded about an individual who is unhappy yet determined in his job. The man thinks about chucking it all and hitting the road (another theme we will soon encounter), but this time the worker decides to stay, and he tempers his existence as the man did in Detroit. He works all day on the job and dulls his pain at night in the bars. "Workin' Man Blues" describes a man with a large family to support, and even though he thinks about other means to exist (welfare), he quickly dismisses that option. He makes his way through the week by drinking a "little" beer at night and singing the lament of folks saddled with unrewarding jobs and family responsibilities that require them to go through life with little hope for possible change.

It's a big job gettin' by with nine kids and a wife
But I've been a workin' man dang near all my life
And I'll keep on workin' long as my two hands are fit to use
I'll drink my beer in a tavern, sing a little of these workin' man
  blues.

I'll keep my nose on the grindstone, work hard every day
I might get a little tired on the weekend, after I draw my pay
I'll go back workin', come Monday morning I'm right back with
  the crew
And I drink a little beer that evening, sing a little bit of these
  workin' man blues.

Sometimes I think about leaving, do a little bumming around
I want to throw my bills out the window, catch a train to
  another town
I go back workin', gotta buy my kids a brand new pair of shoes
I drink a little beer in the tavern, cry a little bit of these workin'
  man blues.

Well, hey! Hey! The workin' man, the workin' man like me
I ain't never been on welfare
That's one place I won't be
I'll be workin' long as these two hands are fit to use
I'll drink my beer in a tavern, sing a little bit of these workin'
  man blues.

Waylon Jennings's "Drinkin' and Dreamin'" contains sentiments similar to those in "Workin' Man Blues." The man in Jennings's song, unsatisfied with his personal and professional life,
is sitting in a bar drinking and dreaming he could drive away and
leave his bills and other problems behind. He regrets that he will
never be able to see Mexico and other interesting places and finally admits he will remain where he is fantasizing about what
life can, or could, but never will, be.

Haggard's concern for the working man and parental responsibility is expressed in more sympathetic terms in a song that was popular in 1974. After being laid off from his job just before Christmas, the man in "If We Make It through December" regrets his inability to buy presents for his little girl. He is unhappy about the timing of his loss of employment but feels that if they can make it through the month, times will improve during the next year.

The working people were certainly eulogized when Alabama listed a number of occupations and suggested that the workers were not being adequately compensated for their labors. "40 Hour Week (for a Livin')" contains a general statement about the amount and quality of work done by the American people and offers no ideas for improving their pay. Hard work—not times—is the emphasis in this song and although it was very popular in 1985, it is not the majority opinion expressed in most of the songs that speak of economic conditions in country music.[7]

In one of these songs, at least, a working man conquers his problem. "Saginaw Michigan" is a rarity for its portrayal of the poor man's triumph over the rich man, and it also stands out for its sense of locale. Although the song is about happy love, it also points up the problem expressed in "Po' Folks." A young man from the wrong side of the tracks is in love with the daughter of a rich man. The girl's father believes that the man is unworthy of her and refuses to allow them to continue their relationship. The disappointed lover goes to Alaska to find his fortune in the gold fields. Just as the man in Detroit was unsuccessful in his search and told his family the opposite was true, the man in Alaska wrote that he was doing exceptionally well. The wealthy and obviously foolish father is taken in by this ploy, and after welcoming the suitor home he offers to purchase the fictitious gold mine. The young man sells his claim, marries the girl, and the father takes off for Alaska, and at least two of the three are happy.

The "poor-but-better" idea compliments the "poor-but-proud" theme. Several of the love songs contain examples of a poor man being superior to a rich one. For instance, sources in two cheatin' songs insist that the poor man is a better sexual partner. A woman marries a rich man but finds money cannot buy sexual skills and continues to yearn for the poor man in Dave and Sugar's "The Door Is Always Open." Jeanne Pruitt's "Satin Sheets" describes a similar situation. A woman chooses a rich husband (who can provide a great sleeping environment) but still longs for the poor man who can satisfy her. John Conlee gives another reason why poor is better in "The Common Man." The common man in this song tells a woman what he thinks of her life and how it compares to his. After asking her to leave her elegant home where he feels out of place and go with him to the local McDonald's he tells her that even his van and dog are common. The assertion that people with great wealth have greater worries is the key reason why the life of the rich does not appeal to him. The problems created by riches are mentioned in these songs more often than the advantages money might bring. The rich are often pitied for their lack of freedom and freedom is too precious to be relinquished either to pursue or gain riches. In fact, living without luxuries is generally more admired than any lifestyle that can be bought.

"Dreams of an Everyday Housewife"

To call these people "working men" is certainly accurate as to gender. Most of the songs that center on working are almost always about men. When a woman is mentioned she is usually a mother, lover, sister, or child, rather than the family breadwinner; she is most often the bread *maker*. Haggard places the woman with nine children in "Workin' Man Blues" and this seems to define the role of other women as well. A few songs mention that the woman is employed outside the home. In a hurtin' love song by Ronnie Milsap, for instance, the source identifies a woman's job in the title. "That Girl Who Waits on Tables," however, is simply a way to identify someone the source has lost. For the most part, the woman waits on the table at home. She is a mother, lover, and wife to the man who is out struggling in a hostile world.

The job that Loretta Lynn describes in "One's on the Way" is the primary occupation for the women in the most popular country songs. Sometimes we get hints that the women may be semi-professional lovers in a few of the honky-tonk songs and some are identified as professionals in a few lyrics that do not make these lists ("She Can't Give It Away," for instance); but from the information contained in these popular songs, the women are working in the home under stresses and strains equal to those the men are facing in their jobs outside the home, although they can't go to the tavern to wash away the problems. In 1980, a few songs describing a more modern lifestyle for women began to appear when Dolly Parton started singing about working away from home. These songs are not enough, however, to dilute the over-all impression that women spend much of their time in the kitchens, bedrooms, and nurseries, and if they take outside employment it requires the same type of skills they use in the home.

"Harper Valley PTA"

We have looked at a few of the predominant views in country music of the way people make a living, how some people react to social movements, how roles of men and women are depicted, and how people and places from the past and home are perceived. There is one other general statement about living that must be mentioned. A few songs observe the irony and hypocrisy often embedded in our behavior and attitudes.

The best known song of this type was written by Tom T. Hall. It probably needs as little introduction as Lynn's "Coal Miner's Daughter" for the recording by Jeannie C. Riley was a great success. "Harper Valley PTA" was first a song title, then the title of a movie, and it went on to be the starting point for a television series. The song describes a woman's reaction to the narrow-minded and hypocritical opinions of members of a local PTA, who disapprove of the activities of a mother who failed, in their judgment, to conform to proper social standards. The mother attends one of their meetings and strikes back by detailing the transgressions of the officers: one is a drunk, one is a lecher and a cheat, one has impregnated his secretary, one is an exhibitionist, and all are hypocrites. She defends her actions (such as wearing short skirts) as insignificant in comparison to theirs. This is the type of response to criticism that many people like to hear. "You're worse than I am" is a common justification. The message fell on receptive ears, for many listeners may also have been or imagined themselves to be the object of unjust criticism. We like to hear about this type of defiance and the fight of a little person against the powers in the social system.

Another song that took a major step toward outlining the way many people live is "Skip a Rope," written by Jack Moran and Glen D. Tubb and made popular by Hensen Cargill. It uses a child's game to make some acute observations about society. Children are overheard commenting on their parents' behavior. The observations become a rope-skipping song.

> Oh, listen to the children while they play
> Now, ain't it kinda funny what the children say?
> Skip a rope
> Cheat on your taxes, don't be a fool
> What was that they said about the Golden Rule?
> Never mind the rules, just play to win
> And hate your neighbor for the shade of his skin
> Skip a rope.

It should be noted that "Skip a Rope" is one of a very few songs on the annual top fifty charts which makes any reference to racial minorities. Although some observers have stated that country music has tinges of racism, this assertion is not borne out in the most popular recordings.[8] Johnny Cash's "The Ballad of Ira Hayes" expresses sympathy for the plight of an Indian who was among the heroes of Iwo Jima, but dies a broken, forgotten man. Tom T. Hall calls attention to prejudice and how it is obviously an attitude that is nurtured in "(Old Dogs—Children and) Watermelon Wine." The man in this song receives advice from an "old grey gentleman" who said: "God bless the children while they're too young to hate."

"Ramblin' Fever"

As we have seen, there are several songs about livin' that can be interpreted as general comments on life. Most are ostensibly concerned with the attitudes and behaviors of one person or a small group of people (such as "Harper Valley"), but the message insists on a broader application. Now we turn to more specific examples of living—living by one person and how several individual experiences may also lead to some general conclusions about the way people are living in country songs.

The first, and perhaps most noticeable, individual way of living found in many country songs is the description of an unfettered lifestyle. Most of the lyrics contain descriptions of an independent, freewheeling person who feels satisfied about the way life is going. Such people are often living less-than-modest existences, but they usually express little interest or need for material possessions. Some even brag about their ability to survive with little physical comfort. Roger Miller's "King of the Road" describes a man who gets by inexpensively, yet is satisfied with life. He is free of responsibilities, attachments, and common cares— and that is what he wants.

The man in Miller's song displays some other characteristics often found in songs where the independent person is making his or her way with few restrictions. They are free to go where they please when they please, and will brook no restrictions of that freedom. Sometimes they serve notice to anyone who mistakenly attempts to form a close personal relationship that they intend to keep moving and living as they wish. Merle Haggard describes this condition in "Ramblin' Fever." The malady that causes this type of behavior is one that the man in the song does not intend to treat, and as far as he is concerned it is a permanent condition.

My hat don't hang on the same nail too long
My ears can't stand to hear the same old song
And I don't leave the highway long enough to bog down in the
    mud
'Cause I've got ramblin' fever in my blood.

I caught this ramblin' fever long ago
When I first heard a lonesome whistle blow
If someone said I ever gave a damn they damn sure told you
    wrong
I've had ramblin' fever all along.

Ramblin' fever
The kind that can't be measured by degrees
Ramblin' fever
There ain't no kind of cure for my disease.

There's times that I would like to bed down on a sofa
And let some pretty lady rub my back
And spend the early morning drinking coffee
And talkin' about when I'll be comin' back.

'Cause I don't let no woman tie me down
And I'll never get too old to get around
I wanna die along the highway and rot away like some old
    highline pole
Rest this ramblin' fever in my soul.

This desire to keep moving and the refusal to settle down is described as free-spirited in Miller's and Haggard's songs, but it is sometimes mellowed with bits of sadness. Johnny Cash's version of Kris Kristofferson's "Me and Bobby McGee" is about a man who is traveling around and has some of the attitudes and behaviors of the men in the two previous songs; however, there is one important difference. In his lyrics, Haggard mentions the pleasant interlude of dropping in to have his back rubbed by a woman, but Bobby McGee is more than a masseuse to the man in Cash's song. Unfortunately, he fails to note this until she leaves him. He enjoys his nomadic lifestyle, but only as long as the woman is there to sing along when he plays his "harpoon" (harmonica). When Bobby deserts him he feels he should go on, but he is not sure that his life is as meaningful as it was before. This type of uncertainty is an unusual element in these songs.

"I Wanna Live"

When a reaction to the free lifestyle is mentioned it is usually one of two extremes. The first type of reaction is to extend the unfettered life to its logical consequences. Surely, to be without attachments can mean being friendless and alone. If one is living without friends, family, and loves, then other people are of little importance. When other people are involved, the "fever" can cause the pain to spread. "My Elusive Dreams," made popular by Charlie Rich, tells how a woman accompanies a man who follows fleeting schemes and plans and drags her all over the country. The man says he knows how his itch hurts the woman and that she refuses to allow him to pursue his pipe dreams alone, but he seems to feel only a little regret for causing her pain and does not indicate that he plans to modify his behavior. He tells how they once had a child and moved the child with them from place to place, but now they are alone and are still traveling. Even though the woman is tired and the man understands that his fickle nature is not bringing him any closer to the fulfillment of any of his dreams, he and she are going on.

In one song, however, a person did stay while the other moved on. George Jones and Tammy Wynette's version of "Southern

190

California" describes a man and a woman with equally strong desires to live in certain places for the lifestyle each prefers. The woman wants to live in southern California to be near the glamour and excitement she thinks is there, and the man wishes to remain in Tennessee where he is quite comfortable and uninterested in seeing the stars and their cars. The last part of the song is a recitation in which the woman speaks of living over the bar where she works and wondering about the man back in Tennessee. Meanwhile, the man is sitting in his luxurious home looking at a faded photograph and wondering if the woman ever thinks of him. Both of these people are unhappy yet determined to live as each wishes, and the pain of an interrupted relationship is insufficient to cause them to change.

The second type of reaction is to become adamant in defense of the way one is living and insist that there will be no change. Sometimes the stubborn stand appears in the form of a warning about how one's lifestyle can affect those who form any type of relationship with an obstinate one. We will see more of this expressed in the next group of songs, but one particular source is certainly open, and what is said should be sufficient to discourage (or perhaps challenge) anyone. In "I've Always Been Crazy," Waylon Jennings indicates that the condition has been long standing and there is little possibility for remission. Another example of a person who has been "crazy" for some time is Charlie Rich's version of "Rollin' with the Flow," in which a man admits that he has already lived longer than he expected (past thirty) and has not changed a lifestyle that others thought he would outgrow. He still has the same wild friends, and he is proud that while other men his age are raising kids he is still raising hell. He appears confident that he will never grow old and will continue rolling along. Jerry Lee Lewis recorded a song that may be more realistic and certainly is a more forceful statement than "Rollin' with the Flow." Lewis's recording of "Middle Age Crazy" portrays a man who is trying to turn back time so he can be what he was—or at least what he thought he was—before he married, started a business, and settled down. This is another country song that was made into a film and it surely points up a universal condition that

191

must be a fascinating topic considering the age of many country music listeners. The song, unlike most in the independent lifestyle group, describes a man who has taken the drastic step of throwing aside normal habits and behaviors. He has lost his enthusiasm for his wife and business and thinks the world is passing him by, so he swaps his business suit for jeans and boots, exchanges his Oldsmobile for a Porsche, finds a new woman to prove he "still can," and, even though he is forty, he thinks he is going on twenty.

The last three songs make an adamant and forceful, if less than admirable, statement about the way people feel toward their own independent lifestyles. Closely related to those who are free, or think they are free, are those who are free some of the time rather than all the time. Instead of displaying a constant and continuing style of living that pervades all of one's life, many songs describe more specific parts of living, such as work and leisure activities.

"Bits and Pieces of Life"

First, let us look at what a group of people known as "good old boys" do best—play. Then we will note what they care for least—jobs. The celebration of work and play separates the good old boys from the free spirits noted above. The truly free individual may play and work at times, but these activities are of short duration and in scattered places. The emphasis, therefore, is on ramblin' and the urge and the consequences of that way of life. The good old boy, on the other hand, is fairly stationary, has semi-permanent playgrounds (although the furniture is constantly being rearranged, if not replaced), the music is loud and important, and the women are often called "queens."

"Honky-Tonk Heroes"

There is a difference between what is known as "honky-tonk music" and songs celebrating the lifestyle of people who frequent the bars and other places known as honky-tonks,[9] and we are more interested in the songs in which the source depicts a lifestyle by describing the activities that take place in, around, and to and from such places. Moe Bandy and Joe Stampley, who have recorded several songs of this type, described the individuals, their behaviors, and their attitudes in "Just Good Ol' Boys."

> Well, I've been kicked out of might near every bar around
> I've been locked up for drivin' a hundred and twenty through town
> Well, I've been shot at and cut with a knife
> For messing 'round with another man's wife
> But other than that, we ain't nothin' but good ol' boys.
>
> Good ol' boys, we're all the same
> Ain't no way we'll ever change
> Mean no harm by the things we do
> Or the trouble that we get into
> Other than a wild hair once in a while
> We can't help it, it's just our style
> And good ol' boys is all we'll ever be.

Perhaps the people who must deal with the good ol' boys wish they would adopt the lifestyle of the ramblin' ones and move out of town. However, they are staying and playing what they see as harmless pranks. The type of behavior outlined in this song is more destructive than that of most of the individuals who are out for a good time. The song, however, lays out several common behaviors and how the boys see themselves and their relationship to others.

Most of the songs describe these people as full of fun and easygoing. They are often direct, sometimes more honest than necessary, and out for little except a good time. "If You've Got the Money, I've Got the Time" was a true honky-tonk song made popular by Willie Nelson in 1976. It was co-written by Lefty Frizzell, who had the first popular version in 1950. The man in

"Just Good Ol' Boys" by Ansley Fleetwood. Copyright 1979 by Brandwood Music Inc. and Mullet Music Corp. Used by permission.

193

the song is suggesting to a woman that if she will provide the money and her Cadillac, he will be happy to go out drinking and partying. Even though he says that if they run out of her money he will make other plans, he exudes enough enthusiasm and spirit that it might be worth paying his way in order to have him around. Some songs take a more serious approach to having a good time. Cal Smith's "The Lord Knows I'm Drinkin'" describes a man who is in a bar with a young woman when he is accosted by what he calls a "self-righteous woman." He admits that the bottle and the table are his and that the young woman is with him, but there is no need for the meddling Sunday School teacher to pray for his obvious sins for he will have a personal talk with God later that night. He is up front about his sins and has enough self-confidence to present his own defense to the Lord. His adamant statements about what he is doing and how he doesn't particularly appreciate a hypocrite telling him how to conduct his business is another common trait in these songs. These good old boys see themselves as slightly different, care little for how others view them, and fail to see that their actions should be of any concern to others.

A few songs contain tinges of concern for others. Roger Miller, who has written his share of off-the-wall lyrics, presents this view in "Dang Me."

> Well, here I sit high getting ideas
> Ain't nothing but a fool would live like this
> Out all night and running wild,
> Woman sitting at home with a month old child.
>
> Just sitting 'round drinking with the rest of the guys
> Six rounds bought and I bought five.
> Spent the groceries and half the rent,
> I like fourteen dollars
> Having twenty-seven cents.
>
> They say roses are red and violets are purple
> Sugar's sweet and so is maple syruple
> Well, I'm the seventh son of seven sons;

194

My pappy was a pistol
And I'm a son of a gun.

Dang me, dang me
They outghtta take a rope and hang me
High from the highest tree,
Woman, would you weep for me?

Just as few songs contain admissions of behavior that is "just a little unfair," at least one song advises a mother of how she should attempt to keep her son from adopting this lifestyle. This song is one of many in which the term "cowboy" is synonymous with "good ol' boy." Waylon Jennings and Willie Nelson collaborated on this recording, which is filled with advice and gives a peek at what the young man would be missing if his mother is successful. "Mammas Don't Let Your Babies Grow Up to Be Cowboys" combines some of the aspects of ramblin' songs and working songs. The second verse points out a few of the things the cowboy likes and why he creates a certain image.

A cowboy loves smoky old pool rooms and clear mountain
  mornings
Little warm puppies and girls of the night
Them that don't know him won't like him and them that do,
  sometimes won't know how to take him
He ain't wrong, he's just different and his pride won't let him do
  things to make you think he's right.

When songs are answered, the responses usually receive less notice than the original. This occurred when Tony Joe White wrote and recorded an answer to this song. His version (with Jennings appearing on the record) was called "Mammas Don't

Let Your Cowboys Grow Up to Be Babies," and it suggested that there was little harm in dipping snuff, driving old trucks, and living the life of a cowboy. Although the audience for White's song was much smaller than that for the original, the song did offer a different view for a few mothers and potential cowboys to consider.

"Queen of the Silver Dollar"

"Good old boys" is a more accurate description than "good old girls" in most of these songs. Women are apt to suffer unhappy consequences when they get attached to a ramblin' man, and the same thing happens with the good old boys. We have seen how Loretta Lynn reacted to a man who returned from a night of carousing and wanted to follow up with loving in "Don't Come Home A-Drinkin' (with Lovin' on Your Mind)." Most of the women are objects of a search in the hurtin' and happy love songs where the men frequent bars, and some of the songs mention the honky-tonk queens or angels. The object of a hunt or the one who is suffering from neglect by a good old boy is the woman most often mentioned in this type of song. Buck Owens sang a song that described a good girl who was driving him wild. "I've Got a Tiger by the Tail" tells of a woman who the man believed was mild and meek, but turned out to be an extremely active individual with a great love for bright lights and parties. As for the lifestyle of women who are hitting the bars and carrying on like most of the men in the above songs, they are extremely rare. Several of the women are singers, or bar girls, but few are the center of attention for the way they are living. The Oak Ridge Boys' version of "Y'all Come Back Saloon," for instance, portrays a woman who knew many songs but was singing primarily for an old cowboy she took home every night.

We have noted how the woman in Shelly West's "Jose Cuervo" adapts to the good old boys' habitat. We have always known that the boys would not be trolling in a barren place and women were always an integral feature of their preserves. However, more of the quarries are arming themselves and some are speaking out. No recording of this nature gained the popularity of "Jose Cuervo," but others found their way onto the weekly charts. The clever woman and the inept man are staples in the music and many of them appear in a situation where the good ole boy is operating. Songs by Lacy J. Dalton and Bobby Bare did not appear on the year-end charts but contain excellent descriptions of the quick (and discerning) woman and her role in the playground. A woman in Dalton's song ("Wild Turkey") is drinking in a bar and demonstrates that she is familiar with a variety of liquors as well as some inept men. Although she is drinking to counter the sorrow caused by a man, she is quick to inform a male predator that her condition does not make her an easy prey.

> Well, I have seen some losers who could make a statue cry
> But, boy if you had feathers I'd swear that you could fly
> Yes, I came in here alone, and yes I've had a few
> But, I'll be damned if I go home with a Wild Turkey like you.

The man in Bobby Bare's song ("Numbers") was just as unfortunate when he encountered one of these independent women in a bar. He started the numbers routine by announcing to all those present that he considered her to be a nine, for in his eyes, there were no tens. After reducing her to an eight because she ignored him, his high self esteem was apparent when he suggested that if they were to become a pair they would total eighteen. She decided she would calibrate his attributes on her own nominal scale. She pointed out that his male chauvinist numbers jive rated a five on novelty, his pot belly rated a ten on size, his outdated and frayed-cuff double-knit suit rated a four, his 1969 homemade convertible rated a three and a third, his smile rated a six (he needed some dental work), and the cheap wine he was drinking commanded only a two, his strutting rooster act a three

"Wild Turkey" by Hugh Moffatt and Pebe Sebert. Copyright 1982 by Songmedia. Used by permission.

and a half, and after she made all the deductions he earned a one—because there was no zero on her scale.

"I'm a Truck"

When these good old boys sober up and go to work there are a few jobs that get the most notice, and two stand out for the large number of references to them in country songs. One specific type of work gained much prominence during the 1960s and trailed off in the late 1970s. David Allan Coe and his friend Steve Goodman said that no country song would be complete without mentioning a truck. We have already seen that the pickup is a favorite means of transportation for a number of people, but when trucks are thought of in connection with country music they are usually of the eighteen-wheel variety. For a few years it looked like Americans were going to make the trucker a folk hero like the Old West cowboy. In the late 1970s, however, the people's love for the trucks and their drivers diminished and the western cowboy reappeared in the form of the rodeo rider. Bobby Bare said he thought the reason why truckers were no longer heroes was "the damn trucks kept getting bigger, the trips kept getting longer, and the unions moved in."[10] It might also be that after CB radio allowed the ordinary motorist to overhear what the drivers were saying, and after a few four-wheelers were blown off the interstate highways by semis playing tag, the automobile driver learned too much about truck drivers and the myth seemed to fade away.

The "truckin'" songs often describe the absence of love on the long hauls ("Six Days on the Road"), the lovers along the way ("Truck Drivin' Song-of-a-Gun"), the special type of person who takes such a job ("I'm Movin' On"), the fantasies that drivers can create during their trips ("The Girl on the Billboard"), and trouble with the police ("The White Knight"). Some songs concentrate on the image of the drivers as strong yet sympathetic persons. "Teddy Bear," made popular by Red Sovine, describes

198

the sympathy of several drivers for a crippled child and includes the use of the CB as a means of communication. The story, which is recited, is about a little boy who uses "Teddy Bear" as his CB handle when talking to the drivers passing on the highway. Sovine speaks as a driver who is carrying on the conversation and discovers that the boy is unable to walk and wishes to ride once again in an eighteen-wheeler like the one his dad used to drive. Teddy Bear's father is dead and the sad story evokes great sympathy for the young man. When he finishes telling his tale, all the drivers who have been listening turn their "hot loads of freight" around, head for the kid's home, and get in line to take turns hauling the boy around the block. The song combines several themes common in trucking songs. The drivers care for the poor, weak, and downtrodden; they are an independent group; and, of course, they love children.

One trucking song describes some behaviors similar to those found in the good-old-boy group. "Convoy," probably the best-selling trucking song, describes a free-spirited man who is bucking the National Guard and the police out of frustration over being assessed a fee he could not pay, and who gets many people to join a caravan to support his protest. The convoy of trucks, minibuses, and other vehicles join together to crash roadblocks and even evade a police helicopter. This is another song that was made into a movie, but the movie was not as successful as the song, even though Kris Kristofferson was the star trucker. The song does point up a phenomenon that began to surface in the mid-1970s. Before that time it was expected that people who violated the law or committed antisocial acts would be caught and punished. The large number of prison songs certainly are filled with this theme, but in "Convoy" a number of people commit several illegal acts and are not caught or punished.

The drivers of the big trucks, who enjoyed much interest in country songs for a time, are beginning to retreat from the public taste. A few songs have achieved a small measure of success since 1976 (a good year for this type of song), but for the most part this occupation started to fade away soon after that time. Just as train songs appear with less frequency than they once did, the truck songs have also tapered off in popularity.

"Play Guitar Play"

The second most often mentioned occupation, and one that became very popular as a topic in the late 1970s, is that of a country entertainer. It is natural to assume that people who write songs will write about the profession. There is the possibility, however, that this topic might be unacceptable to many listeners who would be unable or unwilling to relate to a situation that focuses on writing or performing country music. Singers also run another risk when they use this type of message. A problem with some other genres of music occurs when singers perform for their own, or for the band's benefit. In other words, they sing to the people on stage or to those in the recording studio and the listeners are treated as outsiders. Most country performers have not made this critical error—yet. The technique country songwriters use to write about the life of the pickers without making it appear to be a closed process is to include a theme such as hurtin' love or ramblin' and use the preoccupation with the music as a catalyst, not an end in itself.

Since writing or speaking about communication is sometimes called "metacommunication," we might call singing about country songwriting and singing "metacountry" (owed to Raymond Rodgers).[11] The most prevalent theme in these metacountry songs is found when the source creates discomfort for a loved one through his or her single-minded dedication to writing or performing the music. "Amanda," written by Bob McDill, was made popular by Don Williams in 1973 and by Waylon Jennings in 1979. The man in the song has discovered, to his surprise, that he is getting old. He believes that Amanda deserves a better life, but he is unwilling to change his ways. He loves what he is doing while he understands that most people cannot know how much enjoyment can be found as a member of a "hillbilly" band. It is certainly not a case of sudden infatuation, for he got his first guitar as a teenager and is now almost thirty.

The suggestion that being on the road with a hillbilly band is for a young person rather than one who can still act young is also found in Merle Haggard's "Red Bandana." The man tells how a woman seems to have matured after thirty years on the road while he knows he will never grow up. Making a reference to the woman's attempt to emulate Bobby McGee, the man admits that the woman should be leading a better and more comfortable life. He knows that the woman hates life on the road and wants him to give it up, but he refuses because he still loves it. He says he also loves her, but he obviously cares more for his career. Another song that emphasizes a songwriter/singer's dedication and a woman who endures his ways is "She Believes in Me." Kenny Rogers's version of this song describes a man coming in late at night, speaking to his lover, going to the kitchen for a snack, picking up his guitar, and attempting to write a song, leaving the woman alone in the bedroom. Again, dedication to this profession is causing a woman to wait for a man while he struggles to write a song that will (he hopes) change the world. She has faith in him, but she also cries alone.

These three examples of how dedication to a lifestyle and a particular occupation can cause pain in a lover are typical of the hurtin' songs that emphasize the act of writing and singing country songs. Another example is Tom T. Hall's "Homecoming," which illustrates how the constant traveling and trappings of the profession can drive a wedge between a father and a son.

"How to Become a Country Star"

A few songs center more exclusively on the problems of succeeding in the business. One such song, written and recorded by Waylon Jennings, depicts a man who has been trying to become a star for ten years and has moved to Nashville because Hank Williams achieved fame and fortune there. After getting to Music

City he is unsure that he was given correct information, for he asks: "Are You Sure Hank Done It This Way?" In the last verse he describes the way it must be for many people trying to become stars.

Lord, I've seen the world with a five piece band
Looking at the backside of me
A singing my songs, one of his now and then
But I don't think Hank done 'em this way
No, I don't think Hank done 'em this way.

The desire to be successful in the music business seems to strike a responsive chord with the listeners even when the love theme is absent: Glen Campbell's "Rhinestone Cowboy" and Don Williams's "Tulsa Time" are two examples of individuals who move to New York and California respectively to make it and are just as unsuccessful as Jennings's man in Nashville. What is important, however, is that these people are failing and feeling just like the man making cars in Detroit—thus maintaining a tested theme. We also noted that Jennings's version of "Luckenbach, Texas" was the wish of an entertainer to give up some people's idea of success and move back to the rural environment and out of the rat race. To cover all points on the spectrum, Jennings also recorded "Let's All Help the Cowboys (Sing the Blues)," in which the man is asking women not to refuse the opportunity to love a cowboy so that they (the cowboys) will have something to write about.

The metacountry songs seem to be replacing the truckin' songs on the popularity charts. As the latter group faded, the metacountry songs began having a greater impact. Five metacountry songs were on the top fifty year-end list for 1979, and many more received a large amount of attention. The number of popular metacountry songs tapered off in the 1980s and were almost as rare as those about truckers. Alabama said it was necessary to have a fiddle in the band in "If You're Gonna Play in Texas." Other songs contained references to writing and singing. For instance, the dream in "Long Hard Road (the Sharecroppers Dream)," was a desire to be delivered from a difficult life by a song the narrator had written. However, one of the most realistic songs of the period was a metacountry song. John Anderson's "Would You Catch a Falling Star" must be as poignant and meaningful to pickers as it is to the larger audience. A has-been singer, who once had all the trappings and benefits of a star, is the main character in the song. On his slide from the top the singer is touring in a van rather than a customized bus, playing to small audiences instead of the large crowds of the past, and actively seeking companionship when women used to flock around him wherever he played. Anderson's interpretation of the lyrics makes the "star" an extremely sympathetic figure and the audience can identify with his failure, even if they cannot relate to the occupation. Whether the interest will remain for as long a period as it did for the trucking songs will probably depend on the ability of the sources to relate the specialized lifestyle to the audience. As long as the writers emphasize a lifestyle that is not too far removed from that of the ramblin' man, the good old boy, or the more universal hurtin' lover, there is no doubt that this type of message will remain popular.

"The Prisoner's Song"

If all the "po' folks," "rambler," "workin' men and women," and "good ol' boys and girls" were to be turned out of the jails, prison overcrowding would be solved. Surely, the lifestyles of most of the individuals described up to this point are similar to those of many people who end up behind bars. In real life, as in country music, these people are punished more often than others in our society. Basically, the same reason offered to explain the great emphasis on losing in the love situation (the "Born to Lose" syndrome) is used to explain the fatalistic view of incarceration.[12] It is probably true that the poor, the hell-raisers, the ones who roll around with no permanent employment, and those who have highly individualistic attitudes and behaviors are prime candidates for running afoul of the laws that are written to encourage conformity in society. Many who adopt free-wheeling lifestyles have strict individual codes of conduct that, at times, come in conflict with those written by the people who control the system.

The implicit theme running through much of this music indicates that illegal or antisocial behavior will result in punishment. Most of the people in the songs accept, with little complaint, the maxim, "If you commit the deed you will pay the consequences." "If you play you pay" is *not* one of the rules stressed in the early music, but to ensure that the "play" is worth what you "pay" is a more common concern. During the 1970s a few messages that achieved popularity indicated that you may be able to play and escape paying. "Convoy" is one such message. The hero and his followers violate the law and get away with it. "One Piece at a Time," made popular by Johnny Cash, describes a worker in a General Motors plant who, over a period of several years, steals Cadillac parts by secreting the small items in his lunch box and the larger ones in a mobile home. Unfortunately, the man discovers something that most Americans already knew, which is the parts and designs often change from year to year and the completed automobile has a rather unusual appearance. The man is not caught or punished for his acts of stealing.

A more constant theme is the one found in Jennings's "I've Always Been Crazy," where he says he has been busted for things he did and didn't do. Just being "one step over the line" is enough reason for some people to be punished. Tom T. Hall's "A Week in the County Jail" points out how a number of people view small town or rural police departments where you can be arrested without even being near the line. The man who served the week's sentence did so on a trumped-up charge and found that rebelling against the terrible food wore down as his hunger grew stronger. It took only a week for him to decide to pay the fine he did not owe for something he did not do in order to get out of jail. The opposite view is found in Jerry Reed's "When You're Hot You're Hot." A man is shooting dice when the game is disrupted by the police. When he is brought before the judge, the crapshooter is thrilled to discover that the judge is an old fishing buddy. He tells the man on the bench that he will be glad to pay him an old debt if he is set free. The judge slaps the wrists of the other shooters and throws the book at the source, who reacts by telling the judge what he will do if "his honor," will remove his robe and accompany him outside.

Deeper emotions are found in the songs where people are in prison for more serious offenses. "Sing Me Back Home," written by Merle Haggard (this is also the title of Haggard's autobiography), is the story of a man who is walking to the death chamber. He asks the warden to permit another prisoner to take his guitar and sing him back to an earlier time. This is a more desperate situation than the one in "Green, Green Grass of Home," but it is a similar fantasy. The taking of a life, which placed the prisoner in this strait, is also found in "I Never Picked Cotton," but in contrast to that message, the man in "Sing Me Back Home" covets the lifestyle of his family. He wants to see his poor mother, who did what she could to keep him on the straight and narrow path.

The mother who attempts to raise a son to be a good man is featured in several songs. Johnny Paycheck's "I'm the Only Hell My Mama Ever Raised" tells of a woman who does all she can but fails to keep her son from no-good friends, fast cars, and the other distractions that seem to encourage the criminal intent in these songs. Merle Haggard described the role of the mother best in "Mamma Tried," which involves another uncontrollable young man who is hell-bent on a road to crime and cannot be stopped by a dedicated mother. This song seems to be autobiographical, for in Haggard's book he narrates the behaviors in his early life that ultimately landed him in San Quentin.[13]

The pain in these songs is mostly caused by the loss of personal freedom. The inability to move on, to live the free-wheeling lifestyle so many of these people desire, is found here just as it was in Vernon Dalhart's immensely popular recording of "The Prisoner's Song." There is little regret in the messages, and there remains the tunnel view of those who wish to live their own lives for their own satisfaction with a minimum amount of restriction. Few of the messages mention women other than in the role of mother. Bonnie, of Bonnie-and-Clyde fame, is the only woman who receives top billing, in "The Legend of Bonnie and Clyde." The "wild" women who haunt the habitats of the good old boys are seldom mentioned, and even then they are afterthoughts or part of an imprisoned man's dream. In most instances, the woman is a family member, and the desire to rejoin the family is extremely important to those who have received harsh punishment for their actions.

"One Day at a Time"

The man facing death in "Sing Me Back Home" is attempting to avoid present reality by looking back, but a number of livin' songs are concerned either with a way of life that will increase their chances after death or with living according to how they relate to a supreme being. We mentioned Claude Gray's version of "Family Bible," in which religious precepts were important to one family. In the same year in which Gray's song was popular (1960), there was another song that presents the view that no matter how unfortunate or unforgiving a present existence may be, there is always the possibility that conditions will improve. "Wings of a Dove," made popular by Ferlin Husky in 1960 and 1961, offers such hope for many people.

> When troubles surround us, when evils come
> The body grows weak, the spirit grows numb

206

When these things beset us, He doesn't forget us
He sends down his love on the wings of a dove.

Just as this message is one of hope, others are mixed with the good old days ("Precious Memories," for instance), but most predict how things will be in the indefinite future. Tex Ritter's version of "Hillbilly Heaven" gives his opinion of who will be in the great hillbilly band in the sky. Some sources ask for guidance for how they should live, and describe a relationship between a supreme being and an individual. Dolly Parton's "The Seeker," which she wrote and recorded, describes this relationship in terms of someone seeking instructions and guidance from a teacher.

The special relationship between poor people and their God is highlighted in one of the most interesting songs of this type when Tom T. Hall combines the characteristics of an individual lifestyle and the equally individualistic relationship with the Lord. "Me and Jesus" is another of Hall's statements of, for, and to the "common" yet special man.

Well, me and Jesus got our own thing going
Me and Jesus got it all worked out
Me and Jesus got our own thing going
We don't need anybody to tell us what it's all about.

I know a man once was a sinner
I know a man that once was a drunk
I know a man once was a loser
But he went out one day and made an altar out of a stump.

Jesus brought me through all of my troubles
Jesus brought me through all of my trials
Jesus brought me through all of my heartaches
And I know that Jesus ain't agonna forsake me now.

We can't afford any fancy preachin'
We can't afford any fancy church

We can't afford any fancy singin'
But you know Jesus got a lot a poor people adoin' His work.

Some people are not as certain as the man in Hall's song. "Why Me" questions an individual's worthiness to accomplish the work of the Lord. This song was written and made popular by Kris Kristofferson. He has written many songs that made the charts, but this is the only one on the year-end lists in which he is also the singer. The song is a prayer from a man who wants to know why he was selected to carry out a special task. Kristofferson is the coauthor of another song about a person asking for help rather than clarification from the Lord. The woman in Cristy Lane's popular version of "One Day at a Time" is asking for assistance to get through the trials of everyday life, and this message is one that is heard most often in these songs.

Asking for help to live as a better person, to make it through the day, to overcome insurmountable personal and economic problems, to receive a reward that does not appear forthcoming on this earth, and to clarify perceptions of specific and special relationships are common themes in these songs. Tanya Tucker just asks to go to a familiar place in "Texas (When I Die)," but most people have higher aspirations, and their desires and hopes continue to flow through popular commercial country music.

"I'm a People"

It would require another book to identify all the lifestyles found in country songs, but those occurring most often have been mentioned. Several corollary themes are intertwined within some of the lyrics. For instance, the importance of the family as a group, the problems facing the disrupted or broken home, the problems of shifting from one lifestyle to another, the concern for people as victims, philosophical views of life, bits of history, and even such rare themes as reincarnation ("El Paso City" and "The Highwayman") are indications of the variety found in songs that describe the lives and lifestyles of the people in country music.

A few generalizations can be drawn from individual lifestyles. Drinking is often mentioned in the love songs as a reaction to or cause of a hurt. It is also a specific behavior for those celebrating the good old boy lifestyle, and it can help a person through an arduous task such as digging a grave, but as a primary activity it is seldom found. A few novelty songs ("10 Little Bottles," for instance) are centered on the habit, but drinking is usually used to dull a pain or to persuade someone to get into the proper mood for other social or antisocial activities.

Some changes in themes occurred during the period: the decrease in trucking songs and the increase in metacountry songs; the decrease in songs emphasizing punishment for criminal or antisocial behaviors and the increase in the number of songs containing the same activities but without punishment.

One of the most consistent elements in these songs is the adamant statement defending the way certain people live. Many of these people are satisfied with their lifestyles. Even though they might be sorry for the fact that their way of life hurts a loved one, they still are unwilling to change. Those who are working and know they have little opportunity to improve their lot are, in most cases, planning to continue their jobs. "Take This Job and Shove It" became an anthem for the striking coal miners in 1978, although the man in the song only states that he wishes he had the nerve to say "shove it." The desire to quit is much more common than the act of quitting. The more appropriate and defiant statement is contained in Johnny Cash's version of "Oney," where the working man has caught hell for years from Oney, his foreman. The man in the song explains how he has long hated Oney but has put up with him in order to keep his job. However, at the end of his last day at work before retirement, he plans to take all his pent-up frustrations out on Oney's hide. He has given his plot much thought, for he explains that he is in fine physical condition from hard labor while Oney has gotten soft as a supervisor. The song ends as the final whistle blows and the working man calls out for Oney.

The songs of livin' are as diverse as the people who listen to the music. The most common themes are the ones the audience likes to hear, and perhaps the listeners have also lived these lifestyles, have seen others live them, or have at least been told about them. Perhaps the songs selectively remember the good times and forget the bad; so do the listeners. Perhaps the songs glorify unglamorous events and happenings; so do the listeners. Perhaps the songs make fun of serious events and lifestyles; so can the listeners. It takes an audience who is familiar with how the people in the songs live to appreciate a number of these fine songs.

PART III

The
Country Music
Audience:

*The People
Who Listen to the Folks*

Chapter
6

The Listeners:

When They Came Out of the Closet

The country music audience has suffered from ridicule and out-right defamation from some outsiders. Fortunately, most lis-teners pay as little attention to their critics as the critics do to the music. Criticism of the music—and, by implication, of the people who listen to the music—became less severe during the late 1970s when country began drawing a wider and more diverse audience, but it still continues and has been noted by some observers who know the music best.

John Greenway—in language far different from that found in country lyrics, but easy to appreciate nonetheless—observed why some people feel uncomfortable with the genre. "Like sex and liquor, the human organism takes naturally to the strong rhythms of Country-western music, and so the exigencies of so-cial order require that they be publicly abominated and privately approbated."[1] Frederick E. Danker suggests that "to get inside country music is a problem for those who take themselves as so-phisticated."[2] One reason why the "sophisticates" may have such a problem is offered by Bill C. Malone: "After all, they had never particularly cared for folk music when it was sung by the 'folk' themselves. . . ."[3] Charles F. Gritzner believes there are four major reasons (one was paraphrased earlier) for some people's problems with country music:

1. *Psychologically,* people who rail out against the music seem to do so because they are afraid of it—afraid, perhaps, that it will remind them of where they came from, who they may have been, and what they may still be deep inside.

2. *Historically,* our forefathers arrived on these shores with established notions of what constituted "good" music.

3. *Negative geographical and cultural associations* still persist; country music, regardless of its general acceptance among working class peoples nationwide, still carries a strong association with the rural South.

4. *Aesthetically,* the acceptance or rejection of country music is very much a personal matter; one either likes or dislikes it, usually with considerable intensity.[4]

Some objections come from within the audience. There is a segment of the audience that loves country music and wishes it to remain a message for a small minority. They believe, with some justification, that trying to supply a music that appeals to all the people will dilute or eliminate the unique qualities they cherish; they would like to keep the music a well-guarded secret. This does not mean that they object when Ella Fitzgerald records country music, although they did not rush out to buy her version of "Born to Lose." Those who love the "traditional" music are saddened, and sometimes frightened, when a new generation of artists changes the music from the way their favorite entertainers performed it. These listeners would prefer to have the audience come to the music rather than having the music move to the audience. However, it is both the audience's and the music's movement that has increased the popularity of country music.

Commercial country has been changing since the first recording. As long as the music is living it must change, for the alternative would mean stagnation and death to a form that deserves a better fate. The audience has also changed over the years. It

214

might be in order now to take a look at some descriptions of the country audience, then see what the messages tell us about it, and finally explore the phenomenon of an expanding and rapidly growing audience that came out of the closet dancing the "Cotton Eyed Joe."

"Fair to Middlin', Lower Class Plain Hard Working Man"

Most observers of the early period of commercial country music tell us that the listener was most likely to be a lower-to-middle-class white southerner. Bill Malone has suggested that before World War II the audience could be identified by knowing the performers. The entertainers and the audience "had been subjected to the same cultural, social, economic, and religious influences," and those who made the decisions in the industry concerning the direction of the music assumed that it would not "appeal to urban, middle-class listeners."[5] Malone's assertion that the music "has reflected the social and economic patterns of the people who created, disseminated, and digested it" provides the foundation for understanding the audience by noting what it contained in the music.[6] Dorothy Horstman used this rationale to identify the relatively poor, hard-working, God-fearing, socially isolated folks—who in the 1960s became more affluent but remained concerned about the complexity of a fast-paced, inconsistent world.[7] The problems that many have characterized as indigenous to southern culture and society are offered as reasons for the attitudes and behaviors found in the music.[8]

Perhaps there is some truth in the Country Music Association's claim that the typical country consumer cannot be identified.[9] A shortage of accurate national data is probably the major reason we do not know as much about the listeners as we would like. Age and race are the two demographic variables that seem to have the greatest meaning. Most investigators agree that the audience is almost exclusively white and in the 25–49 age group. Generally, rock is still the music of the teens; many people fifty and over are not disposed to any particular type of music. Some studies note a few teenagers who list country music as their favorite, but these were young people from rural areas or recently transplanted from the South.[10] The same situation is reported for the few black people who prefer country. Some blacks who grew up in the South and Southwest are country music listeners.[11]

The specific traits of the audience are not easy to identify. Peterson and DiMaggio, after surveying ten "partial" sets of data about radio listeners, people attending concerts, those attending the Grand Ole Opry, record buyers, and other information obtained from questionnaires, found that the two variables listed above are the most reliable. They did suggest, however, that the country audiences listed fewer years of education than other radio listeners, were over represented in the lower-prestige occupations, and were moderately affluent (the data they examined were reported from 1968 to 1972). The authors assert that the music is more accurately described as a cultural rather than a social class phenomenon. Their conclusion is important:

> Reviewing all the data that have been presented, it is clear that country music has broken away from its earlier ethnic and regional confines to be embraced by a broad segment of mid-life, working- and lower-middle-class whites. But no twisting of the data can equate country music with a distinct social class defined in terms of income and its correlates, occupation, and education. Not only are country music fans more clearly distinguished by race and age than by social class, but more importantly, many people of the same strata, race, and age do not like country music. In fact the type of Tin Pan Alley music defined in the industry as "easy listening," which includes the sorts of music identified with Frank Sinatra, Tony Bennett, Tom Jones, Carole King, Barbara Streisand, Percy Faith, and the Tijuana Brass, is still preferred by

a larger segment of the working and lower middle class as evidenced by radio station surveys.[12]

"You Can't Fool
a Country Music Fan"

If we accept the assertion of Malone and others that the music tells us much about the audience, we are able to make some additional observations. We know that the music speaks primarily of love. The songs describe adult love relationships during courtship, long- or short-term bonding, and ultimately the disrupted relationship. Most of the love songs deal with fractured relationships that generate pain. The songs usually describe a recently interrupted relationship and the impact that the break has had on the person describing the situation. Reasons for the suffering are often detailed, blame is placed or accepted, and the problem is either deemed irreversible and inescapable or not.

What can we infer about an audience that ensures the popularity of a music so preoccupied with the pain of lost love? When the music was thought of as primarily regional, the assumption that southerners had the propensity to lose was offered as a rationale for this attention to losing in love and life; obviously, no other American people have experienced the type of loss the southerner has known and had to attempt to justify or explain it; therefore, it was assumed that the people were programmed to accept defeat in their personal lives. Whether this regional characteristic can still be applied to the modern audience is questionable since the music has achieved such widespread acceptance. However, most casual observers still view the music as primarily southern, because of the great number of performers who come from the South and Southwest, and they are apt to be unconcerned with or unaware of Peterson's and DiMaggio's conclusions. Because of the dilution of the regional rationale and the finding that the larger number of people in the working and lower-middle class prefer other types of music, individual differences may better explain the audience. In the mid-1970s a theory was offered to explain why certain people choose particular mass media messages for consumption: because it satisfies personal needs and wants. The "uses and gratification" idea has some of the characteristics of "selective exposure," which implies that people select a message that supports their attitudes, beliefs, and behaviors.[13] Although both of these theories have been criticized, there is some indication that they may help to explain the question of taste choices.[14]

"Slow Hurtin' Songs"

No doubt some people use music and other types of mass entertainment to escape from their everyday lives. Those who might be searching for escape or diversion, especially from an unhappy love relationship, should have little interest in country music of the hurtin' type and would be more likely to tune into what some folks call "elevator" music. Most of the country music is not conducive to escapism. We may infer that the people who are so taken with hurtin' love songs care to hear how others are expressing similar problems. It is rational to assume that hurtin' love songs are not used for escape—if they are the audience has greater problems than we ever imagined.

The detailed vignettes of unhappy love often offend the "Progressive Elitist" critics of mass culture.[15] They feel and preach that people should not waste their time on these topics, for no ones lives or loves that way. However, unhappy love is a universal phenomenon and many people find solace in the commonality of their experiences. The following personal experience illustrates how one man seemed to be living in a way that could be described in a country song:

A friend wanted to have a beer party and, lacking space in his small car to haul a forty-gallon keg, asked me to drive him over to the distributorship in my van. We went at mid-morning only to discover that my friend's party was not an isolated event, for a long line wound out of the door of the manager's office. When we finally made it into the office, the manager apologized for her lack of help, and told us that we could save time by going to the walk-in cooler and picking up a keg. As we stepped through the door-way of the cooler, we noticed a rather thin middle-aged man wearing jeans and a short-sleeved shirt sitting on a stack of the stuff that made Milwaukee famous. The man looked up from what-ever he was staring at on the floor and asked if we cared for a beer.

We told him that it was a little early in the day for us to have a beer (an excuse no true beer drinker will give or accept) and we weren't really dressed for the cool temperature, so we would just pick up our keg and go. He said he understood that we were cold, and that he didn't usually drink so early in the morning either, but that today was different. Knowing that he was going to tell us why today was special, we resigned ourselves to hearing his story.

He looked at the kegs that had lured us to the place and said, "I thought I had a real good girl this time. We sure did have some good times together. I couldn't get over to her house last night, so I decided to take her a potted plant this morning. When I got there she wasn't home, so I just put the pot down on the porch and drove off. Down the road a little piece I met her coming home with an old boy she said she wasn't going to see anymore—so, I just went back to her house and got my plant."

Turning his attention back to us, he went on in the same sub-dued voice, "Now, I'm gonna get drunk and be somebody."

This man did not seem to be the type who would be interested in mood-altering music; he was much more likely to select music to reinforce his emotional state. The person who does not wish the music to serve in this capacity certainly considers it a distrac-tion, and this may be one reason why some people harbor such an intense dislike for country. Some of these songs of pain give the impression that the music is more likely to depress rather than uplift the spirits of an audience. Perhaps it is, but more likely it is a reminder of when we—or someone we know—had similar experiences. These songs are extremely effective at keying memories. The music undoubtedly strikes an emotional response in the listeners, but it also does more.

Country music requires a type of imaginative activity that is unnecessary in music of escape. To be fully appreciated, the music requires some solitude. When listeners tune other stimuli out and tune these messages in, the messages can key bits of memories in a person old enough to have experienced the situations, circumstances, and behaviors described in the lyrics. Realizing that this interpretation can be carried to an extreme by suggesting that some music might be used to encourage masochistic behavior, it should be pointed out that this is not a norm. Even though one song might suggest a hint of masochism ("Mamma Spank" tells of how a woman plans to punish her man for his trifling behavior), the "spanking" is designed to fit the childish actions rather than as a means to achieve sexual pleasure. Perhaps at a particular point in a painful period, a few people will feel the need for self-flagellation. But in the music itself this period seldom extends to a more uncomfortable episode than feeding a jukebox to hear songs that remind one of recent pain. A reprieve in the message occurs when the sources indicate that the pain is intense but temporary. Several songs presented hurts that would last forever, and in a few cases it lasted till death; but, for the most part, the songs give the impression that the pain is acute but short in duration. Remember that in "He'll Have to Stay" the pain lasted one day. Hope is also expressed in enough of the songs to assure a person of ultimate relief. Hopelessness is certainly a common element in these songs and it cannot be disregarded. One of the most interesting characteristics of many hurtin' songs is the passivity of the one who is hurting. Lying on the bed, looking at and talking to the walls, walking the street asking for a lost love, having a memory intrude at the most inopportune time, thinking they will die of the pain, all are real to people who put stock in an interrupted relationship; and the shock is enough to restrict many normal activities. Fortunately, the condition is not as permanent as it is noticeable. Life goes on for the sources (sometimes on the next album track), and this is noticed by the receiver. The broken-hearted will continue living and loving (sometimes when the next bit of clothing hits the floor), but at a time of emptiness, loneliness, and despair, this type of assurance is unacceptable.

"I Never Knew (What That Song Meant Before)"

It would seem, then, that the hurtin' love songs serve an important function by reinforcing and explaining a universal condition for adult men and women. Men and women who actively seek reinforcement find the songs an articulation of their trials and tribulations in love relationships. Along with this reinforcement, the songs also serve as expressions of their thoughts and feelings. The expression lets the listeners know they are not alone in their suffering. Willie Nelson's observation that the people can relate to the hillbilly singing a pain song also can mean that the audience wishes their problems to be articulated by someone with Nelson's ability to put their thoughts into the proper words.[16] Nelson does it better than most, but many writers describe pain that listeners are unable to express. Hearing their feelings described in language that is easily understood, the listeners can apply the situation to their own lives—something that would be more difficult with the fantasy themes and abstract language found in the Tin Pan Alley songs.

These listeners also accept the singers as friends—friends who demonstrate their closeness by the self-disclosing statements in the message and the way the message is presented. The listener who prefers this type of close relationship will be attracted to the music; those who would prefer a more normal, public distance will be attracted to music in which the singer sings at the audience rather than to them. This bond allows a singer to be successful with less than a technically perfect voice. The sincerity and emotion in George Jones's voice mean more

221

than his ability to hit and hold a note. The outsider sometimes has difficulty understanding how a singer communicates so effectively with the listener because of what they perceive as offensive nonverbal qualities, just as they have trouble relating to the verbal content. When the pop singers recorded Hank Williams's material, or when the urban folk singers discovered country songs and thought they were in the folk tradition (i.e., not commercial), they were accepted by some people who surely would have appreciated the original singers' versions much more than the "covers" if they had been able to overcome their prejudices toward the vocal qualities of the original singers. Country listeners are more forgiving of a voice, for they accept the source as friend. This special relationship is encouraged by the singers and approved by the audience through the sincerity contract. Outsiders and nonbelievers will not, or cannot, expend the effort that a listener must to accept the source and the message as two people in a face-to-face encounter will if they are to communicate on any other than a superficial level. A person who refuses to make such an effort, and fails to consider the bond that must be established between the singer and the listener, will not care much for the music.

It is probably true that the individual characteristics, rather than the group characteristics, have greater bearing on why the listeners find the hurtin' love songs so attractive. From the music, we know that the listeners are active, involved, willing to develop the special relationship between the source and receiver, and we intuitively understand that they must make an effort to accept the sentiments of the source through the sincerity contract, using the music to reinforce rather than escape from their reactions to shattered love relationships. Basically, they have no problem relating to those hillbillies and their pain songs.

"Love Ought to Be a Happy Thing"

Happy love songs may appeal to those listeners who wish to escape from their everyday existence. They are more likely to be vague in language and circumstances and more closely resemble the pop songs that serve so admirably as background noise. This is especially true of the ones that take a serious approach to happiness, as when the source attempts to tell of a happy love experience in a fairly straightforward manner, yet cannot offer specific reasons for that happiness. Songs celebrating the sexual aspects of a relationship became more detailed in the 1970s. When songs of happy love reveal specific reasons, such as sexual excitement, they may be used as reinforcement in the same way as the hurting songs. Certainly, many of the songs are fun because of their novel euphemisms, their clever metaphors, and words with double or hidden meanings. In addition to the language, the phrasing and other nonverbal techniques can impart surprise meanings and provide enjoyment in their own right.

There are many more popular hurting songs than there are happy songs, and perhaps this reflects some characteristics of the audience. First of all, members of the audience who prefer music to reinforce their moods and emotions are unlikely to be drawn to the happy love songs. The listener who is happy in a love relationship needs no reinforcement; and anyway, the joy in the song is usually so isolated that the listener can find little with which to relate. We may recall a time when we were on top of the world and the reason for being there was quite specific. When a singer describes why he or she is there, that primary reason does not mesh with our experiences as the more easily cued sad happenings do.

The upbeat or novelty songs expressing happiness probably grab attention for their unusual techniques outside or alongside the verbal message. We might be drawn to them for their form, but for little else. The songs of happy love also sometimes aid or abet other activities, such as dancing. When the vocal qualities or instrumental and vocal backgrounds of the song are more attractive, these characteristics shift the music closer to the pop genre than the more detailed and realistic hurting or cheating songs. The inability of the happy love songs to generate great enthusiasm may come from the audience's lack of commitment to the

223

sincerity contract. We are not required to take an active part when listening to a source tell of a happy experience; in fact, we may wonder why the source is so happy and why we have to listen to all that happiness. Perhaps some listeners are a little offended by such a display.

"A World of Our Own"

The reason for the shortage of happy love songs is probably related to what we found in the audience's overwhelming interest in hurting love songs. Happy people probably need less reinforcement in periods of happiness than do people in times of trouble. The unhappy songs are expressed in more detail, and the images are sharper and more meaningful than in the happy ones; thus, a prime attraction of the hurting songs is absent from the happy ones. People can relate to the unhappy story of lost, faded, or slipping love because the situations are more specifically drawn and the sentiment is so universally shared. The happy love song is vague in detail, but specific in that it is happening to the source, and the message is usually aimed at the one who is supplying the happiness; therefore, the listener feels no need to join in the communication process. Some of the happy songs are popular for their clever language (such as Hall's "I Love") and some because of their special situations (Fargo's "The Happiest Girl in the Whole U.S.A.") but, for the most part, they are probably made popular by the same people who ensure that pop tunes are successful. They are songs for escape, they require little concentration, they can be enjoyed with others (especially the peppy dance tunes), and they also appeal to people who prefer the public distance between singer and listener.

"Faithless Love"

The cheating songs contain several of the more important elements of the hurting love songs. In fact, most cheating songs ex-

224

press some degree of pain, a great amount of dissonance, and a certain amount of frustration. The earlier songs were invariably filled with guilt about having to find outside love, but they stressed the necessity for severing companionship as a result of the lack of love at home. The conflicting drives that force one to seek love then affect one after finding it make up a significant part of the descriptions of the cheating relationships. The importance of staying married is stressed, though not always adequately explained. The general assumption is that the marriage should remain intact even if it is unrewarding. Some of the sources use the threat of cheating to create a better attitude in the "cold" one ("Carolyn," for instance); and in a few of Loretta Lynn's songs the affair is a retaliation against the man who refuses to change his behavior.

The reasons for cheating received so much emphasis because the sources (or those gatekeepers who allow the flow of the messages) felt that the audience would not accept cheating for cheating's sake. There had to be a good reason for this type of behavior. Punishment, though not necessarily swift, was explicit ("I Got Caught") or implicit ("Conscience, I'm Guilty") in most of the songs. The illicit love affair was most often used to compensate for the perceived hurt—a hurt usually compounded rather than alleviated by the act. These characteristics are still found in many cheating songs, but during the latter part of the 1970s, there appeared cheating for excitement with women who actively sought out and enjoyed the act and the cheating situation developed into long-term relationships instead of just a series of one night stands. The hypocrisy in such songs as "Margie's at the Lincoln Park Inn" and those that identified society's inconsistent view of this type of love indicated that the audience was more perceptive than the gatekeepers believed. Probably they were always more perceptive, understanding, and receptive than the recording and radio executives imagined.

The songs are attractive because they point out what the audience is experiencing. Cheating may not be as universal as hurtin' love, but as some observers continue to point out, it is widespread. As some national publications have reported, there are

225

people who have become fairly well organized at the cheating game—as is demonstrated by the "cheating bars."[17] If the members of the audience are not engaging in the activity, they still cannot help but notice it. With the cheating songs employing the same self-disclosing of personal information, with the sources telling of pain or strain that encourages the acceptance of the sincerity contract, with the clever language used in describing the situation, the reason for the relationship, and the reaction to that relationship, the audience can relate to these messages just as they do to the hurtin' ones.

The songs of happy cheating employ some of the characteristics of the more popular happy love songs. They are specific in their reasons, they are honest in their approaches, and they are not dealing with the floating fantasies found in pop songs. Since they use both the style and the techniques of the hurtin' songs, with some of the more specific reasoning found in the effective happy love songs, they are the type the audiences attend.

"Roots of My Raising"

While country love songs can answer individual desires for those who prefer their music to be realistic, honest, and filled with personal language and statements related to their love experiences, it may be that the songs of living satisfy similar needs. As some observers have pointed out, working people hope to secure the American dream by hard work and sacrifice, but most realize that they are not going to achieve it.[18] This struggle to achieve security is often found in the songs of living; we find some songs that describe people who wish to strike back at the forces that control their lives and others who say that they must stay with personally unrewarding occupations in order to support their families. Often people drink to dilute the disappointments and frustrations of failing to accomplish their hopes and dreams. Tom T. Hall described why working people do not wish to hear tales of fantasy and what motivates them to tune into these songs:

226

They don't want to hear about Moon over Mankura. They want to hear songs about themselves. And you know, since day one of the Declaration of Independence, the American working man, either through war, inflation, or depression . . . [has] been jerked around from one calamity to another. And so that's where the songs come from. It's not easy out there if you wonder where the next refrigerator payment is coming from, or if your kids are going to eat, or if they're going to close down the plant where you work.[19]

Again, the desire to hear songs about themselves is a key to understanding the country audience. What they wish to hear about themselves are what Hall identifies as the trials and tribulations of the working man. Coupled with this desire is the satisfaction of individual wishes found in the love songs. The situations are normally events that adults encounter: looking back on childhood experiences, problems facing the family as a group, the close-knit and surviving family unit that often faces problems of the working class. One characteristic that identifies people as a group is the sharing of a common and identifiable problem that forces them to work together to survive. As Horstman pointed out, the desire to retreat to a time when life was simpler and less hectic is found in all but a few songs. The immediate family (usually wife and children) is sometimes overlooked, but most often is accepted as a responsibility that either drives the working man on or keeps him locked into an unsatisfying lifestyle.

The myth of the "moving on," truck-driving songs, and the metacountry songs describe lifestyles from two different perspectives. The driving songs are often descriptions of a hard but free life that must appeal to the home-bound listener. The metacountry songs are less free and are usually coupled with the hurting or independent, self-centered individual who is generally obsessed with the life of making music. That free-living and self-centered person who moves on alone (even with a partner) is a way of life that may suit a fantasy in these songs. Certainly, the good old boy and the highly individualistic person who bums around all over the country are not typical of most of the audiences's life-

227

style, but they could illustrate a way some of the audience would like to live. By describing freedom as the absence of personal and family responsibilities, the lives of truck drivers, country entertainers, and hell-raisers allow a fantasy to be brought into focus with specific details. It may still be a fantasy, but it is clothed in realistic lifestyles that the listeners can relate to their own lives.

"Blame It on the Times"

The audience seems to approve, or at least not disapprove, of the prevalent attitudes, beliefs, and behaviors found in these lyrics. We have found a few of the myths about the music to be based on some degree of truth. For instance, the good old boys who are drinking and carousing are happily exhibiting self-centered behavior. They are generally looking for a good time that is more often to be shared with other men. Although they are often searching for women, little time is given to an explanation of what happens when, or if, they find them. When men began talking about the results of finding willing women, their reactions were less glowing than we might have expected. Although some songs with the good old girl as a central character started to appear, the commonly held belief that women occupy the traditional roles of mother, lover, sister, and wife is generally supported. Men are often alone or with a male friend ("Bar Room Buddies"), but women are not taking full advantage of the equal opportunity to live this unrestricted lifestyle. Some women are supporting characters in the songs that celebrate honky-tonk living, but they are usually talked about rather than occupying the center of attention. Seldom do we find a woman who is speaking from the role of the honky-tonk queen, unless she is responding to a man who has mistreated, tricked, or deserted her. Continuing the practice of having the woman characterized by a man in the music, the "new" woman is usually described by the man who encounters her. A few women are beginning to paint their own portraits, but they are still in the small—if striking—minority.

In the cheating songs we often find the "bad" woman who is actively involved with a man, acting as a threat to a happy (if chilly) home, or just serving as the enticement to a weak and gullible man. We receive little information about the bad woman, but from the reactions to her by both the men and the women, we can make some generalizations. She is identified by her living and loving habits: her habitat is the honky-tonk; she actively pursues men for money or sex, and she dresses for the task and the environment. Women are not allowed the same freedom as men to change their role or behavior. A man can move back and forth along the good-bad continuum as if he were in his pickup truck; however, the woman is presumed "good" only until she can be persuaded to be "bad," and once a woman is presumed "bad" she is offered little opportunity to move back up the scale.

There are some inconsistencies in the ways women are portrayed in country music. If they are perceived as active in the search and have the drawing power to lure men into their arms, they are often still the passive creatures who await men in the lonesome songs. In the happy searching song, the quasi-happy ones ("Don't the Girls All Get Prettier at Closing Time"), and the frustrated songs where there is an absent love or lover, the woman is the object of the hunt, not the active, prowling, all-alluring one encountered in the cheating songs. Perhaps the woman, once she slips down the scale, takes on more aggressive characteristics. Perhaps the bad person is always given by the good people more power than is really deserved. Perhaps it depends on the viewpoint of the one describing the situation. We did find the example in Loretta Lynn's "Somebody Somewhere (Don't Know What He's Missin' Tonight)" of a woman with self-determination who desires as strongly as any man, but for the most part this is not characteristic of the women in the hurting and cheating songs. Shelly West introduced a more carefree and independent woman in "Jose Cuervo," however that image appears as infrequently in the most popular songs as the one offered by Lynn. There have been a few metacountry songs about women who are obsessed with the music and end up destroying a personal relationship, but most of these songs have not achieved wide acceptance.

The role of the outspoken woman should be mentioned here. These women are found (usually in the "wronged" songs) where they are threatening to retaliate, are retaliating, or in some way speaking out for what they perceive to be their rights. This is prominent in the messages of Loretta Lynn, but others have also contributed to it. If we could still consider country to be southern music, we might venture to say that southern women are especially able to assert their rights by manipulating men to gain their objectives. The aggressive, outspoken woman is generally admired (or feared) by southern men, according to some observers.[20] A woman who is intelligent and verbally adept can often use the system, and the women in these examples certainly display this capability. Whatever their reasons for accepting this behavior, the audience certainly applauds the outspoken and aggressive women in Loretta Lynn's songs.

Both the outspoken woman and the outspoken man are generally admired. Even though we find people in the hurting love songs who are hesitant to express their desires and wishes, we do find them speaking out forcefully in other songs. The good old boys confident in the way they are living, the wronged women fighting back, the mother telling the Harper Valley PTA what she thinks, and the prisoner who is unrepentant for committing a violent crime are examples of people speaking forcefully to and about those individuals and forces restricting their personal and public lives. Other behaviors are often accepted by the audience. The open unabashed expression of deep emotions—the crying of a man who has lost his woman, the sympathy shown for a crippled orphan, the feeling for the person who has lost freedom, the anger felt toward those who do not fit the mold of the true American—are clearly expressed in the songs and approved by the audience. If emotions and attitudes are judged to be sincere, they are generally approved. The audience will accept the source's attitudes as long as the source appears to approach the sentiment honestly. Whatever the sentiment, it must be warranted by the circumstances, unless intentional irony, sarcasm, or humor is intended.

Some observers fear that a few people listening to the music may attempt to adopt some of the behavior outlined in the songs. Someone may drive a pickup truck with a gun rack in the rear window, drink beer from a long-necked bottle, wear jeans, cowboy boots, and a hat; but this does not mean that the person is living the life that Tom T. Hall or Merle Haggard describe in their songs. When a songwriter describes how real people live and love, the messages may serve as reinforcement but seldom as a way of life to one who is in need of a role model.

"Don't Think You're Too Good for Country Music"

It may be that the way the audience identifies with the source is one of the most telling characteristics of that audience. Many performers during this period, as Malone noted about the ones from the earlier period, are products of the same social and economic environments as the listeners. However, some have successfully fulfilled the American dream while continuing the impression that they are still part of the struggling working class. They are also among the most astute men and women in the entire music profession, and they manage to project the opposite image. Many of them control their product from beginning to end in almost the same way as the oil industry does. They write and sing the songs and they own publishing companies, recording facilities, booking agencies, radio stations, and other parts of the production and distribution elements of the music industry. Even while they are enjoying their great success, some performers give the impression of being much like the members of the audience; most of them are able to cope well with success and appear to be just the same as when they started in the profession. Successful country performers do not allow prosperity to drive a wedge between them and the audience. The audience feels pride in the achievements of the sources and will do what-

231

ever they can to contribute to them. Identification with the artist is one of the prime reasons country fans give for purchasing the recordings of any singer.[21] The intense loyalty of the country fan is commonly accepted in the trade and it serves the performer and the music well.

While the loyalty of the audience is not a trait that can be determined by what is contained in the message, it does help to explain another aspect of the approval of the sincerity contract. It helps to ensure that singers can attempt to do new things with their music that may attract a wider audience without losing the old one (Bill Anderson's disco tune, for instance) and it ensures that there will be a ready market for the product—in contrast to the fickle audiences for much mass appeal music.

People who are intensely loyal to this music will often be obstinate about it. If a radio station does not program their favorite singer, they call and complain; if that fails, they will search out other stations or switch to their own personal playback systems. These fans had to be dedicated in seeking out the music when few stations played it, and some feel that since their favorites are not being played by the new country stations, they will have to return to their private resources once again. The audience is just as outspoken, dedicated, and obsessed as are some of the people in the songs, and they have emerged from the closet without opening the door. However, a major portion of the audience was never bashful in the first place.

"I Was Country When Country Wasn't Cool"

Country music is touted as the music of the 1980s. It was also called the music of the 1970s and the 1960s. Given the fact that if you predict an event long enough you increase the odds of having it happen, those who predicted the current rise and impact of the music have had more evidence to support their claims than have others at any time in the past. The mean age of the American population is rising, thereby increasing the size of the prospective audience—the 25–49 age group that is extremely important to the music. Expanding the base from which to draw listeners at a time when other commercially popular musical forms are in a state of poor health opens up new possibilities for the expansion of the country audience. The audience grew during the late 1970s, as indicated by the increasing number of radio outlets programming the music and the sales of the recorded product.

The new audience for the music is considered by some to be a blessing and by others to be a curse. We have already noted that some people fear the special nature of the music has already changed too much. There is no doubt that the music retains its distinctive characteristics. One has only to listen to the top songs over the years to notice some distinctive changes—both in the styles of performance and in the songs themselves—but there is still much that remains stable in the music. The changes introduced by Ernest Tubb, Tom T. Hall, and others are now considered mainstream but were resented when they were introduced. Just as the music has undergone subtle and significant changes over the years, so has the audience.

"Within Your Crowd"

One has only to attend a few country concerts to get the feeling that the audience is changing. The influx of younger fans is noticeable at the concerts of both progressive and traditional artists. This new audience has been noticed by the recording companies, the concert promoters, and all others actively involved in the business. The younger audience was drawn first to bluegrass, which had a revival on college campuses when young people discovered it. Audiences at the large number of bluegrass festivals are a mingling of old and young. (This music exists only because

233

of festivals and live performances, since radio generally ignores it.) Bluegrass followers have assimilated the young audience better than the more commercial country audience has. One observer, using negative terms to name both the traditional and the new audiences, described the people attending a progressive country concert as "hickies"—a cross between hicks and hippies.[22]

The blessing derived from the new audience is most notable in the increased sales and drawing power for country music. Willie Nelson said that he liked to perform for college audiences because of the enthusiasm and energy that young people bring to a concert. The problems are related to fears of the traditional performers and fans that the new people will have a detrimental effect upon the music. Some of the problems reflect the tendency of any group to distrust outsiders, but it behooves us to look at how the new audience differs from the more traditional audience and how this may affect the message.

When an audience is attracted to music at a later age instead of growing up with it, they bring their prior listening behaviors with them. Those who are disenchanted with rock music and move to the country scene retain many of their habits from their first experience. They are unsophisticated in the ways of the older audience because they have not been associated for long with the traditional behavior patterns. The more traditional country audience is semi-respectful while the artists are performing, for they are interested in hearing the songs. This attentiveness is not a predominant trait in many of the newer audiences, who are primarily interested in the "feel" of the music and the overall atmosphere. It is easy to spot newer country music fans at a concert, for they carry on loud conversations, move about, and seem to pay little attention to the performers. The more traditional audience will sit quietly during the set except when they express enthusiasm as a singer begins a familiar song and at the conclusion of a song when they may show their approval very loudly. The new, young audience will show their pleasure at the end of a song, but exactly what they have enjoyed about it is unclear.

Just as the listener and the pseudo-listener can be separated rather quickly at a concert, they can also be easily identified in the living room. True country fans are interested in listening to the songs; the newer listeners give lip service to the music but will attempt to carry on conversations during its presentation. It is possible that these new fans will develop as others who have been drawn to the music and have found a comfortable home.

While the nonverbal characteristics of the music appear to be the major attraction to many members of the newer audience, it must be remembered that the nonverbal qualities of the performers seem to discourage some of them. The initiated rock audience has no difficulty with that music because they understand the language and artifacts of the music. To an outsider the rock message may appear to be little but repetitive shouts of joy or protest, but to the person attuned to the message, it has meaning. When a member of one audience is exposed to a different music, there is a period of adjustment because the newcomer is seldom prepared to step in at the attention level of the older, more experienced audience. A new listener can easily be distracted from the message by extraneous and unfamiliar artifacts of the sources and the other members of the audience. A person new to country music is often distracted by the nonverbal characteristics of the performers, such as the sequined wagon wheels sewn on Porter Wagoner's brightly colored western suits, and his hair which is of a color and style far different from that of their peers. This confusion is found especially in an audience that has moved from a music scene where the singers dress in costumes that vary from "early Goodwill" to "late ski slope" and where some performers' hair appears to have been styled by plugging a guitar into an overloaded amplifer.

Even though the new audience is unsophisticated in the ways of country music, they will tend to adopt some of the ways of the original audience. It is to be hoped that they will learn about the music's history and discover all that the genre has to offer. When Willie Nelson was asked if he had noticed any strange reactions to his *Stardust* album, he mentioned that a young girl had volunteered the information that she had never cared for country music until she heard him sing "Stardust." It is possible that the people who are so enamored of Nelson will pick up a copy of his *Red Headed Stranger* or *To Lefty from Willie* and discover country music.

The problems with the new audience are probably compounded by the difficulty in assimilating so many people in such a short time. The new audience is so large that it retains many of its original listening patterns. The sudden increase in the number of new listeners troubles some observers who believe that many of them will prove to be fair-weather fans, just following the latest fad. No doubt some members of the new audience will turn out to be as fickle and unperceptive as some of the new radio stations. What will save country music from the fate of disco (a music form that rose quickly and fell fast) is a strong, stable core of traditional listeners. What has to be of concern is the possibility that the rush to embrace the new audience will alienate the older, more faithful audience. By catering to a mercurial listenership, the music industry may damage the support of the majority of the country audience, and when the faddists move on to the next wave, country will have a less secure place to return. But there is hope. Several of the new performers who appeal to the new audience also retain much of what is good for the past, and this is the best sign for the future.

"If Ole Hank Could Only See Us Now"

Two major movements in the eighties affected the music. The "Urban Cowboy" phase took its name from the movie. It did much to increase the size and diversity of the audience, and it altered the message both directly and indirectly. This movie used the music in much the same way it was used in *Nashville,* but *Urban Cowboy*'s impact on the audience and the delivery system was greater. It pushed the music even closer to pop and away from honky-tonk, even though much of the movie took place in a dance hall. The movie became a metaphor and an analogy for the music, but it was based on a faulty assumption: Gilley's is to a real honky-tonk what Sylvia is to Loretta Lynn.

236

The music began to promote those musical qualities deemed to be inoffensive to that new audience attracted to the music and environment presented in the movie. The new music did not offend the new audience, but it did offend many of those who longed to hear traditional music. The greatest impact on the message was felt when the new artists failed to release many honky-tonk songs, a genre that was perceived to be too hard-core country for the audience. The new (and even some experienced) performers who adapted to the music industry's plans to produce mass-appeal music were, for the most part, incapable of producing enough sincerity to sing true hurtin' and cheatin' songs. These two factors combined to lead country farther into the bland suburbs of the music community where it rested on a foundation of songs that had little individuality or honesty. The original fans did not desert the music as rapidly as they should, or could have, for they had their own playback systems, some radio stations continued to play the older music, and real honky-tonks and barrooms did not give up their passions easily.

Two of the most obvious impacts of this movement were the creation of an additional outlet for the music and another playground for the "semi-good old boys and girls." Baby Gilley's opened as fast as discos closed, and a new industry flourished. Since the people who were providing the music for the new audience in the new locations knew as little about the music as the radio people did when they shifted from rock formats to country in the seventies, they made essentially the same mistakes as the disc jockeys made. They played the type of music that was most like that they had been playing (rock or disco), left the power of the amplifiers set at their original volume level, and expected the audience to enjoy the experience the way they did in the film. A naive audience responded favorably in the early days of the movement. What they knew of the traditional country dances was that glimpsed in movies or described on the teaching records that quickly appeared. Most of those who had grown up with the dancing stopped frequenting these establishments after a few trips; therefore, good role models were scarce. It took only a few minutes in one of these places to realize that much of the live

237

music provided by local bands suffered from an absence of competent drummers. Alabama was correct when they said you needed a fiddle in the band if you wanted to play in Texas. What they failed to mention is that it is even more important to have a drummer who understands the special nature of a country dance tune. These new drummers were raised on rock music, just as the disc jockeys in radio and the clubs were, and they brought their limited background to what they thought was country music. Rather than attempting to understand the nuances and subtleties that can be produced by such a forceful instrument, they attacked the drums much like a hyperactive child trying to demolish a toy with a mallet. It is hard to dance a two-step when the drummer is taking four at a time.

The recording companies attempted to satisfy the demand created by and in this outlet. This is one of the reasons for the appearance of some of the groups mentioned in the happy love chapter. The groups and newer artists recorded mostly upbeat songs that were longer, more repetitive, and emphasized instrumentation over vocals. They remained popular a little longer in the bar rooms than they did in the living rooms. Unfortunately, several of these groups bore characteristics similar to the bouncing ball used to highlight lyrics in movie and television shorts. That ball trips across the printed lyrics to indicate words the audience should be singing. Some of the singers and "new" groups seemed to be as off tempo and knowledgeable of the lyrics as these little bouncing helpers.

Another phenomenon that developed from this movement was the use of the term "cowboy" to describe members of the audience. This description also found its way into the message. When the "new" and some parts of the "old" audience did assimilate, they were too astute to assume the name of "hickies," so they took a name from the music and gave it a new meaning. Bill Malone describes what happened in the Austin scene: "Gradually a music culture emerged which enveloped them all, and one which reflected a curious combining of images and symbols: hippie, Texas, and above all, cowboy (a usage which arose from the desire to find an indigenous and binding metaphor)."[23] This term, aided and abetted by the performers, spread to encompass even wider segments of this audience.

The songwriters did not ignore the new audience, performers, or environment. In 1985, when the movement was on the wane, two lifestyle songs that mentioned a few members of that audience were among the fifty most popular songs of the year. The Bellamy Brothers described an important segment of the new audience in "Old Hippie." The man in this song switched to country music after losing his enthusiasm for disco and finding he was too old for "new wave." He had been a serious member of the drug culture, but now alters his mind with only a little of what he grows in the back yard. He is now a jogger—another fad on the decline during this period. He is generally pleased with his present life and happy that he changed his behavior before it was too late. The born-again cowboy did not fare as well in one of Conway Twitty's recordings. In "Don't Call Him a Cowboy," a man is probably trying to denigrate a competitor in a bar when he cautions a woman that she should know a man before she classifies him. Telling the woman that he knows she has heard how a night with a Texas cowboy would be, he warns her that the one standing at the bar is a fake. The hat, custom-made vest, and fancy boots do not tell what he is really like. The man giving the warning insists that the roughest ride the dude has experienced has been in his foreign car. In language that has at least two meanings, he tells her that it is doubtful the man at the bar can make it through an all-night rodeo, and until the man proves himself in the saddle she can't call him a cowboy.

The precise time for the demise of the "Urban Cowboy" phase is as difficult to identify as any other movement in the past. (Tom T. Hall said, "They killed the son of a bitch on Farm Aid.")[24] One of the more favorable outcomes of the recording industry's desire to introduce new talent was that it opened the gates for performers that could and would sing real country songs. This select few, either because of—or in spite of—the companies, proved once again that a large percentage of the country music audience wishes to hear a message that is close to that heard throughout the history of the music. Ricky Skaggs, George Strait, Reba McEntire, Dwight Yoakam, and Randy Travis struggled to record the music they wished to sing. Their success, and the success of others who have been called "traditionalists," has received much notice in and outside the industry.[25] Edward Morris describes how it affected the way the message is delivered as well as the message itself. He observes that "there is a re-emphasis on distinct, up-front vocals and restrained acoustic instrumentation, both foundation stones of country music." The message is changing because the new movement is "sending artists and their producers deep into publishing vaults in search of old hits and even near hits. The trend is also inspiring songwriters to compose songs with an old feel, a practice that was rampant in the folk-music boom of the early sixties."[26]

Unfortunately, as each movement flourishes, another movement tends to wither. The effect of a movement usually has a carry-over, but does not grow as in the early days. Casualties occur when those who wish to fit a mode discover that the mode is declining in popularity. It happens to all who try to ride a trend. The problems are always articulated by those who are attempting to mesh with a group that is receding rather than expanding. There is no way to solve the problems that are generated by this situation, and complaints and verbal attacks help little. Just as those who wished to perform in the more traditional manner could not be heard in the early eighties, those who wished to continue and expand the gate for the non-traditional were concerned with the turn around of the mid-eighties.

An interesting facet of the first, and then the counter movement of the 80s, is the platform many new artists have for expressing their views about them on talk shows and in trade publications. The argument usually runs something like this: "Country music has room for all types of songs and performers. My music does not fit the present mold but should be heard. It is not being heard because the record companies do not know how to classify it and the radio stations will not program it even if it is recorded."

The performers are correct on all these points. Being correct does not mean that the system will change, it just means that the "different" music will not be heard. The success of the traditional performers adds impetus to those who are different from them and want to be heard. The traditional performers fought the system with a product that the audience wanted to hear and eventually that takes precedence over all gatekeepers. The major question those trying to get into the system have to answer is not whether the music is "country," but does anyone other than the performer want to hear it? The audience must always be considered when a message is intended for mass consumption. They are sometimes ignored, they are sometimes offended, they are sometimes infuriated, but the people are always the ultimate judge. If a performer remains cloaked in a cocoon refusing to expand to a larger market, he or she should be satisfied with reaching a small number of people, keeping a day job, and knowing that "I did it my way." If performers wish to expand the audience for their message they must listen to the audience. Many so-called performers listen only to themselves or a few close associates. When a politician makes this same error and relies on family and a few friends for advice on reaching the people, the practice is called "drinking your own bath water." Mass messages must be tested in a larger pool, and, rather than attacking those who restrict the flow of the communication, the performers must try to involve as large an audience as possible. When a source has something the larger audience wishes to hear, many professionals will join in to help deliver that message.

"Wonderful Future"

Although the new audience causes pleasure and pain—just as the music itself does—they are here and growing. Probably of more consequence to the message is where the future songwriters and singers come from and where they take the music. If they come from the newer group, there is the possibility that the

241

music will be diverted in undetermined directions. More likely it will retain the most attractive characteristics from the most active period of commercial country music. As long as people live and love, there will be other people who write and sing about these experiences. To maintain the music in its so-called "pure" form would mean that the audience would have to remain the same, and this of course cannot be. As the audience experiences life from different perspectives, so will the writers and performers tell of it. The music will grow in the direction of the people who chronicle the lives of the audience, so changes are more apt to take place in the lifestyle songs than in the love songs. The music will still be the music of the people, and although it may be experienced and conveyed differently, it is certain that country music will carry the message.

Notes

Chapter 1

The Country Music Process:
How the Folks Send the Message to the People

1. For one interpretation of *Nashville*'s impact and a small excerpt from what Stan Kenton said about country music, see Jack Temple Kirby, *Media-Made Dixie: The South in the American Imagination* (Baton Rouge: Louisiana State University Press, 1978), pp. 158–59.

2. Larry L. Barker, *Communication*, 3rd ed. (Englewood Cliffs, N.J.: Prentice-Hall Inc., 1984), p. 5. For an excellent description of the complex system for producing and marketing the contemporary country music product which demonstrates the similarity between Barker's definition of the human communication process and the country music system and provides a very good view of the constraints of the system, see John Ryan and Richard A. Peterson. "The Product Image: The Fate of Creativity in Country Music Songwriting," in *Individuals in Mass Media Organizations: Creativity and Constraint*, eds. James S. Ettema and D. Charles Whitney (Beverly Hills, California: Sage Publications, 1982), pp. 11–32.

3. Barker, *Communication*, p. 9.

4. Kurt Lewin, "Frontiers in Group Dynamics: II. Channels of Group Life; Social Planning and Action Research," *Human Relations*, 1 (1947), 143–53. A communication model that illustrates Lewin's "gatekeeper" is found in Bruce H. Westley and Malcolm S. MacLean Jr., "A Conceptual Model for Communication Research," *Journalism Quarterly* 34, (1957), 31–38.

5. Paul Hemphill, *The Nashville Sound: Bright Lights and Country Music* (New York: Simon and Schuster, 1970), p. 66.

6. For a description of Ralph Peer's methods for obtaining publication rights and his impact upon commercial country music, see Nolan Porterfield, *Jimmie Rodgers: The Life and Times of America's Blue Yodeler* (Urbana: University of Illinois Press, 1979), pp. 95–101.

7. Jimmie N. Rogers, Raymond S. Rodgers, and Peggy J. Beasley-Rodgers, "The Country Music Message: An Analysis of the Most Popular Country Songs from 1965 to 1980" (paper presented at the Popular Culture Association Convention, Cincinnati, Ohio, March 28, 1981).

8. Personal interview with Willie Nelson, April 27, 1979. Nelson's comments quoted in this chapter are from this taped interview.

9. Loretta Lynn with George Vescey, *Coal Miner's Daughter* (New York: Warner Books, 1976), p. 109.

10. Tom T. Hall, *The Songwriter's Handbook* (Nashville, Tennessee: Rutledge Hill Press, 1987). A valuable source of song lyrics, as well as short items describing why they were written, can be found in Dorothy Horstman, *Sing Your Heart Out, Country Boy,* rev. ed. (Nashville, Tennessee: Country Music Foundation Press, 1986). For two additional books that reprint a number of country lyrics, see Carol Offen, *Country Music: The Poetry* (New York: Ballantine Books, 1977); and Frye Gaillard, *Watermelon Wine: The Spirit of Country Music* (New York: St. Martin's Press, 1978), pp. 191–236.

11. For a perceptive view of the use of clichés in country songs, see Dave Hickey, "Dolly Parton's Songs Have Real Soul," *The Best of Country Music,* 1 (New York: KBO Publishers, 1974), 64–65.

12. Connotative characteristics of words, as well as other important functions of language, are described in John Ciardi and Miller Williams, *How Does a Poem Mean?* 2nd ed. (Boston: Houghton-Mifflin Company, 1975), pp. 101–52. For an excellent description of the use of language in country music, see Paul Ackerman, "The Poetry and Imagery of Country Songs," *Billboard,* March 18, 1978, pp. CMA–22, 42.

13. For some examples of early recordings that contain explicit lyrics, see Nick Tosches, *Country: Living Legends and Dying Metaphors in America's Biggest Music* (New York: Charles Scribner's Sons, 1985), pp. 120–56.

14. Mark L. Knapp, *Interpersonal Communication and Human Relationships* (Boston: Allyn and Bacon, Inc., 1984), p. 37.

15. Rufus Jarman, "Country Music Goes to Town," *Nation's Business,* February 1953, p. 51. Roger M. Williams, when commenting on Hank

Williams's statement concerning the role of sincerity in country music, insisted that "[t]alent and technique are at least as important as sincerity." *Sing a Sad Song: The Life of Hank Williams,* 2nd ed. (Urbana: University of Illinois Press, 1980), p. 107.

16. Ciardi and Williams, *How Does A Poem Mean?,* pp. 205–9.

17. Perhaps the requirement for the country singer to be a good storyteller is a factor of the southern roots of the music. For a description of these southern roots, see Bill C. Malone, *Southern Music/American Music* (Lexington: University Press of Kentucky, 1979).

18. Tom T. Hall, *The Storyteller's Nashville* (Garden City, New York: Doubleday & Company, Inc., 1979), p. 83. Hall did record the song in 1982 for an album to be sold on his concert tour.

19. For some comments about the difficulty a singer faces when working with a song he or she did not write, see David Allan Coe, review of *Mr. Hag Told My Story* by Johnny Paycheck, *Country Music,* July–August 1981, p. 70.

20. For examples of some of these publications, see Bill C. Malone, *Country Music, U.S.A.,* rev. ed. (Austin: University of Texas Press, 1985); Paul DiMaggio, Richard A. Peterson, and Jack Esco Jr., "Country Music: Ballad of the Silent Majority," in *The Sounds of Social Change,* eds. R. Serge Denisoff and Richard A. Peterson (Chicago: Rand McNally & Company, 1972); Chet Flippo, "Country and Western: Some New Fangled Ideas," *American Libraries,* April 1974, pp. 185–89; Douglas B. Green, *Country Roots: The Origins of Country Music* (New York: Hawthorn Books, Inc., 1976); Charles Gritzner, "Country Music: A Reflection of Popular Culture," *Journal of Popular Culture,* 11 (1978), 857–64; Patricia A. Hall, "From 'The Wreck of the Number Nine' to the 'Wreck on the Highway': A Preliminary Comparison of Traditional Folksong and Commercial Country Song Composition and Composers," *Journal of Country Music,* 6 (1978), 60–73; Horstman, *Sing Your Heart Out, Country Boy;* Larry King, "The Passions of the Common Man," *Texas Monthly,* August 1976, pp. 98–101, 123–30; George H. Lewis, "Country Music Lyrics," *Journal of Communication,* 26 (1976), 37–40; Offen, *Country Music: The Poetry;* and Steven D. Price, *Take Me Home: The Rise of Country and Western Music* (New York: Praeger Publishers, 1974).

21. The first in this analysis was developed for a study of the top ten songs from 1965 to 1974, conducted with Peggy J. Beasley-Rodgers and Raymond S. Rodgers and first reported at the Popular Culture Association in the South Convention, Tampa, Florida, October 9, 1975. For in-

formation about content analysis as a research tool, see Ole R. Holsti, *Content Analysis for the Social Sciences and Humanities* (Reading, Massachusetts: Addison-Wesley Publishing Company, 1969).

22. For background on these channels, see Malone, *Country Music U.S.A.;* and both Charles K. Wolfe, "The Birth of an Industry," and Douglas B. Green, "Depression and Boom, in *The Illustrated History of Country Music,* ed. Patrick Carr (Garden City, New York: Country Music Magazine Press/Doubleday & Company, Inc., 1979), pp. 30–101. For a detailed history of the recording industry, see Roland Gelatt, *The Fabulous Phonograph: From Edison to Stereo,* rev. ed. (New York: Appleton-Century, 1965).

23. Green, *Country Roots,* p. 22.

24. John D. Stevens and Hazel Dicken Garcia, *Communication History* (Beverly Hills, California: Sage Publications, 1980), p. 137.

25. Betty Franklin, "Country Cashes In," *Forbes,* October 13, 1980, p. 181. It was in 1980 that country music passed a significant milestone in sales, garnering 14.3 percent of the recorded music market, which meant $526.5 million in sales according to the National Association of Recording Merchandisers (NARM). John Lomax III, "Nashville Lowdown," *Country Rhythms,* February 1982, p. 73. Lomax reported data from NARM that country music sales were 15% of all the sales in 1982 ($538.8 million); however, it was 9% in 1986 ($415.6 million). "15 Years of Country Record Sales," in Robert K. Oermann, "Country Music Sings New Tune." *The Sunday Tennessean,* April 19, 1987, p. 10D.

26. For a comparison between country and rock audiences' buying habits and the costs to produce both types of albums, see Otis White, "The Nashville Sound: Pickin' and Grinnin' for Fun and Profit," *South,* May 1980, pp. 40–49.

27. For a brief synopsis of arguments against the crossover trend in country music, see Robert K. Oermann, "Old vs. New Country: The Battle Is On," *Country Rhythms,* September 1981, pp. 24–27.

28. The performers who forced the retreat from "pop-country" were often identified as the "new traditionalists." For a description of the music in the early eighties and the return to the traditional in the mid-eighties, see Don E. Tomlinson, "Country Music: What Price Progress" in *Mass Media and Society,* ed. Alan Wells (Lexington, Massachusetts: Lexington Books/D. C. Heath and Company,1987), pp. 177–186. For a view of the effects of these new performers upon the music see a special report composed of brief articles by Ken Tucker ("Why Ricky, Reba,

and George Are Hard at It"), David Gates ("Are You Sure Hank Done It This Way?"), Bill C. Malone ("CMA Awards: Wins of Change?"), Robert K. Oermann ("What Goes Around Comes Around"), and Paul Kingsbury (Dwight Yoakam: Honky-Tonk as Cutting Edge"), "The Old Sound of New Country," *Journal of Country Music,* 11 (1986), 2–14.

29. For views of this type of music and the people performing it, see Jan Reid, *The Improbable Rise of Redneck Rock* (New York: DeCapo Press, Inc., 1977); and Michael Bane, *The Outlaws: Revolution in Country Music* (New York: Country Music Magazine Press/Doubleday/Dolphin, 1978).

30. Lynn with Vescey, *Coal Miner's Daughter,* p. 14.

31. Jack Hurst, "K. T. Oslin Tries Another Kind of Commercial Success," *Chicago Tribune,* July 7, 1987, Sect. 5, p. 3.

32. For a concise description of the financial intricacies of recording contracts see, John Lomax III, *Nashville: Music City USA* (New York: Harry N. Abrams, Inc., 1985), p. 195. For a breakdown of earnings derived from the sale of an album, see Mark Mehler, "Where Does Your Money Go?", *Country Music,* March 1980, pp. 22–23.

33. Kenny Rogers and Len Epand, *Making It with Music: Kenny Rogers' Guide to the Music Business* (New York: Harper & Row Publishers, Inc., 1978).

34. For a historical review of country music radio, see Richard Price Stockdall, "The Development of the Country Music Format" (Unpublished Master's Thesis, Kansas State University, 1979).

35. George O. Carney, "Country Music and the Radio: A Historical Geographic Assessment," *Rocky Mountain Social Science Journal,* 11 (1974), 19–32.

36. For a more detailed description of the way country music is promoted see Lomax, *Nashville: Music City USA,* pp. 189–91.

37. There is a possibility that the smaller stations located in rural areas may offer more variety in the music because they are used as test markets for some new record releases. For a study that mentions the test market possibility but found little difference between the music played on city and rural stations, see Lyn Thaxton and Charles Jaret, "Country Music and Its City Cousin: A Comparative Analysis," *Popular Music & Society,* 6 (1979), 307–15.

38. For some programmers' observations about the virtues of reduced playlists, see Tom Rowland, "Country Radio: Instinct Meets Research," *Cashbox: Country Music Special 1981,* October 17, 1981, pp. C–34, 46.

39. Richard A. Peterson, "The Production of Cultural Change: The Case of Contemporary Country Radio," *Social Research,* 45 (1978), 292–314.

40. Richard A. Peterson and Paul DiMaggio, "From Region to Class, the Changing Locus of Country Music: A Test of the Massification Hypothesis," *Social Forces,* 53 (1975), 497–506.

41. Donna Halper, "Stations Sprout, Country Blossoms in New Musical Field Day," *Billboard: World of Country Music,* October 17, 1981, p. WOCM–26.

42. Wilber Schramm, *Men, Messages, and Media: A Look at Human Communication* (New York: Harper & Row Publishers, Inc., 1973), p. 167.

43. Richard A. Peterson, "Has Country Lost Its Homespun Charm?" *Chronicle Review,* May 29, 1979, pp. 22–23.

44. James Lull, "Popular Music and Communication: An Introduction," in *Popular Music and Communication,* ed. James Lull (Newbury Park, California: Sage Publications, 1987), p. 22.

45. Moira McCormick, "Many at Coin Meet See 45s as Strong Survivor/CD Jukeboxes Are Getting Big Play," *Billboard,* November 21, 1987, pp. 1, 81.

46. Is Horowitz, "Fewer Jukebox Licenses Issued Despite Pressures," *Billboard,* March 1, 1980, pp. 1, 59. The official number of boxes were reported to be 250,000 in 1987. McCormick, "Coin Meet," *Billboard,* p. 1.

47. The sales manager for Warner Bros. Records stated that fifty to sixty percent of their country singles were sold to jukebox operators. Marc Cetner, "Labels, Retailers Reexamining Role of Singles in Current Market Climate," *Cashbox,* October 10, 1981, p. 14. The jukebox industry was reported to have purchased forty-six million 45s in 1986. McCormick, "Coin Meet," *Billboard,* p. 1.

48. "AMOA Jukebox Award Winners Announced," *Cashbox,* October 17, 1981, p. 33.

49. The growth of TNN and CMT is described in Gerry Wood, "Country Music Networks Flourish/TNN, CMT Build Subscriber Bases," *Billboard,* June 20, 1987, pp. 1, 76.

50. Jonathan L. Freedman and David O. Sears, "Selective Exposure," in *Advances in Experimental Social Psychology,* ed. Leonard Berkowitz (New York: Academic Press, 1965), II, pp. 57–97.

51. For a description of how the form of a song may affect an audience, see Irving J. Rein, *Rudy's Red Wagon: Communication Strategies in*

Contemporary Society (Glenview, Illinois: Scott, Foresman and Company, 1972), p. 74.

52. Bill C. Malone, *Country Music, U.S.A.: A Fifty-Year History* (Austin: University of Texas Press, 1968), p. x.

53. John Grissim, *Country Music: White Man's Blues* (New York: Paperback Library, 1970), p. 242.

54. For an excellent description of the reporting systems, tabulating practices, and inherent problems related to the *Billboard* country charts see Lomax, *Nashville: Music City USA*, pp. 191–95.

55. For a quick review of the role of BMI and ASCAP and the way they collect fees and distribute proceeds, see Rogers and Epand, *Making It with Music*, pp. 133–35.

Chapter 2

Hurtin' Love:
Most of the Folks are Hurtin' Most of the Time

1. Dorothy Horstman, *Sing Your Heart Out, Country Boy*, rev. ed. (Nashville, Tennessee: Country Music Foundation Press, 1986), pp. 147–48. For some classic hurtin' songs from the early period of commercial country music, see pp. 149–96 in the same source.

2. Bill C. Malone, "A Shower of Stars: Country Music Since World War II," in *Stars of Country Music: Uncle Dave Macon to Johnny Rodriguez*, eds. Bill C. Malone and Judith McCulloh (Urbana: University of Illinois Press, 1975), p. 435; and Ann Neitzke, "Doin' Somebody Wrong," *Human Behavior*, November 1975, pp. 65–69. For another view of the treatment of women in country songs, see Barbara Sims, "'She's Got to Be a Saint, Lord Knows I Ain't': Feminine Masochism in American Country Songs," *Journal of Country Music*, 5 (1974), 24–30. For a perceptive look at how women singers have objected to their stereotypical roles in the music, see Mary Bufwack and Bob Oermann, "Women in Country Music," in *Popular Culture in America*, ed. Paul Buhle (Minneapolis: University of Minnesota Press, 1987), pp. 91–101.

3. "The Way to Love a Man" (#10, 1969), "Singing My Song"

249

(#29, 1969), "He Loves Me All the Way" (#10, 1970), "Run, Woman, Run" (#23, 1970), "I'll See Him Through" (#30, 1970), "Good Lovin' (Makes It Right)" (#9, 1971), "We Sure Can Love Each Other" (#19, 1971), "Bedtime Story" (#30, 1972), "Reach Out Your Hand" (#42, 1972), and "Till I Get It Right" (#21, 1973).

4. Jimmie N. Rogers, "Images of Women as Indicated in the Messages of Loretta Lynn," *Studies in Popular Culture*, 5 (1982), 42–49. Lynn's "sassy point of view" is also described in Bufwack and Oermann, "Women in Country Music," pp. 97–98. For an annotated discography of Loretta Lynn's records, see Laurence J. Zwisohn, *Loretta Lynn's World of Music*, University of California: John Edwards Foundation Special Series No. 14 (Los Angeles: Palm Tree Library, 1980).

5. Loretta Lynn with George Vecsey, *Coal Miner's Daughter* (New York: Warner Books, 1976), p. 38.

6. Lynn with Vecsey, *Coal Miner's Daughter*, p. 14.

7. Nietzke, "Doin' Somebody Wrong," p. 66.

8. Patricia Freudiger and Elizabeth M. Almquist, "Male and Female Roles in the Lyrics of Three Genres of Contemporary Music," *Sex Roles*, 4 (1978), 57.

9. Lynn with Vecsey, *Coal Miner's Daughter*, p. 201.

10. Jimmie N. Rogers, "If You See Me Getting Smaller I'll Be Gone: Changing Images of Women in Dissolving Relationships as Depicted in Country Music" (paper presented at the Southern Speech Communication Association Convention, Houston, Texas, April 3, 1986).

11. For a view of how women in the music use sexuality within the framework of marriage, see Ruth A. Banes, "Southern Women in Country Songs," *Journal of Regional Cultures*, 1 (1981), 62–64.

12. Personal interview with Willie Nelson, April 27, 1979.

13. Kris Kristofferson, jacket notes, *The Silver-Tongued Devil and I*, Monument PZ 30679, 1971.

14. Russell Nye, *The Unembarrassed Muse: The Popular Arts in America* (New York: Dial Press, 1970), p. 347.

Chapter 3

Happy Love:
Some of the Folks are Happy Some of the Time

1. For some examples of how sexual love is described in country music, see Stan Leventhal, "Sex and Country Lyrics: The Sound and the Fury," *Country Rhythms,* February 1982, pp. 46–48.
2. Dorothy Horstman, *Sing Your Heart Out, Country Boy,* rev. ed. (Nashville, Tennessee: Country Music Foundation Press, 1986), p. 126.
3. Horstman, *Sing Your Heart Out, Country Boy,* p. 125.
4. Russell Nye, *The Unembarrassed Muse: The Popular Arts in America* (New York: Dial Press, 1970), p. 347.
5. Personal interview with Willie Nelson, April 27, 1979.

Chapter 4

Cheatin' Love:
Some of the Folks Cheat Some of the Time

1. Douglas B. Green, *Country Roots: The Origins of Country Music* (New York: Hawthorn Books, Inc., 1976), p. 177.
2. Dorothy Horstman, *Sing Your Heart Out, Country Boy,* rev. ed. (Nashville, Tennessee: Country Music Foundation Press, 1986), p. 198; and Green, *Country Roots,* p. 177.
3. Carol Offen, *Country Music: The Poetry* (New York: Ballantine Books, 1977), p. 41.
4. Jimmie N. Rogers, "Images of Women as Indicated in the Messages of Loretta Lynn, " *Studies in Popular Culture,* 5 (1982), 42–49.
5. Green, *Country Roots,* p. 177.
6. Horstman, *Sing Your Heart Out, Country Boy,* p. 202.
7. Jimmie N. Rogers, "Audience Attitudes as Indicated by Cheatin' Messages in Popular Country Songs," *Studies in Popular Culture,* 3 (1980), 2–10.

Chapter 5

Livin':
Most of the Folks are Livin' When They Are Not Lovin'

1. Charles F. Gritzner, "Country Music: A Reflection of Popular Culture," *Journal of Popular Culture*, 11 (1978), 862.

2. One author believes that "home" is the most prevalent theme in the music. Steven D. Price, *Take Me Home: The Rise of Country and Western Music* (New York: Praeger Publishers, 1974), p. 141.

3. For a study of "rednecks" in the music, see Raymond S. Rodgers, "Images of Rednecks in Country Music: The Lyrical Persona of a Southern Superman," *Journal of Regional Cultures*, 1 (1982), 71–81.

4. For a view of the ambivalence found in country songs of war and patriotism, see Dorothy Horstman, *Sing Your Heart Out, Country Boy*, rev. ed. (Nashville, Tennessee: Country Music Foundation Press, Inc., 1986), pp. 255–57.

5. Mel Tillis comments on "Ruby, Don't Take Your Love to Town" in Horstman, *Sing Your Heart Out, Country Boy*, p. 207.

6. Stephen A. Smith, "Sounds of the South: The Rhetorical Saga of Country Music Lyrics," *Southern Speech Communication Journal*, 45 (1980), 164–72.

7. Stephen A. Smith and Jimmie N. Rogers, "Political Culture in Country Music: A Revisionist Interpretation," in *Politics in Familiar Contexts: Projecting Politics Through Popular Media*, eds. Robert L. Savage and Dan Nimmo (Norwood, N.J.: Ablex Publishing, in press).

8. Jens Lund, "Fundamentalism, Racism, and Political Reaction in Country Music," in *The Sounds of Social Change*, eds. R. Serge Denisoff and Richard A. Peterson (Chicago: Rand McNally & Company, 1972), pp. 79–91. For a study that does not uphold the assertion, see Jimmie N. Rogers and Stephen A. Smith, "Country Music and Organized Religion: Mediated Cultural Criticism," (paper presented at the International Communication Association Convention, New Orleans, Louisiana, June 1, 1988).

9. For an excellent description of honky-tonk music, see Douglas B. Green and Bob Pinson, "Music from the Lone Star State," *The Illustrated History of Country Music*, ed. Patrick Carr (Garden City, New York: Country Music Magazine Press/Doubleday & Company, Inc., 1979), pp. 125–33.

10. Bobby Bare, introductory remarks to "Rest Awhile," *Lullabys, Legends and Lies,* RCA CPL2–0290, 1973.

11. Sometimes when a country music songwriter borrows an idea from another, he or she sets it off in parentheses following the title, thus making it a subtitle—(owed to John Prine), for instance. "Metacountry" is a term that was first mentioned to me by Raymond Rodgers, and he is given credit in the country music style of footnote.

12. Horstman, *Sing Your Heart Out, Country Boy,* p. 278.

13. Merle Haggard with Peggy Russell, *Sing Me Back Home: My Story* (New York: New York Times Book Co., 1981).

Chapter 6

The Listeners:
When They Came Out of the Closet

1. John Greenway, "Country-Western: The Music of America," *American West,* 5 (1968), 32.

2. Frederick E. Danker, "Country Music," *Yale Review,* 63 (1974), 392.

3. Bill C. Malone, "The South, and Americanism," *Mississippi Folklore Register,* 10 (1976), 57. This is an interesting article because the author was unaware that it was to be published. See a letter from Malone in *Journal of Country Music,* 7 (1978), 124.

4. Charles F. Gritzner, "Country Music: A Reflection of Popular Culture," *Journal of Popular Culture,* 11 (1978), 862–63.

5. Bill C. Malone, *Country Music, U.S.A.: A Fifty-Year History* (Austin: University of Texas Press, 1968), p. 362.

6. Malone, *Country Music, U.S.A.: A Fifty-Year History,* p. 360.

7. Dorothy Horstman, *Sing Your Heart Out, Country Boy,* rev. ed. (Nashville, Tennessee: Country Music Foundation Press, 1986), pp. xx–xxi.

8. For views of the distinctive southern experience, see C. Vann Woodward, *The Burden of Southern History,* rev. ed. (Baton Rouge: Louisiana State University Press, 1968); Patrick Gerster and Nicholas Cords, eds., *Myth and Southern History* (Chicago: Rand McNally College Pub-

lishing Company, 1974); and Paul M. Gaston, *The New South Creed: A Study in Southern Mythmaking* (New York: Alfred A. Knopf, 1970).

9. John Lomax III and Robert K. Oermann, "The Heavy 100 in Country Music," *Esquire,* April 1982, p. 65.

10. John P. Robinson and Paul M. Hirsch, "Teenage Response to Rock and Roll Protest Songs," in *The Sounds of Social Change,* eds. R. Serge Denisoff and Richard A. Peterson (Chicago: Rand McNally & Company, 1972), p. 224.

11. John D. McCarthy, Richard A. Peterson, and William L. Yancey, "Singing Along with the Silent Majority," in *Side-Saddle on the Golden Calf: Social Structure and Popular Culture in America,* ed. George H. Lewis (Pacific Palisades, California: Goodyear Publishing Company, Inc., 1972), p. 58; and Paul DiMaggio, Richard A. Peterson, and Jack Esco Jr., "Country Music: Ballad of the Silent Majority," in *The Sounds of Social Change,* p. 49.

12. Richard A. Peterson and Paul DiMaggio, "From Region to Class, The Changing Locus of Country Music: A Test of the Massification Hypothesis," *Social Forces,* 55 (1975), 503.

13. Jay Blumer and Elihu Katz, eds., *The Use of Mass Communication: Current Perspectives on Gratifications Research* (Beverly Hills, California: Sage Publications, 1974).

14. For a quick review of both theories and an alternative concept, see Dennis K. Davis and Stanley J. Baron, *Mass Communication and Everyday Life: A Perspective on Theory and Effects* (Belmont, California: Wadsworth Publishing Company, 1981), pp. 152–55.

15. For a description of six evaluation positions on mass culture, see Michael R. Real, *Mass-Mediated Culture* (Englewood Cliffs, N.J.: Prentice-Hall, Inc., 1977), pp. 16–18.

16. Personal interview with Willie Nelson, April 27, 1979. Nelson's comments quoted in this chapter are from this taped interview.

17. For two reports on the Palms Danceland in Dallas, Texas, see Diane K. Shah with Lea Donosky, "Best Little Dance Hall," *Newsweek,* January 22, 1979, p. 81; and "Cheating Hearts," *Time,* October 2, 1978, p. 37.

18. McCarthy, Peterson, and Yancey, "Singing Along with the Silent Majority," pp. 60–61. For additional information about the pursuit of the American Dream, see Stephen A. Smith and Jimmie N. Rogers, "Political Culture in Country Music: A Revisionist Interpretation," in *Politics in Familiar Contexts: Projecting Politics Through Popular Media,* eds.

Robert L. Savage and Dan Nimmo (Norwood, N.J.: Ablex Publishing, in press).

19. Cynthia Gorney, "Masters of the Country Music Lament: The Bitter-Sweet 'Story Songs' of Tom T. Hall," *The Washington Post,* November 19, 1979, pp. E 1, E 11.

20. Sharon McKern, *Redneck Mothers, Good Ol' Girls and Southern Belles: A Celebration of the Women of Dixie* (New York: The Viking Press, 1979).

21. Information from an Arbitron study commissioned by the Country Music Association in October 1976. Study furnished by the Country Music Foundation Library and Media Center.

22. Associated Press, "Exit Rednecks, Enter 'Hickies,'" *Southwest Times Record* (Ft. Smith, Arkansas), August 28, 1975, p. 7E.

23. Bill C. Malone, *Country Music, U.S.A.,* rev. ed. (Austin: University of Texas Press, 1985), p. 394.

24. Personal interview with Tom T. Hall, September 27, 1985.

25. For some views of the impact of the "traditionalists," see Martin Booe [*Los Angeles Daily News*], "Country Music Getting Better, Not Worse," *Arkansas Gazette,* June 7, 1987, p. 17 G; and Stephen Holden, "Country Music's Young Turks Do It Again," *New York Times,* June 28, 1987, p. H 21. For descriptions of the impact of both movements in the early eighties, see Bill C. Malone, *Country Music, U.S.A.,* rev. ed., pp. 369–415; Don E. Tomlinson, "Country Music: What Price Progress" in *Mass Media and Society,* ed. Alan Wells (Lexington, Massachusetts: Lexington Books/D. C. Heath and Company, 1987), pp. 177–186; and a special report by several authors in "The Old Sound of New Country," *Journal of Country Music,* 11 (1986), 2–14.

26. Edward Morris, "To Publisher's Glee, Acts Mine Golden Country Songs," *Billboard,* December 26, 1987, p. 1.

Index

257

263